LIFE CHOICES AND LIFE CHANGES
THROUGH IMAGEWORK
The art of developing personal vision

M
A
N
D
A
L
A

Life Choices and Life Changes Through Imagework is a guide to both the principles and the practice of using imagery as a self-help tool. The wide range of easy to follow exercises, along with the method of constructing these for oneself, covers every area of life from self-image to self-presentation, from relationships to work, from health to creative problem resolution, and from dealing with resentment and loss to managing money and time. The book is as much for individuals who want to realise more of their potential, as for experienced psychotherapists, counsellors, and management consultants looking for new ways to help clients manage and transform their personal and professional lives.

Imagework does not depend on our ability to see inner pictures, nor does it require a willingness to 'think positively', or to espouse any particular belief system. The approach represents a unique synthesis of major imagery, visualisation, and counselling techniques with the author's own discoveries during years of psychotherapy, counselling, lecturing, and training.

Dina Glouberman, PhD, founded and directs three international training centres on the Greek island of Skyros: The Skyros Centre, a personal development holiday centre, Atsitsa, a holistic health and fitness holiday centre, and The Skyros Institute, European Centre for Holistic Studies. She is also a Senior Lecturer at Kingston Polytechnic in Surrey, England, and Founder-Director of its new management and personal development training centre, Vision for Change. An individual, family, and group psychotherapist of many years standing, Dr Glouberman specialises in the use of imagery for personal, professional, and management development, and runs imagework training courses in the UK, Scandinavia, and Greece. Originally from the USA, and now living mainly in the UK, she is married and has two children.

In memory of my mother, father, and brother
– Sara, Isaac, and Emmet Glouberman –
whose individualistic, truth-seeking, and loving spirits live on in my life and illuminate the pages of this book

LIFE CHOICES AND LIFE CHANGES THROUGH IMAGEWORK

The Art of Developing Personal Vision

DINA GLOUBERMAN

MANDALA

UNWIN PAPERBACKS

London   Boston   Sydney   Wellington

First published by Unwin® Paperbacks,
an imprint of Unwin Hyman Limited, in 1989.

Unwin Hyman Limited
15–17 Broadwick Street, London W1V 1FP

Unwin Hyman, Inc.
8 Winchester Place, Winchester, Mass 01890, USA

Allen & Unwin Australia Pty Ltd
8 Napier Street, North Sydney, NSW 2060, Australia

Allen & Unwin New Zealand Pty Ltd in association with
‘   the Port Nicholson Press
Compusales Building, 75 Ghuznee Street, Wellington, New Zealand

British Library Cataloguing in Publication Data

Life choices and life changes through imagework:
The art of developing personal vision
1. Personal success
158'.1
ISBN 0-04-440483-2

Typeset in Palatino 10 on 11½ by
Computape (Pickering) Ltd, North Yorkshire
Printed and bound in Great Britain by
Cox & Wyman Ltd, Reading

CONTENTS

PREFACE

We live in a culture where we are valued more for what we achieve in the eyes of others, than for finding our own inner eyes. I, like most other people I know, used to spend much of my life running like a rat on an exercise wheel in a cage, trying to keep up with the inner and outer expectations that dominated my life. Every now and then I would kick the exercise wheel, or rattle the bars of my cage, but this merely delayed me: I would eventually go back to the wheel and run even faster to make up for lost time. Whether I was doing something that I really wanted to do, or something I didn't, the inner result was the same: even my most creative desires were transformed into expectations that ended by oppressing me.

In real terms, I *was* trying to do rather a lot. Over the last ten year period I have co-founded and run with my husband two health holiday centres and a training institute on a Greek island, maintained a full time job as a lecturer, developed a psychotherapy practice, facilitated courses in imagework, and co-parented two children. Trying to meet the demands inherent in having so much responsibility was, for many of these years, painfully difficult for me, especially since my creative urges are not matched by equivalent organisational skills. No matter how fast I ran I couldn't really keep up, and the more exciting my life looked to others the worse it felt to me.

Imagework is the method I developed and used to enable me to survive and grow. When I found out how powerful images could be, I used every technique of imagery and visualisation I could find or make up and I used them daily. It was my line of communication with my inner world, and my one most important tool; not only to find an inner calm, integrate all the bits of me, heal my past hurts, improve my relationships, become and stay healthy, and contact my spiritual self, but also to plan projects, work more efficiently and

consistently, make sound decisions, present myself better, and generally gain access to more resources than I knew I had.

At first, I was just looking for a way to live more happily in the cage. And indeed it worked – people who hadn't seen me for a long time would tell me I looked younger and more dynamic than I had ten years ago. But while I was becoming more effective and more confident about meeting all the expectations that were built into my life, I was also discovering my own view of the world, my own sense of the meaning of life, and my own priorities. I was, in fact, developing my personal vision. I was able to see the cage for what it was, open the door, and walk out onto my own life path. The external facts of my life are not so very different, but I am now choosing my path, and looking forward to the surprises ahead.

Using images in the way I do and teach others to do would seem to many people to be weird, odd, mad, or just impractical. To me, the dismissal of imagery – and the failure to build imagery training into our educational systems – is itself an oddity of technological societies. Imaging is as natural as thinking in words. It forms a central part of every ancient culture we know of, is the first language of the child, and has been used successfully by at least a small number of creative and effective people in every professional and business field I can think of.

I myself could not now go back to the world I lived in before I learned to use my inner images, any more than I could go back to a world without words. Images and words taken together are the way in which I now guide my life and make it work for me. And since I am naturally a verbal rather than a visual thinker, with a distinct inability to create full colour pictures in my mind, I believe that if I can use images effectively, anyone can. Over the years I have taught numerous people to do so.

I have chosen to create a new term, 'imagework', to refer to the self-help process that I have developed. The commonly used term 'visualisation' conjures up the idea of creating visual images, which many people, including myself, find difficult to do. Images can be sensed, felt, heard, smelled, and even tasted as well as seen. Furthermore, the term 'visualisation' has developed a whole range of associations of its own which are not all relevant to my approach. The term 'imagework' actually describes exactly what I do – work with images.

Writing this book has been a true labour of love and, somewhat to my surprise, a greatly enjoyable one too. I hope that through it I can offer and share some of the hard won insights of these years of experimentation, and encourage more people to find their unique path in life and walk down it with pleasure. Perhaps I am also going a little way toward repaying my own debt of gratitude to the language of imagery by reminding others of this lost heritage, and encouraging them to reclaim it.

ACKNOWLEDGMENTS

It is a pleasure to have the opportunity to say 'Thank you' for all the loving support and help I got in writing this book. My only regret is that while I'd like to write all the names simultaneously, the appropriate technology does not seem to have been invented yet. But thank you all, all at once.

Lois Graessle nursed me through this book from beginning to end, reading draft after draft, and offering loving encouragement and practical suggestions at every stage. Bryan Andrews, Yannis Andricopoulos, John Clarke, and Evelyn Hunter also painstakingly read earlier drafts of this book and offered absolutely invaluable editing help, advice, and support. Without such good friends and colleagues, this would have been a very different book, and writing it would have been a much lonelier experience. I cannot thank them enough.

A big thank you also to Charles Handy, Gaie Houston, John Grinder, John Rowan, Paul Rebillot and Rupert Sheldrake for their encouraging words which appear on the cover of this book, as well as for all helpful comments and suggestions.

My special gratitude goes also to Marion Russell, of Unwin Hyman, who not only commissioned this book and thereby made it possible, but also, by encouraging me all the way through and never doubting that a real book would appear at the end of all the struggle, made me believe in it too. And a warm thanks to Gillis Mackinnon whose cartoons have introduced real images into a book on imagework. And too, thanks to all the members of the Unwin Hyman team.

George Target, who got me going on this book in the first place by being so enthusiastic, taking the idea so seriously, and giving me that essential push at the beginning also deserves a very heartfelt thank you.

Many people's stories and insights appear in this book, usually with their names changed and identifying characteristics eliminated. But you will know who you are, and I thank you all.

I remember also with loving gratefulness as well as with lots of vivid images all those people who have worked with me, trusted me, grown with me, and helped imagework to grow and develop over the years, including clients, members of my original Open Circle growth groups, participants of Skyros Centre and Atsitsa, members of my Visualisation and Life Choices course, trainee therapists of the Institute of Psychotherapy and Social Studies, participants of the various workshops and courses I have facilitated at colleges, companies, centres, and local authorities in this country and abroad, and generations of BA Social Science and Certificate of Qualification in Social Work students at Kingston Polytechnic. We did have some amazing times together.

My father, Isaac Glouberman, who died in November, 1988, was a tireless, loving, and proud supporter and participant of every crazy venture I have gotten involved with, and he spent many hours discussing this book with me and offering every bit of help he could. The last letter I got from him before he died included a cheque to help me 'buy' time from my college to enable me to concentrate on writing. I'd like to give my deep inner appreciation and love an outer expression here.

My husband and children, Yannis, Ari and Chloe Andricopoulos, need a special deep appreciation for their willingness to stand by, encourage me, and tolerate all the results of having a wife and mother who was totally absorbed in writing. And for loving me through it all. And, in the case of Ari and Chloe, for letting me hog the Apple Macintosh computer.

More unusually, I also want to thank all my inner images and guides, some of whom appear in the book, and many of whom don't. I can truly say that without them this book could not have been written.

1

THE DOG, THE CARROT, AND THE SAMOVAR

One afternoon last summer, I sat down for a moment on a rock by the Aegean sea with a colleague, Alice, and we chatted about our work. When Alice asked me to tell her about imagework, I offered to demonstrate. I suggested that she allow an image to emerge that represented who she was or what she needed to know at that moment in her life. An image emerged of a tree in autumn, still full of fruit, but some of the leaves beginning to turn. The tree had a sacred feeling about it, a good deep ancient feeling. I asked her about the history of being that tree, and she remembered the time when she had been a sapling, and the tree had been more flexible, and had swayed with the wind.

I asked what was next for the tree. 'I need', Alice said, 'to develop a scent so that the bees will come and I can pollinate.' Then she laughed and called me all sorts of names, having suddenly realised that while she had started thinking of herself as a mystical middle-aged being, she really wanted to develop her female scent, find a partner, and have children. The whole experience took only a few stolen moments, but that evening, as I watched Alice dancing, her whole body language was different, and she looked ten years younger. Alice had just had first-hand experience of the power of the imagination.

CHOOSING A LIFE

Imagination is the ground of our being. Whatever we create in our lives, whether it is an omelette, a multinational corporation, or a love affair, begins as an image in our minds. Deeply held symbols, of which we are not necessarily aware, structure our thoughts, feelings, attitudes and actions. It is perfectly possible to operate all our lives without ever investigating these internal images or programs, but then we will have very little choice about who we are and where we are going.

Imagework is, in its broadest sense, a method of tapping into, exploring, and changing the images that guide our lives. It enables us all to develop personal vision – the ability to understand our present situation, and to identify and bring about the future that fits us best. The approach is applicable to every aspect of life, from self image to self presentation, from relationships to work, from health to creative problem resolution. All of these are underpinned by that unique human capacity to make, often unconsciously, images or models of how things are and how things should and could be.

Most of us choose our life rather the way we choose a new suit. A limited number of styles and sizes are available on the rack, changing somewhat from year to year, designed by mass market designers who seldom have our interests in mind. We pick the one that seems about right, guided by unexamined images which arise from fashion or familiarity. Sometimes we even let someone else pick it for us. When the choice doesn't really 'work', we either blame ourselves for being the wrong shape and try desperately hard to get ourselves right, wear that model until it moulds itself to us and feels familiar (although it may never really suit us), or search hopefully and longingly for another style or size on the rack that will be the perfect fit.

The purpose of image work is to help you to create for yourself a truly *haute couture* existence – a life that is made to measure for you, that fits you as you are rather than as you feel you should be, feels good as well as looks good, enhances your natural gifts, and makes your unique statement in the world.

2

In a sense, imagework could be considered a psychological equivalent of Yoga, a way to become and stay healthy in the deepest and widest sense of the word. Like Yoga, it is a wholly natural activity which does require a little training and practice. Imagework does not depend on an ability to see inner pictures, nor does it demand a willingness to 'think positively', or to espouse any particular belief system. Used occasionally, it is enlightening, but used regularly imagework can be truly transformative, and can give us an enduring sense of being at peace, at one with ourselves and with the universe, and in charge of our lives.

This book is a guide to using imagework as a self-help tool in everyday life. It is as much for individuals who are seeking to develop their own potential, as for experienced psychotherapists, counsellors, and management consultants looking for new ways to help clients manage and transform their lives.

3

WHY IMAGERY?

Why do we need imagery? What is wrong with words? The simple answer is that words and images represent two equally natural but very different modes of thinking. From everything we know about creative thinkers, successful achievers, and healthy happy people, there is no doubt that the most productive way to think and to be is to use both. Words are our socially structured way of thinking logically, analytically, and realistically, and of communicating effectively with others. Images are our personal idiosyncratic way of thinking intuitively, holistically, and metaphorically, and of communicating effectively with ourselves. By training ourselves to utilise and to integrate the two, we can bring together imagination and logic, and bridge the gap between inner and outer reality, so as to be both effective and creative in the world, and harmonious and peaceful within ourselves.

Unfortunately, while verbal language is emphasised and developed every day in school, imaging has the status of a forgotten art, almost totally ignored in conventional education and training. Why should this be? In a recent seminar discussion I had with college students, the realisation emerged that while their education had been relatively useful in helping them to understand and deal with the material and social world, no time had *ever* been set aside in the curriculum for understanding and dealing with themselves more effectively. Were this not so, this book would be superfluous, for its contents would figure alongside reading, writing, and arithmetic on the standard curriculum of school children.

WILL I BE ABLE TO DO IT?
(It's as easy as falling off a log)

Many people say that they cannot see pictures in their mind, and believe therefore that they are no good at creating images. The common use of the term 'visualisation' to describe the exploration of inner images exacerbates this doubt, because it

4

seems to imply a kind of inner seeing: this is one reason why I have chosen to use the word 'imagework' rather than 'visualisation'. In fact, everyone can create images that work for them, just as everyone can dream, and you get better and better with practice. It is simply that we all do it slightly differently.

Asked to picture a rose, you may be unable to 'see' the rose, yet you will have a 'sense' of the image – which may be partly visual but perhaps more strongly based on smell, feeling, sound, taste, or a combination of these. You will almost certainly be able to tell what colour it is, even if you cannot literally 'see' the colour, and in any case you will find that you can smell the fragrance, or hear the snip of a scissors cutting off the stem, or feel the petals. In the many imagework courses I have taught over the years, I have found fairly consistently that while no one has *ever* failed to have images, about 20 per cent of the participants do not see vivid pictures. This 20 per cent happens to include me.

Imagine this: I am holding a peach in my hand, a big, ripe, juicy, furry, unwashed peach. I hand it to you. What colour is it? Can you press your thumb in it and feel how soft it is? Do you like the furry feeling? Smell it. How does the smell make you feel? Perhaps it is a good idea to wash it. You turn on the tap and the tap squeals. Can you hear it? You wash the peach, feeling the cool water flowing over your hands. You turn the tap off and it squeals again. The peach now feels smooth and wet. You have an irresistible urge to taste it. You bring it to your mouth, and take a big bite out of it, and the juice dribbles down the side of your mouth.

If that did not produce a complete blank, then you can create images. Perhaps you don't like peaches. Try imagining your bedroom and walking into it. Or remember the house you lived in as a child and explore it. Or go for a walk in the woods on an autumn day, feeling the leaves crunch under your feet. Or listen in your mind to your favourite music. Or go skiing, skating, or swimming. Or fall off a log.

Creating images is easy because imaging is simply a normal mode of thinking, and moreover one that emerges in infants long before verbal language does. Imagework is basically a training in using images more effectively to understand and change our lives. It includes developing the receptive ability to tune into the images that guide us, and the active ability to create new images that enhance our health, happiness, and creativity.

How is this different from daydreaming? While daydreaming is a light hearted escape from everyday life that requires only the desire to be somewhere, someone, or something else, imagework is a focused activity designed to illuminate and improve everyday reality. With imagework, unlike daydreaming, however far we travel into the world of the imagination, we always bring back a gift to the everyday world in which we live.

AN IMAGE OF IMAGEWORK

It seems appropriate to find an image to describe imagework. This image comes to me:

I am, and have always been, a sailor, and have visited many strange places. I have always felt at the mercy of the elements, and have never quite understood why I have chosen this kind of life. One day I get hold of some diving equipment and for the first time I penetrate the world beneath the surface of the sea. I discover that what I thought was weather is really the heaving of sea monsters. I make friends with the sea monsters, while respecting their power and danger. They pledge to help me with my journey as long as I consider their wishes and concerns. By the time I climb back in my boat I am laden with gifts they have offered me. As I resume my journey, every now and then I don my diving equipment, and continue with my explorations under the sea. I get to know not only the monsters, but also their various friends and enemies. I begin to feel one with the sea. I learn now how to choose my journeys wisely, and to chart my course with their help. Each voyage now seems to have a kind of magical meaning that adds to its pleasure, and makes me grateful to be a sailor.

This book could be considered a diving manual for people who do not wish to sail on the surface of life, nor to feel adrift and purposeless, but want to understand and work with their deeper intuitive self and make constructive life changes. Imagery is the only diving equipment we need, along with some lessons about diving safely and effectively. As we learn how to understand and transform what we thought was our fate, there may be some monsters to confront. But what a magical gift it is to have the monsters on our side.

IS THIS JUST THE LATEST FAD?

Imaging is as ancient as human society. Pre-civilised people probably thought mainly in pictures, and may well not have completely differentiated between realistic perceptions, dreams, myths and visions. As psychiatrist Carl Jung[1] described their vivid world: 'Plants and animals then behave like men; men are at the same time themselves and animals also, and everything is alive with ghosts and gods.'

As language and rational thought developed, imagery, no longer a part of everyday life, became the province of specialists, as indeed it is today. Ancient priests, philosophers, saints, mystics, shamans, artists and psychics, not to mention psychologists, psychotherapists, and a few modern doctors are some of the specialists who have worked with imagery to help facilitate healing, power, wisdom, creativity, religion, spiritual development, personal growth, and loving relationships.

Healers of all kinds, for example, have traditionally used imagery to aid the natural healing process. Egyptian followers of the god Hermes believed in curing disease by visualising perfect health. Greek healers suggested to patients that they dream of being healed by the gods. Shamans visualise going on a journey and finding the sick person's soul.[2] In the same tradition today, Drs Carl and Stephanie Simonton[3] pioneered the use of imagery with cancer patients who, by visualising their cancer and their healing process, can encourage their bodies to heal.

Sigmund Freud[4] and Carl Gustav Jung[5] are probably the most well known of the modern day explorers into the inner world of images. Sigmund Freud, the father of psycho-analysis, considered images to be the natural language of our unconscious mind, and described the exploration of dream imagery as the 'royal road to the unconscious'. His technique of working with images, called 'free association', involved teaching patients to relax and allow their minds to follow a chain of images without censorship. Freud's view of the unconscious was that it is a rather primitive, frightening, regressive and animalistic world which contains all the thoughts and images we have pushed out of conscious awareness because they seemed dangerous or unacceptable. This picture of the unconscious still frightens many people, and stops them from exploring their inner self.

Carl Jung, Freud's famous colleague, had the very different belief that the unconscious is an untapped source of human creativity, inspiration, and spirituality. He too saw imagery as the passport to the unconscious, but viewed it more as a way of retrieving the 'sunken treasures' hidden there and pro-moting the healthy development of the human spirit. He developed the technique of 'active imagination', a method of inviting images to appear, amplifying them, and interacting with them, and considered the years he spent pursuing his inner images to be the most important in his lifelong journey toward self realisation.

Jung expected his patients to carry out the process of active imagination on their own, after an initial training by the analyst, and in this way to take responsibility for the dialogue between conscious and unconscious and therefore for their own psychic growth.[6] He was thus a pioneer in understand-ing and valuing the power of using images, not only as a part of psychoanalysis and therapy, but as an easily accessible self-help method.

The therapeutic uses of imagery are now recognised to some extent by most branches of psychology and psychotherapy, whether psychoanalytic, behaviourist, humanist or transpersonal. Some approaches specialise in guiding people through standard images or scenes, such as meadows, hilltops, caves, or meetings with wise beings and guides, which are universally powerful and meaningful.[7] Others use the person's own symbols or dream images as the basis for personal exploration.[8] Still others are aimed at harnessing the unique features of imagery in order to reduce stress and make specific positive changes in peoples' lives.[9] Imagery is also being applied effectively not only in psychology and psychotherapy, but in medicine, sport, education, business, creativity training, and spiritual development. Virtually any human activity can be facilitated in one way or another by engaging imagery.

Unfortunately, despite the plethora of theorists and practitioners now using imagery and visualisation, these are still conventionally considered an 'alternative' approach and not integrated into conventional medical or educational institutions. I recall a brief stay some years ago in an ultramodern teaching hospital: I was horrified by that very common practice of handing out sleeping pills automatically and indiscriminately to patients, including young adolescents. People who needed to spend considerable periods in hospital often developed a lifelong addiction to these pills. The obvious, and inexpensive, alternative of offering classes to train people in the use of imagery for relaxation and sleep, not to mention for speeding up the healing process, was simply never considered and was scoffed at when suggested.

There was one woman on my ward whose multiple health problems had necessitated long and frequent stays in hospital. She was now addicted to sleeping pills as a direct result, felt that she did not ever seem to get really better, and was generally depressed about her future. As I talked to her about how she could help herself through imagery and encouraged her to experiment with it, she felt hopeful for the first time in years. She thought I must be some magical healer sent to her by her guardian angels, because she had never heard of such a thing in the many months she had spent in a wide variety of hospitals. It was a potent reminder to me of how long a way there is to go before the ancient and universal art of imaging, along with other holistic non-technological methods, makes significant inroads into modern institutions.

THE IMAGEWORK APPROACH

My own approach to imagery has been influenced by most of the theories and practices in use today. A few stand out as having made a particular impact upon me in my development of the theory and practice of imagework.

Freud, and even more so, Jung, provided profound and comprehensive theories that served as an indispensable starting point and context. Fritz Perls' Gestalt Therapy, approach[10] constituted my first introduction to the power of utilising images to reveal deep meanings and new perspectives; I can still remember the awe I felt more than twenty years ago when I first used the Gestalt Therapy approach to dream symbols and saw the meaning of dreams unfold before me. Bandler and Grinder's NeuroLinguistic Programming[11] has had a far-reaching influence on my work, for it has dramatically refined and streamlined the use of imagery, providing a technology which specifies the sensory channels we use, and the precise steps to take so as to make powerful life changes quickly and easily. Silva Mind Control[12] impressed me in another way, because it offers a practical course in using imagery that appeals to people from all walks of life, and emphasises the power of imagery to facilitate not only one's own personal effectiveness, but also one's ability to connect with and heal others. Finally, it was the Findhorn spiritual community in Scotland, and in particular their philosopher David Spangler,[13] that introduced me to important principles of 'manifesting' or making happen what we sense is right for us and for others.

In the following pages I have synthesised these and other approaches, as well as the results of many years of my own personal and professional exploration and experimentation, into a comprehensive but simple do-it-yourself framework. My intention has been to clarify the underlying principles of imagery, and to indicate why and how we can use imagery to understand and change our lives in a way that always respects the subtle relationship between our conscious minds, our unconscious selves, and the world we meet as our fate, and which does not depend on any particular psychological or spiritual beliefs.

Chapters 2 and 3 are a discussion of the theory of image-work, which you may choose to read before, in the middle of, or after the more practical chapters. Chapter 4 to 16 offer a wide range of exercises, along with the principles behind them, which can help you to understand who you are, where you are going, who is going with you, and how you can make sure you get there. Chapter 17 is a do-it-yourself chapter showing you how to create your own custom made image-work experiences.

WHAT CAN IMAGEWORK DO FOR ME IN MY LIFE?

Introducing imagework into your life can be as exciting as the introduction of words into the life of a young child, for it is equally powerful and versatile and the more you use it, the more possibilities open up. Once you get the hang of it you will create your own personal way of using it but to begin with, let me give you some examples of the ways I use imagery every day to make sense of and enhance my life.

While some or all of the following examples may sound strange to you right now, do have patience. By the time you have mastered the contents of this book, they will not only seem perfectly normal, but you will wonder how you did without all these inner images. So do come back to read this again when you have finished the 'course', and see if I'm right.

11

WHEN I:

need to renew my energy in the middle of a long day

I take a few moments out to imagine being on a tropical island, or going for a cool swim in the sea, or taking a trip to a mysterious new dimension, or having a shaft of light flow through and around me. I return to my work feeling refreshed and relaxed.

want to become more organised, or more peaceful, or thinner

I first try out the 'new me' in my imagination by getting a picture of how I will be after I have made this change. I may, for example, imagine spending a day being a highly organised person. I can then find out exactly how this feels, what techniques I use, what attitude change I have made in order to be organised, and how it is possible to introduce more structure into my life without giving up my intuitive strength. Once I have become comfortable with this new picture of myself and have ironed out the difficulties in advance, I find myself naturally filling out the picture in reality and becoming the new organised me.

cannot resolve a problem

I create an image of the problem, and then view it from a variety of perspectives. The image itself helps me metaphorically to understand the nature of the problem, and the more perspectives I view it from the clearer the solution becomes. If my problem with starting a new project is represented as a bird trembling on a windowsill, for example, I can begin to understand the fear that is stopping me from moving. If I then take a kind of aerial view and look down upon the image from above, I may see that there are other birds trembling on other windowsills who would love to join me. Or that there is a haven not far from where I am that I can aim for in the short term.

Another approach I use is to consult an internal 'expert'

who I have created inside me and who can often suggest a solution that simply never occurred to 'me' before. My experts range from fictional detectives – especially Inspector Maigret and Hercule Poirot – to Albert Einstein, King Solomon, and old mangy streetwise dogs and cats. Each one suggests how they would solve the problem from their perspective: Inspector Maigret, for example, tends to sniff out situations and tell me what the atmosphere is, while Albert Einstein turns the problem inside out and shows me a whole new way of looking at it.

shop for clothes
I ask a particular internal expert, who seems to be an elegant Egyptian queen, what to buy. I know from experience that whatever she approves of is bound to have style, whereas I, left to my 'own' devices, often get it wrong.

am confused about my feelings and don't know what's bothering me or what to do about it
I invite an image to emerge – a boat in a storm, perhaps, or a tree without water – that is always a perfect metaphor for my situation and helps me to see what I need to do. As the boat, for example, I might realise that I must bring myself back to a safe shore before I try to go anywhere, or as the tree, that I should take care of my own needs if I want to have plentiful fruits to offer to others.

Or I may talk to the 'child in me', an image of myself as a small child, and find out in this way what early situation I am being reminded of, and how I can deal with it in a more adult way. Or I might take the position of an observer and view myself from the outside so as to sense or see what is not obvious to me from the inside.

begin a complex or difficult day or face an important event
I project myself to the end of it, imagining that it is the end of the day, or the interview, or the lecture, and I am feeling wonderful. I discover what the good feeling is and how I

achieved it, and in this way uncover my real priorities and the best way to pursue them. This is a method not only of harnessing the famous power of 'hindsight' *before* the event to see where I need to focus my energy, but also of having an underlying anxiety-free sense that it will turn out okay.

Thus, if before going to an important interview I imagine that it is the end of that interview and I am feeling good about it, I may find that my positive feeling is that I made contact with the interviewer, and felt we both had something to offer each other. I 'look back' and see that I did this by really enjoying the encounter rather than attempting to make a good impression. I can then walk into the interview looking forward to creating a relationship rather than to presenting an impressive picture. This doesn't mean that I know what will actually happen, but only that I am clear where I want to end up. Even when things do not go according to plan, I can keep in mind what it is I want to achieve, and I am even able to maintain the background feeling that somehow or other I will survive and learn something.

am having a relationship problem and feel stuck
I may imagine the person sitting opposite me, tell them how I feel, and then switch roles to try and see and speak from their point of view, continuing the conversation until something within me is resolved. In this way I can both express and let go naturally of feelings of hurt, anger, loss, or resentment that are poisoning my life or keeping me from trusting people. Or I may switch to the observer or wise counsellor position to notice what is happening between us, or visualise how the relationship would be if I could wave a magic wand over it, and in this way find out what specific changes I am wanting.

have an important decision to make
I go into the future – one month, five years, or even thirty-five years on – and imagine being a future me who is contented with how she is living: How did I manage it? What decision *did* I make? What is, in retrospect, most important to me? These

images of the future always come with a feeling of surprise, and yet also a deep recognition that on some level I have always known this.

am finding it difficult to fall asleep
I go to my 'House of Sleep' where I have a special bed, or I lie on a cloud made of the essence of fruits and flowers, and pleasantly drift off, or I begin to create a dream, and before long I am asleep.

fall ill
I talk to my body and ask for images that will help me understand what is going on, and then work on creating healing images to guide me gently back to full health. Or I go to my inner 'House of Health' to get professional advice from the health consultants there. They not only give suggestions about diet or exercise, but also about what attitude toward my life I need to develop if I want to stay healthy in future.

need to understand or help others
I tune into the other person, and invite images to emerge that are relevant to their situation and then share these with them. Or I imagine stepping into their body to find out what is going on. Or I consciously direct healing or loving energy toward them or towards my image of them. Or, more often, I teach them an appropriate imagework technique that will be more useful than I am.

need something that I don't or can't have right now
I experience it in my imagination with full pleasure – the relaxing holiday, the wise counsellor, the circle of loving friends – and in so doing I let go of my need to demand that the world give me exactly what I feel I need and begin to rely on my own resources. This is not to say that I can live my life in my imagination, but rather that by offering myself these very real experiences as and when I need them, I can be open and

welcoming to the surprising gifts that others, or the world, actually want to drop in my lap.

was about to write this book
I did some imagework to clarify the way ahead. I met, in my imagination of course, a dog, a carrot, and a samovar that helped me so much that I named this chapter after them. The whole story is in Appendix One, but suffice it to say that the dog, who seemed to represent the first chapter, 'told' me exactly what should go in the chapter, and even gave me the headings in order, the carrot provided me with ideas about the flavour and tone colour of the book, and the samovar encouraged me to contact my own bubbling creativity. I was very grateful for their support and guidance, as you will be to your images when you learn how easy it is to get them working with you and for you.

As may be obvious to you now, imagery is a mode of thinking, planning, and carrying through that I incorporate into every aspect of life. As one of my students put it: 'Imagework can be used by anyone anywhere: on the tube to work; up a tree; on the beach; in the middle of an argument; or while devouring an ice cream.' Besides all the specific benefits I gain, utilising imagery regularly over the years has transformed me from feeling myself to be a leaf wafting through the air, uncertain of where I was going and whether I would survive, to being a solid tree with deep roots that reach into an underground source, with enough sun, water and good earth to supply my needs, and lots of birds and animals in my branches.

I believe it can do the same for you.

PART ONE

The Theory of Imagework

2

IMAGERY
Reaching the parts that words don't reach

A little girl in California was swimming in the sea when a shark surfaced and ate her. Later her mother found among her daughter's belongings the series of drawings she had been doing in the few days before her death. These drawings clearly showed a little girl more and more submerged each day under a wave; in the last picture she was totally covered by the wave. The girl's mother came to believe that her child had unconsciously known about her own impending death, although consciously she had had no forebodings at all. This gave the mother a little peace.[1]

Did this child really sense the future? If so, how could she both know it and not know it? Why would the sensing of the future express itself in images rather than words? And do children have a connection with some inner wisdom that adults have lost? Elisabeth Kubler-Ross, who worked with the mother of this child and is a world expert on experiences connected with death and dying, claims that there are numerous examples of people, especially children, having unconscious knowledge of impending events to which their imagery is often the key.

For a host of reasons scientists are only now beginning to understand, imagery does seem to have a set of unique qualities which include a powerful ability to connect us with parts of us that words do not reach – in particular thoughts, feelings, intuitions, and body functions, that are normally unconscious. It seems also that babies and young children do have some ways of understanding the world that many adults have lost, and that imagery is the language that best represents and connects us with this early world of childhood.

THE UNIQUE QUALITIES OF IMAGES

To understand the unique qualities of imagery, let us use the following example: The word 'free' is an abstraction with a socially agreed upon set of meanings found in any dictionary (e.g. 'not in bondage', 'at liberty', 'not fixed'). It can be used in sentences like 'I want to be free of this relationship' or 'I will join you at the beach when I am free' or 'I have never really been free.' To understand it better I might think or talk about it, and might reach some important and complex insights, or even a systematic approach to the meaning of freedom.

Compare this with the image of a bird in a cage that people often think of when they are concerned about their freedom. To fully understand this image, I don't talk about it but rather I become it: I imagine that I am the bird. (You may want to do this too). This is what I discover:

> *I feel myself flying around, my wings beating, in panic, wanting to get out, feeling I will be caged forever. I sense that I have been in this cage as long as I can remember, and know that soon they will bring the food and feed me. I suddenly realise that the door is not locked, and, perhaps, has never been locked. I hover near the door of the cage, not daring to fly, suddenly fearing the open spaces, anxious about not being cared for and fed, terrified of the loneliness. Finally I fly out. I feel the wind against my body and I marvel at the beautiful view. I have never felt so wonderful in my life. Night begins to fall. I begin to feel frightened and alone. I wonder where I am going and what I will do. I long to return to the cage but don't know the way back.*

This image is tangible, rather than an abstract concept. It is a personal statement of my unique experience at that very moment, rather than a social category. And yet it probably has an intuitive meaning to you even if you don't know me, and the general theme is one that many people I have worked with have come up with spontaneously.

The image is difficult to analyse as it expresses a global whole: at one and the same time it describes my desire and my fear, the way I cage myself, and the implications of my choices, and all the levels of what leaving the cage might mean for my mind, body, and spirit. Unlike the word 'free', you cannot put it into a sentence; it is in itself a sentence, or even an essay, or a volume.

Because the image is metaphoric rather than literal, it is concerned with relationships, rather than objective facts. It doesn't point clearly to any particular freedom, and it might refer at one and the same time to my spiritual freedom, my freedom from my present relationship, and my desire to leave the city and live in the country. Nor does it specify an objective time: it may represent the way I felt when I left home twenty years ago, or my sense of what lies ahead twenty years from now. Either is experienced as being right now.

Thus images, in contrast to words, can be described as tangible rather than abstract, holistic rather than analytic, personal and idiosyncratic rather than socially constructed, spatial rather than temporal, and metaphoric rather than literal. They also enable us to live through any experience, past, future or totally imaginary, as if it were happening in the present.

By following through the image of the bird, I am able to discover what I only half knew and could not have formulated, and get a clearer idea of what I really want and what that will cost me. If I were to enter into the other aspects of the image – the cage, the air, the scenery – I would get more perspectives on my situation. As Jung[2] put it, 'The essence of the symbol is not that it is a disguised indication of something that is generally known, but that it is an endeavour to elucidate by analogy what is as yet completely unknown and only in the process of formation.' A thousand words are not enough to explore all the tender newborn concepts that the image struggles to let us know about.

IMAGERY AND THE UNCONSCIOUS

There is something about this metaphoric, holistic, deeply personal and yet at the same time highly universal language of imagery that seems to make it ideal as a bridge between our conscious mind and that aspect of our self that is normally considered to be unconscious. It is as if there is a domain of image making between the conscious and the unconscious, a safe territory with a shared language, that enables our conscious and unconscious to communicate with each other and negotiate lasting and farsighted, peaceful agreements. This is the domain where personal vision can emerge.

What is the unconscious? Is there a vast dark cavern inside us that is full of monsters that we don't dare know about? It is more useful and accurate to think of the unconscious not as a place, but as a quality. Even when we personify it for familiarity's sake and call it 'the unconscious', what we are really referring to are all those aspects of ourselves and of our experience of which we are, for whatever reason, presently unaware, and to which we find it difficult to gain access even when we wish to do so.

Up to a point, unawareness is a great gift. In order to get anything done, or to maintain any constancy and structure in our lives, we need to be able to focus the light of awareness on the problem which is at the forefront of our consciousness, and to leave all the rest in shadow.

But it is crucial to have a choice in the matter. Otherwise, it is rather like having at one's service a powerful computer, yet knowing how to utilise only one program, and being entirely ignorant of the merits or even existence of other programs. Although it is commonly thought that the unconscious is by definition unknowable (rather the way I feel about the workings of a computer), this is not really so. There is in fact a great deal of it that is knowable, and which we don't contact simply because we have never learned how. This is where imagery comes in.

THE UNCONSCIOUS BODY

You can tell yourself to stand up, and then do it, but normally you cannot instruct yourself to salivate, or to have your heart beat faster, or to activate your immune system in quite the same way. These latter functions are part of what is called the autonomic nervous system and are usually viewed as being unconscious. This only means that we cannot affect them with words. Images are another matter.

Try telling yourself 'I want to salivate'. Does it work? Now try an image: imagine vividly sucking on a big juicy sour lemon, rolling it round in your mouth while your whole face screws up. Any saliva?

What if you want to relax? Telling yourself, 'I must relax' tends to have the opposite of the wished for effect on your heartbeat, metabolic rate, and blood pressure as you grit your teeth and try to relax. But picture yourself sitting peacefully on the grassy banks of a lovely clear river, and then running happily into the water and paddling around before stretching yourself out in the sun, and allowing the warmth to seep right through you. If you have imagined this vividly, you have just done wonders to all your physiological stress indicators. The autonomic nervous system does not usually listen to instructions given in words, but it does like images.

In healing illness, imagery can be used to gain messages from the body as to what is going wrong, as well as to create images that will transform the functioning of the autonomic nervous system. The imagery of cancer patients, for example, has been shown to enable clinicians to predict how fast growing their tumours are and what their prognosis is, and doctors have also found that helping patients to change their imagery is a more or less direct way of enlisting the body's natural potential to heal itself.[3]

Not only the functioning of the autonomic nervous system, but even the way we hold our bodies, stand, and walk is an expression of our unconscious images, and is often not under our conscious control because it is now so habitual. You have probably noticed that if you watch someone else's posture and movement, you can often guess pretty accurately what their image of themselves is. And as in the case of our autonomic nervous system, if we change our internal images, our body tends to follow suit.

THE UNCONSCIOUS AS DUSTBIN

Thoughts, feelings, memories, and general psychic energy are also often unconscious, or inaccessible to the rational verbal mind, but accessible through imagery. Some of these contents are, as Freud underlined, unconscious because from infancy on we are forced to exclude from awareness certain aspects of ourselves, and we do this by 'repression' – the act of forgetting, and forgetting that we have ever known and forgotten it.

These aspects of ourselves are probably the most difficult to gain access to because we positively do not want to know about them. Freud's technique of free association to dream imagery is designed to trip the conscious mind almost by accident into this repressed unconscious, but even so, rather a lot of interpretation by the analyst is usually needed to understand what is going on, and often there is a great deal of resistance on the part of the patient to accepting these interpretations. Imagework, being a self-help tool, is not primarily directed toward this repressed unconscious, although it can sometimes lead us into hitherto resisted understandings when we are ready for them.

THE UNIVERSAL UNCONSCIOUS

In addition to this repressed unconscious, there are also vast unconscious potentials that we may never have known which

can be contacted through images. Jung's theories are relevant to understanding this aspect of ourselves because he developed the view of the unconscious as an untapped reservoir of meanings that both date back to the primordial history of the human species, and hence are shared by all humans whatever their personal experience, and also project forward into our evolutionary future.

Jung believed that besides our personal unconscious there is also a transpersonal 'collective unconscious'. Its contents, called archetypes, include ancient symbols – like mother, death, rebirth, the hero, power, God, the devil, the persona, the shadow, the inner male and female, and the self that appear in dreams but can also be found in myths and fairy tales of cultures we may have had no contact with but whose ways of thinking we naturally share. Through this more universal unconscious, we can also tune intuitively into a spiritual dimension that tells us 'from whence we come and where we are going'.

More generally, Jung believed that we are often unconscious of our ability to reach intuitively beyond the limited understanding of our personal self into a domain of more universal knowledge. Jung tells many stories of people who had dreams or images that told them of events which they could not have known about in their normal frame of understanding. Some, as in the case of the little girl whose pictures seemed to foretell her death, were events in the future, while others seemed to involve tuning, with some extra-sensory awareness, into the feelings and thoughts of other people who may have been far away.[4]

It is as if with imagery we can open a window into a dimension which does not respect the boundaries of past, present and future, nor the boundaries between people, and we can connect directly with experiences that are not part of our personal history, or indeed that have not yet happened. Young children, who, as we will see, have not yet developed these boundaries, may well be more easily in touch with this dimension.

In doing imagework, people often have images that, while having personal significance for them, also turn out to be related to the feelings or thoughts of other people, or to correspond to something they have not yet experienced in the real world. Alice, learning imagework in a group, came up with an image of a daisy, and suddenly saw a sunflower to the left of the daisy; as it turned out, Jane who was sitting on her left, had been picturing a sunflower. This ability to pick up images from other people is in fact so common that examples of it occur in every group I have worked with.

For Carol, another imagework student, the image of a totem pole emerged; when she went a few days later to a museum she had never been to, she found the same totem pole. Similarly, Keith had an image of a swan, and arrived the next day at a French village whose emblem was that particular swan.

More significantly perhaps, Ellen came to me to decide whether to go to a homeopathic or conventional doctor, and the image of a peacock emerged during her exploration. When she went to consult with the homeopath, he had a little gold peacock sitting on his desk, and this helped her decide to go and see him, a path that turned out to be absolutely right for her. Tony, looking into the future that was right for him, imagined himself speeding down a motorway in a powerful automobile; a few months later he rang me to say, 'Remember that road? I've actually been on it, and in that car.' Not only had he literally driven on that road, but also metaphorically Tony's life began at that point to zoom ahead in terms of success and power.

Many people do not believe it is possible to reach beyond our everyday personal knowledge in this way. I myself do, because I have experienced it, and have witnessed others doing so too. But you may not. This doesn't really matter, because we have so far to go in contacting and making use of our vast untapped personal resources that we can totally transform our understanding without ever having to presume that we have reached beyond our personal self.

THE EVERYDAY UNCONSCIOUS

Aside from the boiling cauldron of repressed instincts, and the great reservoir of universal wisdom and intuition, there is a rather more mundane but equally profound aspect to the unconscious which I like to call the 'everyday unconscious'. This is the whole world of thoughts, assumptions, and intuitions that we *almost* know but cannot quite formulate or utilise – that could perhaps be described as being at the tip of the tongue of our mind. While our work with imagery can connect us with all the aspects of the unconscious, the everyday unconscious is the main province of imagework, and the easiest aspect to make contact with.

One way to look at the role of imagery in this regard is that an image tends to represent not the foreground, but the background of an experience, and thus brings to the fore the assumptions or mental attitude that lies behind the event that our conscious mind may be grappling with. For example, I phone my friend, who cannot see me this evening, and I find myself feeling not only disappointed but very angry. Why? I cannot figure it out. So I turn to imagery. I find within me an image of myself as a baby bird looking for companionship while all the other little birds are excluding me. I realise that I am experiencing a background hurt which is an old one about feeling left out. My friend, by being busy, became one more member of the group who doesn't need me around. I now remember how excluded I felt at the party I went to the night before, and understand that last night's event touched off these old feelings, and today's phone call reinforced them. My anger at my friend was a reaction to this hurt. Understanding the context of my anger now, I am able to reflect and to recognise that my friend probably was simply busy. I phone another friend who invites me to drop by.

Another way of looking at this aspect of the unconscious is that it is as if we have a vast range of files, but have not been taught how to retrieve all the information: as though we were taught to retrieve alphabetically by author, but are not aware that we can also retrieve by subject, by date, and by style.

Some of our inner files, like those from early childhood, are inaccessible because they are stored in imagery or in body sensations rather than in words. Other files are out of reach because they don't fit our notion of ourselves or our way of thinking at that moment. The images that we create and use can then be seen as keys to hitherto inaccessible information and ideas, with each image opening up another file or set of files. The files were not Top Secret, but simply our knowledge of the filing system was inadequate.

OPENING FILES

Fritz Perls[5] founder of an approach to self-exploration called Gestalt Therapy, used imagery in just this way to open files we have not been able to get to in our normal approach to life. In Gestalt Therapy one might find oneself having a conversation between one's right hand and one's left hand, or between the train and the train track seen in a dream, or between oneself and one's long deceased mother. You would allow an image to emerge on the empty chair or cushion opposite, talk to it, sit in the seat opposite and 'be the image', and respond. It has never ceased to astound me, however many times I have experienced and observed it, that by physically shifting seats and in this way taking on another viewpoint, we can gain access not only to a whole new perspective, but even to concrete information that one would have sworn one didn't know.

I remember Jan who complained that she could never remember appointments, and that this made her boyfriend furious because he always did. For example, she had no idea what time she was to meet him tomorrow. 'Ask him', I said. So she pictured him on an empty chair, asked him, and switched into 'his' seat to be him. 'Four o'clock' she said promptly the very instant she sat in his seat.

If this idea is hard to grasp, it is worth thinking about how we operate in different roles in our everyday life. A friend asks you a question and you expand upon the answer with great authority and enthusiasm; then you walk into an examination hall, sit down to read exactly the same question, and your mind goes blank and you feel stupid and useless. All your acquaintances comment on how patient you are when they make mistakes, but when your spouse makes a roughly similar one, you explode instantly. You are an expert at helping other people to solve their problems, but your own look like hieroglyphics to you. My driving instructor could never understand why I kept failing my driving tests when I was such a good driver while he was in the car. 'I'd love to be a fly on the wall,' he used to say mournfully each time I failed once again.

Different roles thus serve as channels for different attitudes, knowledge, feelings, and actions. When we restrict ourselves to a particular role we restrict ourselves to a particular set of potentialities. Change the role, in reality or in your imagination, and you change your potentialities. Try the empty chair technique yourself. You can't understand why your mother is ignoring you: ask her on that chair opposite, and then sit there and find out the answer. You want to know what the interviewer wants: switch roles and be the interviewer and find out.

More generally, not only specific roles, but even our habitual ways of thinking, including our verbal language and concept of self, guarantee certain limited channels. We literally do not have the ability to think of anything that doesn't fit in with our normal view of ourselves and the world. But the more perspectives we can imagine, the more channels we can open up.

Be wise: ask the wise old person inside for his or her view. Be a great judge of character: find out what Hercule Poirot, Miss Marple, or Inspector Maigret has noticed. Be a great lover: ask Aphrodite to help. Find out the best way to sleep: go to the House of Sleep and consult the experts there. Have hindsight before you do something stupid: put yourself forward into the future and look back. Find out what others think of you: take the perspective of looking down upon yourself, then from the right and from the left, and see what you look like. When you have finished exploring all these perspectives, you can get back to your own standpoint and decide what to do.

Childhood Files

The world of early childhood is one of the most difficult aspects of our unconscious mind and body to gain access to through our normal verbal means. Most adults are in a position now where we have forgotten almost everything we experienced in that period of our early infancy before we learned to use words.

Freud characteristically attributes this so-called 'infantile amnesia' to repression, i.e. to pushing down the unacceptable memories of being an instinctually free child. Psychologist Ernst Schachtel[6] however, points out that it may well be that old filing problem. Our childhood mode of thinking was so different from our adult mode that we simply cannot get to it.

It is as if when we learned language, we created a new filing system, and forgot the old one which was based on images and body feelings, not realising how much vital understanding and knowledge is stored under the old filing system and is now totally out of reach. Words are wonderful for expressing an abstract systematic, logical world with socially defined and shared meanings. But as infants and young children we lived in a very different world, and imagery, not words, was our first language. The language of imagery with its concrete, holistic, personal, and timeless qualities is ideally suited to mirror the reality of the young child.

The world of infancy, like the world of images, is a concrete, tangible one – we didn't learn about the world, but rather lived it and sensed it directly. We used the traditional five senses to feel, hear, see, smell, and taste the world, and also our sixth sense of intuition to pick up the currents of feelings around us.

We had no concept of time, and whatever happened was always now and forever, until the next thing happened. Unable also to step back and observe and abstract, we were totally immersed in a sea of experiences in which all things were connected, and everything was possible. The boundaries of inner and outer, mind, and body, self and other, or past, present and future had not yet been drawn. There was only experience.

Our world was also wholly personal. We took it for granted that things were as they seemed, and did not even guess that there was an 'objective' world upon which others might be imagined to have a different perspective. As infants in the first half year of life, if we lost sight of an object we didn't search for it because it had stopped existing as soon as it had gone out of sight. Similarly, as very small children, if we covered our eyes, we thought no one could see us.

Indeed the world was not 'out there' at all, but rather was experienced wholly as a relationship. Our rattle was not an object out there; we knew only the act of rattling which included baby, rattling, and rattle, in one. Mother, equally, was not out there, for it was only the relationship of mother – baby that we understood.

Our lives then were totally active, committed, and involved at every moment. We did not separate ourselves from anything else; we were the world and the world was us. Play was our work, for we were not trying to achieve anything in the future, but were simply engaged in living and in creating meaning. And our first symbols were images, active images of relationships rather than of objects, of rattling rather than of a rattle, of mothering rather than of a mother out there.

We then developed verbal language, and in so doing, gained access to a whole new world view. Our first words were rather like images – private sounds with their own personal, active meanings that may have only been understood by our parents, who knew that 'cover' meant orange peel as well as lid, and that 'da-da' meant daddy, and the cornflakes daddy ate for breakfast. Slowly but surely our private language gave way to the language of the culture. A whole set of possibilities now opened, rather like rubbing an Aladdin's lamp.

We were now finally able to learn about the world from a distance. We could talk about the cup when it was not even in the same room. We began to recognise that there was a world outside of our own direct experience, and that it had certain objective properties that were not as they seemed to us. Things could look bigger or more and yet not really be so. We gained access to time, and eventually to abstractions and systems. We became able to communicate in a complex way, both in speech and in writing, not only with parents but with teachers and with society in general. We learned to be in control of our speech, our thoughts, and our actions. We became, in fact, socially and intellectually skilled members of society.

The Double-edged Sword

But every advance is a double-edged sword. Objectivity also led to alienation, to a world that was indifferent to us. Gaining access to past and future also permitted us to spend most of our time shut out of the vividness of the present. Abstraction enabled us to feel unreal, and socially structured category systems limited our thinking to socially acceptable grooves. Becoming skilled communicators allowed us to lie to others. Thinking in words gave us the ability to lie to ourselves. We faced, in other words, the danger of loss of innocence, the fall from Eden. If you have ever sat in a public place and compared the facial expressions and stances of children and adults, you will know what I mean.

Here the importance of choice becomes crucial. Were we able to continue choosing both these modes of being, or to integrate them and create a whole new mode, all would be well. As adults, we would still be able to play with our friends on grassy fields with all the innocence of the child, and do our accounts with the knowhow of the adult. We could take care of our relationships with the spontaneous direct unconditional loving and commitment of the child, and the skill and judgement of the adult. Likewise, our new business project could be approached with the intuition, involvement, and daring we had as children, and the seasoned experience we have gained since. We truly would be moving forward into a mature understanding of ourselves and the world.

However, quite early in our childhood, our culture, in the form of parents and teachers, intervened to value one mode of thinking and being over another. We learned implicitly that developing and becoming 'grown-up' is like climbing a ladder with the concrete personal and active world of the child at the bottom, and the abstract, social, systematic world of the adult at the top. The faster we climbed it, the more intelligent and mature we were considered to be. Jean Piaget[7], whose theories of cognitive development are the bible of modern educationalists, describes this ladder brilliantly, taking the view that it is absolute and universal.

In fact this particular ladder, which is based on skill with words and numbers, could best be seen as one *branch* of a tree of development. It is only selected and made the basis of psychological tests and other means of evaluation because it happens to be the ladder of initiation into our particular culture. Other branches include sound/music/rhythm, movement/dance, and psychological intuition as well as imagery. All are distinct modes of thinking and being, and each has its special contribution to make, yet all have been undervalued in our educational system. Imagery, which may be the most versatile of these symbolic systems, has been particularly neglected.

At a certain point in our childhood, then, most of us sensed that facility with words and numbers was the way to achieve value, status, and applause. Imagery, along with other non-verbal skills, took a back seat.

OUR VERBAL SELF

As adults, verbal language – words in sentences – is the main tool we use, both in thinking and speaking, to make sense of the world and of ourselves, and to give ourselves the feeling that we are rational, purposeful beings. We have developed, in fact, a verbal self.

As we have seen, this verbal self cannot represent all of us. The abstract systematic logic that words are so good at is much more suited to express the adult rather than the child in us, the logician rather than the poet, the conscious rather than the unconscious part of us.

The specific language we think in, also directs us toward the particular kind of rationality understandable and acceptable to our own culture. The grammatical structure and word meanings of any language contains within them the assumptions about reality that are prevalent in that society.[8] For example, a language that allows us to 'save', 'waste' or 'lose' time, and grammatically describes 'ten minutes' with the same structure as 'ten books', will give us the impression that time is a set of quantifiable objects. As we will see in chapter 15 on time and money, this strange view of time may be the basis for many of our difficulties.

Verbal language, then, forms a kind of groove for our thoughts and gently guides us in certain directions, making some kinds of thoughts easier to say and think than others. Other feelings, understandings and desires are there, but because words do not open those files, we simply don't think about them. Nor do we know that we are not thinking about them: our verbal self is totally unaware that it has gaps in its understanding and information. And the worst of it is that because the verbal self has been entrusted with the task of making sense of ourselves to ourselves, when it isn't privy to our real motivation it just makes up a story, which we naturally believe.

Hypnotists know this trick of the verbal self very well. Picture this common stage demonstration: a hypnotist puts his subject into a trance and tells him that when he emerges from it he will forget what he has been told, but when the hypnotist scratches his nose he will get up and open the window. The subject is brought out of the trance, and in a few moments, the hypnotist scratches his nose and the subject gets up and opens the window. 'Why did you do it?' asks the hypnotist. 'Because it was suddenly cold,' answers the subject confidently. The audience roars with laughter. The subject looks bewildered.

One well-documented naturally occurring example of this process is the case of a man referred to as PS, who had a 'split brain', i.e. a severed connection between his two brain hemispheres. His left (verbal) hemisphere literally did not know what the right (imagery and non-verbal) one was doing. PS, or at least his verbal self, didn't seem to find this a problem. What the verbal self didn't know, it was quite prepared to make up.

In one experiment, the experimenters flashed a picture of a chicken claw into the visual field of his left hemisphere, and a snow scene into that of his right hemisphere, and then asked him to point to a picture related to what he had seen. Quite correctly, he chose a picture of a chicken with his right hand (which is connected with the left hemisphere) and a shovel with his left hand (connected with the right hemisphere). They then asked him, 'What did you see?' His response, which because it was in words was based only on what the left hemisphere knew about, was 'I saw a claw and picked the chicken, and you have to clean out a chicken shed with a shovel.' This was given not as a guess, but as a statement of fact that he never thought to doubt.[9]

The more we restrict ourselves to using verbal language in explaining ourselves to ourselves, and in directing our activities, the more likely it is that we will have a misleading picture of who we are and what we truly feel, believe, and want. This account of ourselves will be skewed in the direction of the conscious, rational, technologically-minded, and socially skilled adult aspect of ourselves that we are encouraged by our culture to identify with, and we will not know that this is not the whole story. Our thoughts, and our lives, are likely to continue to be selections from that mass-produced rack offered to us by society.

Now You Have a Choice

But unlike PS we do have a choice. If we learn to use the language of imagery to symbolise our experience, and integrate its understandings into our verbal thought processes, we can begin to get a sense of self that represents the whole person.

Creative thinkers and doers are always multi-modal in their approach. Einstein, for example, always thought in images and then translated his understandings into phrases like $E=MC^2$. Dream images have been reported time and again as the basis of major discoveries, with an enormous amount of more conventional knowledge and experience having led up to the ability both to have and to interpret the crucial dream. Effective business managers, after gaining the necessary background knowhow and figures, typically use intuition to reach decisions and then report these decisions in words and numbers. Healthy people, physically and mentally, similarly have been found to combine a childlike active imagination, innocence and playfulness with adult empathy, judgement, and skills. One way to look at it is that words and logic are excellent as technological tools, but we need imagery to create the vision that this technology serves.

Most creative people feel that they have developed their approach despite, rather than because of, their educational experience. Few of us have had the benefit of the kind of multimodal educational system which would help us to develop that potential for effective vision which lies within all of us. But if our schooling has not offered us this opportunity, it is not too late to offer it to ourselves.

The moral of the story then is: what you don't know *can* hurt you. You cannot possibly be understanding yourself and guiding your life successfully when you know so little about your true needs and goals, and have access to so small a portion of your potential to reach them. Learning the language of imagery is really simply taking back your birthright, that original language that you knew so well so long ago, and developing it with your adult skills for the purposes of your adult life.

This doesn't mean discarding words, for words too have their own power, and just as a picture is worth a thousand words, so a word is worth a thousand pictures. Indeed, it is only with words that we are able to discuss imagery in this chapter. Why not use both imagery and words, and develop an adult sense of self that is really wise, creative, effective, playful and authentically you?

═══ **3** ═══

LIFE CHOICES, LIFE CHANGES, LIFE CHALLENGES

Choosing the images we live by

One rainy afternoon during one of the most painful and difficult periods of my life I sat in a café wondering how I'd managed to land myself in such a mess. How did such a terrible series of accidents and mistakes happen to me? Suddenly, in an abrupt shock of self recognition, I saw that I myself, or at least the deep unconscious me, must have chosen this life. I was horrified. How could this be? Yet it must be so. At that moment I understood what it meant to take responsibility for one's life. I also decided then and there that my unconscious was not totally reliable as a guide, and that I'd better take my lifeboat off automatic pilot and start to help with the steering.

The unconscious has many faces: dustbin and reservoir, childish fantasy and wise vision, coward and hero, destroyer and creator. We have seen in the previous chapter how important it is for our conscious selves to dip into the unconscious to benefit from its resources and to understand its intentions. But it is also true to say that the unconscious needs the conscious light of awareness as well as the influence of life's challenges to create the life that is really right for us.

To make fully conscious and effective life choices, we need to learn to use images as a bridge between our conscious and unconscious selves, as well as between our inner intentions and our outer actions. To put it another way, we need to tap into and understand the images or programs we live by now, and create new images that will take us into the future.

THE PROGRAMS WE LIVE BY

Through the years, we have created deep programs or patterns or models that tell us what the world is like, what we are like, and how to relate to and operate in the world. These programs are by now usually habitual or unconscious, even if they were once consciously chosen.

These programs we live by range from the sublime to the ridiculous, from the deepfelt inspiration of our organism to the childish decisions about life we made much too prematurely. Our present day choices are guided by these inner programs, and these choices could be said to constitute who we are in the world now. Before we decide to make changes in our lives, we need to understand and respect our present self. This means finding out about all the programs that we are now unconscious of.

Images can be considered to be the symbolic expression of these programs; indeed some theorists even believe that our programs literally are images.[1] Think how your whole experience of life and decisions about how to deal with it would vary depending on whether you had a deep implicit image of the universe as a disappointing mother, an efficient machine, or a playful demon.

Sigmund Freud went so far as to say that all our behaviour is unconsciously determined, or, in other words, that all our choices are based, at least in part, upon unconscious images that derive from the past but control our present and future. Since Freud viewed the unconscious to a large extent as the receptacle for our unwanted and unacceptable memories, images, and instincts, it is rather as if what we thought was a dustbin is in fact the in-tray of our inner managing director.

Jung, almost more than Freud, believed that our lives are dominated by our unconscious – both the personal and the

42

more universal collective unconscious. In his view, not only our actions but even our destiny flows from the unconscious, for much of what meets us as fate is somehow an expression of those aspects of the unconscious that we have not explored and integrated with our conscious selves. If so, whatever happens to us, no matter how clearly it seems attributable to chance alone, can be seen as a challenge to our conscious self to dip into our unconscious and learn a new lesson, or formulate a new program for living.

Where do we keep these programs? Scientists are still proposing and refuting theories as to where they are. One way of looking at it is that they are in our body – in the ways we carry ourselves and move and relate to the world.[2] Another is that they are in our brain: the right hemisphere of the brain, the neo-cortex, the limbic brain, or the entire brain functioning as a 'hologram' such that each part represents and is connected to every other part, have all been candidates.[3]

Rupert Sheldrake,[4] a leading and very controversial biologist, suggests that the guiding images are not in the brain itself, but rather that our brain, like a televison set, tunes into fields of memories, images, and thoughts around us that shape our minds and bodies. These guiding fields evolve and change, affected by the experiences of past and present members of our society and of our species. The reassuring implication is that if enough of us transform our own images in positive directions, we may have a beneficial effect on the image fields of our culture and of our world more generally.

WHERE DO OUR IMAGES COME FROM?

Many of our guiding images emerge in infancy and early childhood, at a time when imagery is the dominant mode of thought, and they guide not only our thoughts but our body functioning and our whole way of being. For example, if you have an image of the world as a disappointing mother whose milk is promised but never comes, this may stem from a time in your early childhood or infancy when you were abruptly taken away from your mother's breast, or inadequately fed, or disappointed in other crucial ways.

This image may be a contributing cause to an ulcer, as your stomach acids are unconsciously working in an angry frustrated expectation of nourishment. It may also affect the way you stand and walk (protective of your heart), the way you think about other people (expecting them to disappoint you, and feeling hopeful and furious at the same time), the occupation you choose (perhaps you become a scientist because you feel that in the laboratory you are safe from such disappointments), and many other major and minor aspects of your life. The image is deeply personal, and may never have been expressed in words, thought about consciously, or discussed with anyone.

It may also be, as Jung indicates, that some images come from the infancy and childhood of our species, and express ancient knowledge that has been lost from our rational technological minds. Thus, the very concept of 'mother' is, according to Jung, an archetype, a human symbol which babies are born having a predisposition to understand because people have always had mothers. A whole range of potential attitudes are naturally available to the baby and child, ranging from mother as witch to mother as goddess, inherited as surely as the ability to walk upright. While the general approach may be inborn, however, the details are filled out by our own personal history.

Other images simply result from our day to day experience of living. They represent the lessons we have learned about ourselves and about reality and the choices we have made and are a convenient shorthand that make it unnecessary to re-invent the wheel every day. A 'good little willing donkey' for example may represent the technique you have evolved to get appreciation and sympathy from others and this will serve to guide your thoughts, actions, expectations, and communications.

Fortunately, compared with the deep structure of language, images are relatively accessible. They can literally be looked at, understood, worked through and transformed. Thus while they contain our programming rules, they are available to us as self programmers to explore and to change.

RECEPTIVE AND ACTIVE APPROACHES

To discover our inner programs, we begin with the receptive stance of being open to images from our unconscious. We ask the unconscious for an image appropriate to a certain issue or question, or to our life in general, and the unconscious, as unerringly as a computer, seems to be able to oblige. Exactly how to do this will become clear in the chapters ahead.

To take an example from business life: Jack, the head of an innovative market research firm, was working with me on trying to see where his company was going, and the image of his company that emerged was of a schizophrenic monkey. The monkey was running around in a jungle, frightened of predators, head and body not integrated, and not knowing what to do next. It had not always been in this position; at one time the jungle was full of bananas and no predators, and the monkey simply gorged itself greedily. But now there were fewer bananas and lots of predators, and the monkey was in this terrible state.

What could the monkey do? Jack's answer came quickly. It could move to a part of the jungle where there were few bananas, but few predators. The monkey would have to work hard to find the bananas but at least it would feel safe. Life would be even better than in the old days, because the monkey was no longer so greedy.

This worried businessman understood immediately the seriousness of his firm's state of chaos and lack of integration. Times had changed, and they were having to compete much more fiercely for the market which had once been wide open. He was in fact operating on the basis of a model that was no longer appropriate in his present environment. More importantly, the image told him how he could solve his problem best. Fewer bananas but fewer predators was the answer for

him. He is now working on developing a less lucrative but also less competitive corner of the market in which he has a unique expertise.

Thus while a balance sheet is often referred to as a snapshot of a business at a given moment of time, imagework offers pictures of a very different order that can sometimes be far more helpful. In this case, Jack asked for an image that represented his company at this point in its life. He could have invited an image of the best business consultant in the world who could look at his situation and advise him. Or he could have created an image of the House of Business, where he could go and get advice. Or put himself forward in time five years with the instruction: 'It is five years from now and I am happy with how the business is going. What am I happy about? What did I do to get here?' Or worked with a dream he had had about his business. Or even put himself back into a childhood situation which felt similar, found out how his method of dealing with situations emerged then and didn't change with adulthood, and tried out in his imagination a totally new way of coping.

All these methods, and many more, detailed in the pages ahead, are ways of setting up an effective consultation between the conscious and unconscious so that we can understand our present patterns and see where to go from here.

SENSING GOALS AND SETTING GOALS

Creating an image of our present situation is often the best way to see our next step, as in the case of Jack and his schizophrenic monkey. Sometimes, however, we may wish to invite images that are more directly about the future. As we have seen in the previous chapter, images seem to have the power not only to sum up our past and present experience, but also to sense what lies ahead. The images that emerge through working with imagework can tell us as much about what we are about to become as about what we have become.

By discovering within us the images that point to the future, we can learn to sense goals rather than to set goals: to sense the rightness of any particular pathway for us, and then to encourage it to emerge. A story that comes to mind here is of Michelangelo chipping away at a rock. '*Ai signore,*' calls a little boy. 'Why are you hitting that rock?' Michelangelo turns around and shouts back, 'Because there's an angel inside and it wants to come out.'[5] Our future self is so like this angel yearning to be set free from the stone.

One of the easiest ways to use imagery to call up our future goals and choices is to imagine that the future has already happened and that we have already made the choice: 'What was it I did?' we can then ask, rather than 'What should I do?' It's rather like one of those children's mazes where if you start from the beginning you go down lots of false paths, but if you cheat and start at the end, it is delightfully easy to see the answer. By putting ourselves into the future, we cheat, and use the advantages of hindsight before the event.

When I was still in my teens, a college professor asked us to do just this: he instructed us to put ourselves forward into the future and write our obituary. I wrote a long and detailed story of my life, much of which has turned out to be accurate, including the fact that I left the USA, lived in another country, and married someone from yet another country. The countries were different, but the essential relationships were correct.

Most interesting of all was the fact that according to this obituary, I wrote a book about how to integrate psycho-therapy into the educational process rather than considering it to be something you do for people with problems. As I was writing this bit of the obituary I remember feeling puzzled, for I was planning at that time to be a psychotherapist and believed in the traditional approach to helping people.

Yet as it has turned out, my commitment to imagework is precisely about using tools I have gained through doing psy-chotherapy as adjuncts to everyday life, and the view that this should be part of the educational domain, rather than solely being a branch of medicine or healing. How did I know? Was it a self-fulfilling prophecy, an image that encouraged the pathway I took even when I was not consciously thinking of it? Or was my intuition telling me something about the nature of my deeper self that my rational conscious mind did not know? Or, indeed, was I actually intuitively tuning into the future?

Whichever it was, and perhaps it was a combination of these, I am still astounded at my ability at the age of nineteen to predict what I would come to do, after long struggle, in my thirties and forties. In writing this book, I find that the knowledge that this work is so central to me that I sensed it long ago immeasurably strengthens my commitment to it. Imagework seems to be the angel that was wanting to emerge from me.

PRACTICE MAKES PERFECT: THE LAZY PERSON'S WAY

The receptive process of tuning into images that serve as messages from our unconscious is usually sufficient to enable us to make new changes and choices, either through seeing our present pattern and finding the way forward, or by directly tuning into our future selves. But at times, even when we are pretty clear about what we want to do next, we find it difficult to take the step. We then need to help ourselves by actively creating and practising new images of ourselves. This is a way of preparing ourselves for the enormous leap involved in doing and becoming something new.

Any new plan or project, whether it involves creating a new business, a new life, or a new approach, is really also a change in ourselves. If I want to write a book for the first time, I need to be able to see myself as the kind of person who writes books. If I want to move house, I need to be able to imagine myself living happily in a new environment.

Change is not always welcome. It may be threatening and frightening because the 'new me' is an unpredictable stranger who I can neither identify with, understand, nor control in my usual ways. It may be disturbing, if I have unconscious negative assumptions about the 'new me' even when the change superficially looks wholly positive. It may in fact feel rather like jumping blindly into an abyss. Working on our images first gives us a map of the territory we are about to encounter; it may help us to see that what looks like an abyss in the dark is really a lovely grassy field.

Funnily enough, the importance of stopping to prepare or even practise an image before acting even holds for the times you are lying in bed and wishing you could get up, wondering why other people seem to jump out of bed so easily. It certainly holds for all the plans, and projects, and self-help schemes, and diets that you have never carried through. Your image of how you are – lying snugly in bed, or lazily not doing your work, or eating too much and feeling bad about yourself – is probably clearer, more familiar, and/or unconsciously more attractive than your image of how you believe you want to be. If you work on your image rather than on making yourself do something, the desired action follows naturally.

In my case, I found that getting up in the morning was

impossible because it just meant work to me. My image was of getting out of a nice warm bed and doubling over with a heavy burden on my back. When I learned to lie in bed and visualise being up and having a lovely cup of tea, I found myself out of bed in an instant.

To understand the power of imagery to facilitate change it is important to realise that when we create images we are not simply running an internal home movie of pretty pictures. We are actually experiencing what we are imagining; the experience is real, even though there is no objective event corresponding. You may not literally have gone for a swim, for example, but if you have fully imagined it, you will look and feel more refreshed, relaxed, and energetic, and real and measurable physiological changes will reflect this.

I remember a fascinating experience when I was being guided through what was called a 'video feedback' session in which I looked at myself on the video screen and actually talked to myself. At one point, feeling sad that I, or my image on the screen, looked old and worn out, I said, 'But you're not seventeen any more', thinking of how it was to be seventeen. Later my guide pointed out to me, laughing, 'And of course at that moment you looked seventeen.' When I played back the film I discovered that amazingly enough this was true. At the moment I was thinking of being seventeen, the years fell away, and I had the innocent, characterless face of a young teenager. I have never forgotten that face, nor ever needed to be convinced again that I am what I imagine.

A good way to think of it is that energy follows thought – what we do follows in the pathway or fits into the thoughtform created by our imagination. We need to be careful about what we imagine, for we may unknowingly become it. I notice that this even works when I cut a slice of bread. My habitual expectation that I will cut it crooked leads me to do so. If I remember to stop a moment and imagine a beautifully sliced piece of bread, this slice appears as if by magic.

Like anything else, sometimes once is not enough and we

need to practise. The more we strengthen our image of how we want to be, and the more habitual it becomes, the easier it is to step into it. An experiment with basket-ball players in America conveys this point rather dramatically.

The players were divided into three groups of equivalent standard. Those in one group practised normally, those in the second did not practise at all, and the players in the third group did not practise physically but spent an hour or two each day mentally shooting goals. At the end of the experiment, the normal practice group was only very marginally ahead of the mental practice group, and both were more than 20 per cent better than the no-practice group.[6] This is why I often call imagework the lazy person's way to life change.

THE WORLD WE MEET AS FATE

We don't live in a vacuum, but rather in a complex, challenging, difficult world which is sometimes beautiful and exciting but may also seem painfully confused, heartbreaking, and unfair. The world we meet as fate is as responsible for our images as our images are responsible for our world. The world therefore must be seen as a partner in the imagework process.

While we often talk of self development, in a sense the self does not need developing, because our true inner self could be said to be perfect as it is. However, the self needs to live in this world, and therefore to work out the most appropriate, efficient, and harmonious relationship with the world. It is really the relationship between ourselves and the world that is imperfect, and needs development.

The process of creating our relationship to the world is rather like negotiating an obstacle course. Every obstacle we meet in life, personal or impersonal, requires us to adjust by developing an attitude or approach or image that helps us to understand and deal with it. Every so often we need to rethink these adjustments. This process of rethinking adjustments to the world is what is usually referred to as self development, and this is also what we are doing when we use imagework.

The net effect of the imagework should be not only more useful attitudes to the realities of everyday life, but a more effective way to make appropriate changes in these realities.

But no matter how many adjustments we rethink and change, and how much inner and outer work we do for ourselves and for others, there will still always be factors affecting our fate which remain beyond our conscious control. These factors have been attributed variously to our unconscious, the universe, God, the Devil, the spirits, or the luck of the draw. Changing our attitudes does have an influence on our fate, but it is just as common for our fate to put pressure on us to change our attitudes.

The fact that nothing is ever totally under our control is not necessarily a bad thing. As the saying goes, power corrupts, and absolute power corrupts absolutely.

RESPONSIBILITY AND BLAME

As we begin to confront in ourselves the extent to which our unconscious choices dominate our lives, and particularly when we find that it is possible to change some of these choices, it is easy to confuse taking responsibility for our lives with blaming ourselves. If it was my own choice that got me into this mess, doesn't this mean that I am to blame?

Illness is a good example of this. In the good old days, when things got too much and you went under, you could relax and be ill, because you knew that at least, unlike depression or anxiety or any other psychological phenomena, this just couldn't be construed as being a personal weakness. Then the word got round that illness was meaningful. Germs could not be to blame; why had you caught the illness and others hadn't? You'd phone up and say you were ill, and your colleagues would wonder why you were ill. This, too, was now your fault for not living better. There was no escape.

Blaming yourself is really a splitting process whereby the 'good', or clever-after-the event part of you splits off and blames the 'bad', 'mad', or 'stupid' rest of you for the mess you have made. Anyone could have done better. Why didn't you? This blaming is not a solution, but part of the problem – for it implies that the conscious self is in a position to 'know better' and to attack the unconscious self rather than work with it. The blaming also tends to hold us in a vice of attack and defence that prevents us from moving.

Taking responsibility for your life really means recognising that you – all of you – made a choice that was almost inevitable given who you have been and your life pattern. There is nobody to blame and nobody to do the blaming. And not only did you choose your path but in some sense your path chose you – for we mustn't forget the part that the world plays. Further, these situations are likely to recur until some shift, internal or external, frees you from that pattern and moves you onto another. To facilitate this shift, it is best to thank your unconscious for doing its best, even thank the world for offering you the challenge it has, and then work together to find some alternatives.

In a sense, then, taking responsibility is the opposite of blaming, for it means recognising that as long as our pattern was unconscious we had no choice. It is only at the moment that we acknowledge our past lack of choice that we open up to real choice. Having fully understood our patterns from the past, we can begin to create new patterns that are more appropriate for our present and future.

ME, MY UNCONSCIOUS, AND THE WORLD

As you begin to utilise imagery in this way, you are essentially setting up new lines of communication and therefore new sets of relationships both within yourself and between yourself and the world. What attitude should you take in these new relationships?

It is helpful to begin by thinking of the unconscious as if it were another human being with whom you have an intimate connection, who basically loves you and wants the best for you, and who speaks the language of images rather than words. This person is old, wise, and powerful, and has infinite resources to place at your disposal, and yet can also sometimes be very childish, obstinate, and destructive. He or she is in many ways living in the past, and refusing to give up attitudes that may no longer be sensible.

To communicate with this being you need to learn the language of images, and begin to express your questions, beliefs, needs and wishes directly, as well as to listen carefully. Be appreciative when you get the response or help you asked for, and accept gracefully when you don't.

The exchange does not go one way. You with your youthful maturity and up-to-date logical thinking have a great deal to offer this being, who may, however, take some time accepting and integrating your contributions into a long established pattern of beliefs. Convincing your unconscious, for example, that the world is no longer a disappointing mother and is now a challenging playmate may take some doing.

Be prepared for a joint democratic effort, in which you consult each other in the setting as well as execution of tasks. No technique your conscious self chooses to use will work all the time, and furthermore, just at the moment you need help most you may well be disappointed. At that moment, when you *have* to get an answer, you are more likely to be in such an agitated state that you will be unable to relax fully, you may be making demands rather than requests from the unconscious, and you may even confuse wish-fulfilling images that your conscious mind has created with true responses from your unconscious. It is as if your unconscious, like lots of people you know, is determined to be a free agent and hates to be pushed around or to have to fit in with your expectations.

When this happens, don't consider this a reason to end the relationship, but rather an opportunity to review it, to learn how to distinguish between demands and requests, and between wish-fulfilling images and the 'real' thing, and then to begin afresh with a slightly different attitude. The fact is that if you could actually get all the answers you wanted, and reach all the goals you set yourself, you would not be gloriously enlightened but simply insufferable.

The third partner in this venture is the world. Your images are not 'in your head' but all round you and are embodied in your relationship to the world. Whatever changes you make within yourself should eventually express themselves in some external form – in new attitudes and behaviour, different life choices, or even a shift in the pattern of your 'fate'.

The real events, things, and people you become open to through these internal and external shifts will function in a kind of feedback loop to reinforce or extend the changes in yourself. Changes in your images and thoughts that make no impact at all even in the long run on your life are slightly suspect; changes in your life that have no effect on the way you experience yourself and your life are ultimately unimportant.

Before long you will discover that you are beginning to accept life's challenges, make fully conscious life choices, and carry through with real life changes.

PART TWO

The Practice of Imagework: Basic Course

=== 4 ===

HOW TO DO THE EXERCISES
Putting imagework to practice

Imagework is first and foremost not a theory but a practice. This chapter offers a general summary of the principles of doing imagework – how to guide yourself, others, or a group, what basic steps are involved in most imagework exercises, and what attitude to take to the process. Chapters 5 – 17 are the practical part of the book, offering specific exercises, and the principles behind them, on a variety of life themes and problems: chapters 5 – 11 could be considered a basic course in imagework, while chapters 12 – 16 offer further topics to explore, and chapter 17 is the summary do-it-yourself chapter.

You may not wish to read the chapters in order, but it is advisable to begin with this chapter and the following chapters 5, and 6: the present chapter outlines the general principles of imagework; chapter 5, teaches you how to relax; and chapter 6 guides you through a basic imagework exercise. Chapter 17 is a good place to end, because it reviews the various imagework structures so that you can make up your own exercises whenever you have a problem to solve or a skill to improve. I would advise you also to skim through the rest of the chapters just to get an idea of what is available; then you can go back and do the exercises that are most relevant to you at any particular time.

Trying to explore every aspect of your life is a daunting

proposition, and there will be some areas which appeal to you more than others. Start with whatever feels easiest and most useful to you, and extend yourself later to areas that are less familiar. As long as you take your time, and only try out new areas when you want to, imagework will be a pleasure to look forward to rather than yet another heavy responsibility in your life.

CLEARING A SPACE

When you are about to do an exercise you need to prepare the space and time within which you can work. A quiet space where you can expect not to be disturbed, with the telephone off the hook or on the answering machine, and an intention to take time for yourself are a good beginning. You may already be in the habit of doing this because you have a similar routine in place for an activity you consider important, be it yoga, a bath, or sex; if not, then this is not a luxury but a necessity, and it is long overdue. For many people, just getting to the point where they feel they have the right to take time for their inner selves is a giant step towards taking better care of their lives. Once you have become really familiar with a particular exercise (or with imagework generally), you will find that you can do it anywhere: in your office, on the underground, lying on a beach, or waiting in a queue.

All the exercises can be done on your own, or with someone you trust, taking turns guiding and being guided, or in a group. If you are working with a partner or guiding a group, read the exercise instructions at least once before you start, so that you are familiar with the general direction in which you will be moving. If you are working on your own, it is even more important to familiarise yourself with the exercises before doing them, because you will want to be in a relaxed and receptive state and not worried about what comes next. It is an excellent idea to put the instructions on tape, leaving lots of gaps between instructions and questions to give yourself a chance to respond.

RELAXING, AND INVITING AN IMAGE

The first step after reading a chapter and reviewing the exercises is to relax. Take the time to learn relaxation, not only because it is crucial for your health and well-being, but because it will enable you to enter more deeply into your images. Once very familiar with the work, this relaxation step can be shortened and even left out altogether because you will automatically know how to relax enough to allow images to emerge.

Not everyone finds the idea of relaxation relaxing; some people in fact get tense as soon as the word 'relax' comes up. But relaxation does not need to be based on physical rest. Some people relax more when they jog, or rock climb, or ski, or make love. Whatever activity makes you feel at one with yourself and the world is relaxing, and you may find that during or after doing it is the best time of all for imagework.

After relaxing, the next step is to learn to invite images to emerge. This really means learning to step aside and allow yourself to do what is really natural and simple – to think in images. If I were to say 'think of a fruit', an image or word representing a fruit would certainly pop into mind, and you would say 'banana' or 'orange'. This totally normal everyday process is really all I mean by inviting an image.

Even this most natural process can become a problem if you feel, as you may already be feeling, 'I won't be able to do this,' or 'I'm sure I'm no good at imagining,' or 'Trust me to spoil everything at this point', or even 'I've got to get this right (teeth clenched); I've got to try hard and make sure it works.'

Imagework is not a test that you can fail. Everyone can create images, and you yourself are doing it all the time. If no image comes up now it will pop up some other time when you are using less effort. In fact, even if you don't get any image you can still do imagework – some of my best work with people has resulted when they told me they couldn't see anything, and I suggested that they step into the nothingness.

I cannot emphasise enough how important it is to welcome

61

the first image that comes, whether it seems immediately
· desirable or not. I know now from long experience that
many of the people who say that they can't get an image or
that their image is not working for them really mean that
they got an image they didn't like and discarded it, and
then got into trouble. Every image is useful, and the less you
like it, the more useful it is likely to be. If you get a number
of fleeting images, just choose the one that has most power
for you.

Whatever image comes up, do thank the unconscious. This
may seem an odd thing to do, but it reminds us to be grateful
for our images, and to be open to whatever comes up or
doesn't come up for us. It is useful to think of the unconscious
as a person who, just the same as everyone else, loves being
appreciated, and is more likely to help you in future if the help
it gives is acknowledged.

GUIDING THE IMAGEWORK

Once the image has emerged, either for you or, if working in pairs, for your partner, you need to guide it with understanding, care, and love so as to make the best conscious use of this gift from your image-making domain. You will find clear instructions about what sort of questions to ask yourself or your partner, and what directions to move in within the various chapters. Basically, guiding imagework effectively involves learning how to combine staying in contact with the reality of the image, with using structure and reason to provide a context, meaning, and direction.

The approach you take could be likened to an adult taking the hand of a child and exploring an exciting world together, mutually respecting the qualities each brings to the adventure. Think of the person, or the part of you, who is guiding the process as the adult who provides the overall direction and structure, and brings a mature, loving, judgement, understanding and caring to the situation, but who sees the child as a valuable person and partner in the endeavour. The child is the one who is being guided, daring to step into the world of the unconscious as long as there is a safety line coming from the adult, daring to admit when the 'emperor has no clothes', and offering startling insights for the adult to make sense of.

You are playing the adult role when you give the instructions, ask questions, sense the meaning and context of the imagework, and reflect and apply it effectively to everyday life. You take on the role of the intrepid child when you 'become' the image, and respond to questions and guidance by sensing intuitively the deep answer inherent in the special reality of the world of the imagination, rather than the intellectual answer the adult has always given.

Remember this cardinal rule as the adult: *Speak in a language that a five-year-old can understand*. This should not be confused with talking down, which in my view you needn't do with children of any age, but rather means expressing your thoughts in simple language. Sophisticated language tends to kill feelings and promote intellectualisation and distance. To put it another way, to the extent that the language of imagery is the language of childhood, by using words that are too adult you force the child to grow up in order to answer the question. This principle of using simple language actually holds, in my view, whenever you are dealing with people on a deep level: the simpler the language, the more of the personality you will engage. And do try, too, to speak to the image as if it were present in the room with you – whether it is a dog, a stone, a wise person, your mother, or Hercule Poirot – responding to it sensitively rather than by formula.

As the child, make sure you have established the tangible reality of the image for you – e.g. feel the ground under your feet, or sit as the person sits – before you try to respond to any questions. Learn to distinguish between responses that are glib and habitual, and those that really emerge from sinking into the concrete image and finding the truth, palatable or unpalatable. As a general rule, pause first and then discover the answer.

Learn also to value the surprise of finding out what you didn't know. Writers of fiction often talk of how their characters take over and do what they want to do rather than what the author expected. As the child you need to be just like one of these characters; as the adult you need, like the author, to be prepared to go along with your characters wherever they lead you.

When fully experienced, an image is not in your head but in your whole being. So do feel free to use not only your mind but also your body to express the image. Carrying thoughts into an active form – moving as the image-being would, or making sounds to express the feelings, or grimacing as you experience something painful – is an excellent way to enhance the power of this work.

If you are working on your own without a partner, it is a good idea in the beginning to set out separate chairs facing each other so that the adult and the child can each have his or her own chair. This means that while doing the exercise you move back and forth between the chairs depending on which role you are playing.

Eventually you will learn to carry on the process on two levels in the same seat, as adult and child at once. In so doing, you will begin to heal the splits that we all have between the inner adult and child, mind and body, rationality and emotions, logic and intuition, and you will become more able to approach situations with all your varied resources. But even so, whenever you get a bit stuck or need extra energy in your imagework, it is best to return to using separate chairs because this can make your imagework easier and more powerful.

The principle of using different chairs also holds when your imagework involves a conversation between two or more people or images. Generally, it is easiest if each character has his or her own chair, and that you actually move when you want to enter a new role.

While you are working with the image, you are really inviting the unconscious to reveal itself. When you have come to a natural conclusion in the work, congratulate your conscious and unconscious selves for their team-work. Then it is time to reflect, and to utilise the resources of your conscious, rational mind to make sense of the experience, map it back onto your life, draw conclusions, and consider what concrete action you wish to take. Hopefully, once your image of what you need to do in the future is totally clear, you will find yourself following this inner plan naturally and with a minimum of inner struggle. You may wish to do some of this reflecting while still at your deep level of focused relaxation, and some later on, after you have emerged.

Even if you feel you have worked through an image, don't discard it as being of no further use. If you keep it on the 'back burner' and dip into it every now and then when you have a moment, you may well find that you are gaining greater insight and moving on in your understanding as the days go by. An image's work is never done, so to speak.

To summarise, the basic general structure of the imagework, with appropriate variations for the different types of exercises, is:

Preparation: Clearing a space and relaxing
1   Inviting an image
2   Studying and exploring the image
3   Working toward resolution
4   Appreciating
5   Reflecting
6   Looking forward
7   Emerging

It is a very good idea also to keep an imagework journal and write about or draw what you have experienced and learned. If you make concrete decisions based on your imagework, write these down too and check them off as you do them. You may also want to set yourself distinct imagework objectives in it, and work on each in turn, for example: relationships, work, creativity, health, money, and spiritual life. Creating sculptures or dances is another way to express the imagework. By doing any of these planning and follow-up activities, you will certainly extend the power and permanence of the insights you have achieved.

The more you give your imagework a concrete form, the easier it is to hold on to the images and work with them. You will also create a wonderful record of the 'inner safari', as one imagework student called it, that you are about to take.

WORKING WITH A GROUP

Working with a group can be a very powerful experience, because the energy of the group focused on the same task, or focused on working with one person's image, is a wonderful amplifier. Over the years I have had to develop methods of using imagework in large groups in a way that keeps the group together and yet enables people to have their own deep experiences. It is not always possible to focus on each individual's images in turn without eventually boring everyone else. Nor is it desirable, in my view, to spend the whole session guiding people through private experiences that they only later share with the group.

These are the three basic methods I use to do imagework in a group:

1   *Taking the whole group through the exercise*: To work with the whole group at once, take the group through the exercise but only do one step at a time, with the group or pairs sharing after each step. Have the group relax, and then take them through the first step. Ask them to signal by raising one finger when they have 'achieved' that step so that you know what is going on with everyone and can judge the pace appropriately. When the first step is over, suggest that people keep their eyes closed but to share what is happening, either with a partner, or with the group as a whole in an informal way. Sharing with a partner creates an intimacy which facilitates trust and depth. Sharing with the group makes possible a group involvement in each other, and can create a really exciting atmosphere. It also allows for a kind of public statement of intentions which is often a first step toward carrying through changes in your life. A combination of both is best. After the sharing, continue to the next step.

2   *Demonstrating and then pairing off*: In this case, work with one person at a time in the middle of the group to demonstrate how the exercise works. Two examples are probably sufficient. Then summarise the structure, and have people divided up into twos, or threes and work with each other. If people are in twos, they should take turns guiding and being guided, giving each other equal time. If in threes, the third person is the observer, learning by watching the interaction, and coming in to be helpful where appropriate; this is an excellent way to learn imagework. In this case, of course, you need to give enough time so that all three play all three roles and each has equal time.

At the end of each guided experience, members of the pairs or threesomes should give each other feedback on their experience of how it went, being as specific as possible as to what worked well and what didn't work so well; there is nothing like honest feedback to facilitate learning and growth.

3 *One at a time*: Go through the group, asking each member in turn to present their image, and guiding them through it briefly. Keep reminding the group that as one person presents an image, everyone else should also be picturing it, going into the landscape of the imagination with them. Encourage people to ask questions so that everyone is involved, after reminding them of the general principles of asking questions sensitively and effectively as described above. It is also lovely if at the end of a process people send the image-being or person special wishes for the future; these can often be both apt and very moving.

All of these three methods are best performed by experienced group leaders, as a great deal can happen at once. A self-help group with members taking turns being the guide can, however, be very effective, as long as you make sure that everyone takes shared responsibility for helping each other through the images.

CELEBRATIONS

One last bit of advice: celebrate. You are about to embark on a wonderful adventure, on which you will meet some incredible friends and guides. And should you come up against any problems as you get started, think of the words of the Chinese book of ancient wisdom, *The I Ching* or *Book of Changes*[1]: 'Difficulty at the beginning works supreme success.'

=5=

RELAXATION AND SLEEP
I need a holiday from myself
(Or: As I sit here doing nothing I'm changing)

I never used to know that I had a right to rest. I always took for granted the fact that I was not living a worthwhile life unless I was working, or, if not actually working, at least worrying about not working. I suspected that it was dangerous, boring, useless, and highly immoral to stop before I dropped.

In any case, I believed implicitly that life is an exam that is always too difficult. It never even occurred to me that life might not require all my resources all of the time. If things seemed easy for a little while, it was only because there was a trick in there somewhere. Needless to say, I regularly operated in top gear until I collapsed, either exhausted or ill, and when I recovered I began again.

I can picture myself some years ago standing on an escalator at the airport on my way to run an imagery workshop in Norway. I suddenly realised that I was in a state of high anxiety. What was all this anxiety about? I had run similar workshops before; I couldn't quite see what the problem was.

On reflection, I discovered that my problem on this occasion was that *I wasn't worried enough*. It all looked too easy – what could the hidden trick be, my unconscious had obviously wondered, as it spurred me on with an anxiety attack to keep watch on all sides. As soon as I reassured my unconscious: 'Slow down, you don't need to use all your resources,' the anxiety evaporated. I could just imagine my unconscious sighing with relief: perhaps there was such a thing as an easy exam.

Learning to rest is really at the heart of imagework. Imagery promotes relaxation, and relaxation promotes imagery. When you create images, you enter into an altered state of consciousness and you relax naturally. Conversely, the more relaxed you are when you work with images, the deeper and more powerful your images are likely to be. This is why it can be so difficult to get an image just at the moment you feel you desperately need one; unless you stop and relax first, you may simply be too keyed up to be receptive.

In a broader sense, the whole of this book can help guide you toward true rest. As you uncover your false assumptions, finish your unfinished business, replace your 'I should's' with 'I want to's' and find a way of life that suits you, relaxation will come naturally. In the meantime, however, gently retraining body, mind, and spirit to rest is one of the most crucial and most straightforward by-products of imagework.

Relaxation is crucial because, as is now pretty widely known, it is actually dangerous, boring, and useless, though perhaps not immoral, *not* to rest. Aside from the emotional and spiritual pain of never resting, there are direct physiological implications.

A stressful situation, i.e. one that calls on us to carry out some action or adapt to some change, provokes the body to prepare for fight or flight. What is called the 'sympathetic' branch of the autonomic nervous system is dominant, and the heart beats faster, the metabolic rate increases, blood pressure increases, we use up more oxygen, we send more blood to our muscles and less to our organs, and we increase our cortisone levels.[1] This is nature's way of saving our lives in emergencies. It may be exciting or painful depending on its intensity and on our own tolerance levels. But it must be temporary.

When it is resolved, and it is time to relax, the opposite or 'parasympathetic' branch of the autonomic nervous system needs to take over, and the body must return to normal functioning – heart beat slowing, metabolic rate decreasing,

and so on. Mental and physical health and balance rely on this natural alternation of challenge, excitement, and stress with peaceful relaxation, reflection, and regeneration.

But life never seems quite like that. Situations go on and on, with no clear action to be taken, nor any clear resolution that leads to rest. There is always a long list of things to do, problems to solve, unfinished business that seems unfinishable. And deeply held beliefs often make it unacceptable to rest unless one is forced to do so.

Many people live in a state of chronic stress, always feeling tense and threatened, and becoming more and more out of balance. Energy decreases, the ability to cope and to resolve problems is weakened, and illness threatens. Hormonal imbalances may occur, the immune system may be suppressed, and aging is accelerated. Like an elastic band that is constantly being overstretched, we lose our elasticity, and every now and then we snap.

The trouble with suggesting that people learn to relax is that those of us who need it most are often also those that honestly believe we are too busy to stop right now – perhaps next year, or when the next project is finished. Then, when we are lying awake unable to sleep, or so tense that we cannot think, we may be ready to stop and try anything; but unfortunately it is at these moments that it is most difficult to begin to learn to relax if no relaxation habit has already been set up.

Luckily, the deep connection between relaxation and imagery means that we can, so to speak, kill two birds with one stone. The form of relaxation advocated in this book is a kind of active relaxation, intended to increase our ability to cut out external stimulation, and use our resources as fully as possible.

Since no matter how busy you are, you are aware that you must sometimes stop and think, understand your present situation, and plan your next step, you will quickly learn that you have no time *not* to relax and focus deeply if you want to be effective rather than simply to look efficient. A cartoon on my wall given to me by one of my imagework students puts it well: 'As I sit here doing nothing I am changing – even though it doesn't look like it.'

In fact, since sleep brings dreams, also of immense use to the project of understanding and planning your life, you can truly say that you are never idle. (This may or may not be something to boast about, depending on your point of view about life.) If you are relaxing regularly, you will also find that you feel happier and more peaceful, have more energy, and are less prone to illness – so it can't be bad.

Learning to relax and learning to encourage sleep are similar processes. In both cases you need to let go of tensions, create appropriate images, and sink into a deeper state of consciousness. The difference is that in the case of sleep you need to go deeper, and to create images that are conducive to sleep, while in the case of relaxation you want to stay alert enough to be able to focus, and your imagery needs to be suitable for that purpose.

There are many methods of relaxing and of getting to sleep,

and you may well have tried a few already. I will suggest here a basic method with a few alternative and optional steps so that you can experiment and find what works best for you. I will also list a number of short forms: if you can just spend a moment doing a 'quick relax' as many times a day as you think of it, you'll be amazed at the result. Remember also that each step of the longer relaxation method can be used as a self-contained 'quick relax' too.

I would also like to remind you that you may already have ways of relaxing that work for you, and these may not involve sitting down. If going for a brisk walk or a jog in the woods, or tuning into Beethoven, or swimming a few lengths is your way of relaxing, then do use those methods instead of, or in addition to, the following. On the other hand, when you cannot get to the woods or the pool or the record player, imagining them may be just as powerful.

RELAXING: BASIC FORMAT

The following relaxation method is based on a sequence of relaxing steps. You prepare by clearing a space in your life. You then begin by sighing, rolling your eyeballs up and then dropping them – this strange eyeball rolling is said to increase the alpha waves in the brain and in this way to aid relaxation – and then you send a breath to all the parts of your body. You then relax body and mind step by step, and imagine pulling a dark heavy screen down through you and allowing a light feeling to come up, concluding with letting your mind or spirit float up and out.

Then you use images that invite relaxation and, if you wish, deepen the relaxation by counting down, and also create a relaxation cue that you can use in future. Now totally relaxed you do your imagework. Some people find it useful first to create a spiritual context for the imagework, by invoking a higher power or consciousness than one's normal conscious self. When you are ready to emerge from this relaxed state, you count up from your deeply relaxed state to a more active one.

The steps, then, are:

Preparation: Clearing a space
1 Beginning to relax
2 Relaxing body and mind
3 Allowing a dark heaviness to descend and a lightness to rise within you
4 Images to invite relaxation: Stepping into a relaxed
   you or creating a sanctuary
5 (optional) Counting down to deepen
6 (optional) Creating a relaxation cue
7 Doing your thing: imagework time. (optional: after
   creating a spiritual context)
8 Emerging

RELAXING: BASIC EXERCISE

Preparation: Clearing a space: Take a moment to give yourself permission to rest. Mentally or physically clear a space which is your personal territory and is not to be intruded on by worry, phone calls, or other internal and external demands. Be aware that if a real emergency came up, you would be able to respond totally appropriately, but otherwise, nothing else needs to be dealt with right now. If there is anything you feel worried about, you can settle your mind by simply writing it down to look at later.

1 *Beginning to relax*: Sit quietly, and focus on your breathing for a moment. Give a few long loud sighs, feeling that each sigh starts at the top of your head and goes down through you, coming out of the soles of your feet. Whether your eyes are open or closed, roll your eyeballs up toward the

ceiling, then let them drop. Notice any tension in your body and then let go of it. Imagine that you are sending a breath of peace to every part of your body. Remind yourself that you have nothing to do, and no place to go, and nothing you need worry about just now.

2 *Relaxing body and mind*: Focus on each part of your body in turn. Feet, legs, etc. First be aware of how they are, saying hello to them. Now tense them and feel how that feels, and then relax them, and let the breath of peace go there. Then say, 'My foot is heavy and relaxed, and as my foot relaxes I feel a deep sense of peace through me.' Or just 'Heavy and warm, warm and relaxed'. As you move on to other parts of your body, mention the earlier parts too: e.g: 'My shoulders relaxed and peaceful, my torso and legs, relaxed and peaceful, my feet, warm, relaxed and peaceful'. When you get to your face and head, include your scalp, the muscles around your eyes, your lips, tongue and throat.

Let the relaxation go into your mind. Imagine that there is a little person in your head, sweeping all the thoughts and worries into a small pile of dust. You can feel their brush tickling your brain folds. Then blow it all out. Now this little person has a paint pot full of white light, and paints the inside of your brain with white light.

3 *Allowing the dark heaviness to descend and the lightness to rise*: If your eyes are not already closed, let them close, and feel your eyelids to be like a dark heavy blind you couldn't raise if you tried. Imagine that you have a dark heavy blind at

the top of your head, and pull this blind down through your body, and let the heaviness sink into the ground. Allow a feeling of lightness to emerge from the ground through your body and into your mind. Let your mind or spirit feel light, and float up, as if through a hole in the top of your head, and float out, like a cloud on a summer afternoon.

4 *Images to invite relaxation*: (Either of the following works beautifully. Try both. Note that while the first is quick, straightforward and powerful, the second involves creating a safe place or sanctuary, which is also deeply enjoyable, gives you an internal haven, and can be a starting point for other imagery work.)

Alternative A: Stepping into a relaxed you: Think of a time when you have been completely relaxed and feeling good about yourself, or an activity that makes you feel like that. This may be quiet, like listening to music, or active, like skiing. When you get a picture of yourself feeling that way, step into the picture and match your breathing to the breathing of that relaxed person.

Alternative B: Creating a sanctuary: In your imagination, go to a place where you've been happy or where you could be happy: a real place or an imagined one. And if you like, you might build a house there, made of whatever real or imaginary material you want. And in this place there is a feeling of deep peace and you can stay there for days and days, although it may be only a minute in real time.

5 *Counting down to deepen*: (optional: If you want to go even deeper) Give yourself this sug-

gestion: 'I'm going to count down from ten to one, and with each number I'll feel more and more relaxed but still alert, more and more in touch with my inner self. Ten . . . deeper and deeper, nine . . . more and more relaxed, eight . . . etc.' As you are counting down you might find it useful to picture yourself walking down steps to a river, with the top step being number ten and ending up at nought with a dip in the river.

6 *Creating a relaxation cue*: (optional, but very useful so that you can have a quick cue to relax you in future). When you feel completely at peace, allow an image to come up, or a word, that represents this feeling, and touch together your thumb and forefinger of either your right or left hand. Say to yourself: 'As I repeat this word or image and touch, I feel more and more relaxed and at peace, and each time I use it in future it will bring back this wonderful feeling, and the more I use it, the better it will work.'

7 *Doing your thing*: Once relaxed, it is time to do your imagework, or any thinking, planning, or even daydreaming as appropriate. Some people find it a good idea when they do imagework to create a spiritual context for this exploration by calling upon and trusting a power or consciousness that is higher than one's own conscious self – God, the Goddess, Mary, an evolved spiritual Master, one's own higher self, or whatever or whomever feels right. This can give you a wonderful sense of safety and peace, and can save you from one of the easiest pitfalls to fall into – getting too hooked on your own personal power. So if you

wish to, spend a moment invoking this higher power or consciousness, and ask them to protect and guide you as you enter the realm of the imagination.

8 *Emerging*: When you have done your imagework, or any other thinking or imagining, and want to emerge from your deeply relaxed and focused state, suggest to yourself: 'I'm going to count up from one to five and with each number I'll feel more and more awake, but still relaxed, and when I say five I'll open my eyes feeling relaxed and alert, feeling better then before, as if I've had a long refreshing sleep. One etc . . . ' Note that it is best to begin the 'reflecting' and 'looking forward' steps of the imagework before emerging, and then to continue them as and when it is appropriate during the day.

SLEEPING: BASIC FORMAT

If you want to sleep rather than simply relax, try the following sequence. Begin with clearing a space, and then follow steps 1, 2, and 3 above: beginning to relax, relaxing mind and body, and allowing the dark heaviness to descend and the lightness to rise. Then try out one of the various alternative images to invite sleep suggested below, and if you are not asleep yet, count down to deepen your state into sleep.

Preparation: Clearing a space
The steps then are:
Steps 1, 2, and 3 as for relaxation
4   Images to invite sleep
5   Counting down to deepen

Going to Sleep: Basic Exercise

Preparation: Clearing a space: Give yourself permission and encouragement to sleep. Like a parent with an anxious child, remind yourself that everything can be better solved in the morning after a good sleep. If you wake up in the middle of the night with a thought or a worry, do write it down; often it is your creative unconscious waking you up to remind you of something. But, having written it down, tell yourself that this is not a good time to take it any further. Again, like a parent with a young child, gently encourage yourself to go back to sleep.

1, 2 and 3: Follow steps 1, 2 and 3 as for relaxation.

4   Images to invite sleep:
Alternative A: Stepping into the sleeping you:

Imagine yourself being deeply asleep, perhaps just before waking in the morning. Step into the picture and match your breathing to the breathing of that sleeping self.

Alternative B: Creating a sanctuary: Go to a place where you've been happy, or could be happy, and totally blissfully safe, a real or imaginary place. Create a house there specially for you. Find a peaceful place to sleep: perhaps under a tree, or inside the house, or on a cloud. (I sometimes sleep on a cloud made up of the essence of fruits and flowers). Breathe in the atmosphere. Curl up and sleep.

Alternative C: The House of Sleep: Allow an image to emerge of your personal House of Sleep. Go inside. Find your special bed there. Notice if you have any comforting things in your bed to help you to sleep. Perhaps there are some special people or spirits there (my House of Sleep has the 'angels of sleep'), who help you to sleep by their warm presence, or by singing to you, or by reminding you that you have nothing to fear. Curl up and go to sleep, feeling totally safe.

Alternative D: Creating a dream: Suggest to yourself: 'If I were sleeping I would be dreaming . . . ' and make up a dream and live out the dream.

Alternative E: Be Creative: Think of the image that would work best for you personally to allow you to sleep.

5   *Counting down to deepen*: Suggest to yourself the following: I'm going to count down from 100 to one, and with each number I will feel twice as sleepy as I did before, until I fall fast asleep. If I skip any numbers, they will still count in the same way.

(If you get to the end and you are not asleep, just start again.)

A QUICK RELAX

Sometimes we need to be able to relax at a moment's notice. In this case, any of the steps above can be used separately to encourage relaxation. Use the one that works best for you, or simply the one that occurs to you at that moment. Or try one of the following:

1 *Relaxation cue*: Use the relaxation cue you developed in Step 6 of the relaxation method.

2 *Tightening and lightening*: Screw up your whole body as if you were a raisin compressed into the tiniest possible area. Let go. Screw up your face and head. Let go. Let your mind or spirit be light and float up and out.

3 *Alice in Wonderland molecules*: Imagine that your molecules are moving closer and closer together so that you become a tiny figure. Then imagine that your molecules, including those that make up your head and your thoughts, expand further and further apart until you fill the room. Come back to normal.

4 *Imagining your tension*: Allow an image to emerge to represent your tension, and then relax the image. A blown up balloon – and then you let the air out? A scrunched up kite – and then it opens out and flies? Just ask for an image of your tension, and then change it.

5 *Energy centring*: Notice where the centre of

energy in your body is at present. Pull it down deep into the centre of your body.

6 *Golden light*: Surround yourself with golden light.

7 *Imagining the background*: Become aware that your thoughts or consciousness have a background to them. Go into that background, which you may experience as being at the back of your skull. Really feel it. Allow an image or stream of images to emerge that represent this background, and float along with them.

8 *Problems outside, clarity inside*: Say to yourself: 'What's stopping me from relaxing?' Whatever problem or body feeling or background awareness comes to mind, allow an image to emerge of it, and put it outside of you. Promise it that you will deal with it later, but not right at this moment. Ask the question again and again, and in each case create an image and put it outside you, until you feel you are totally clear.

9 *Breath waves*: Breathe in to expand your diaphragm, and then fill your chest, in a natural rolling motion, and then let go. Do this ten times, preferably lying down.

APPLICATIONS

Doing things better: Relaxation enables you to do anything better. It is a good preparatory step not only to imagework but to everything else in your life. So when you are about to do anything at all, and particularly when it is something important to you, take the time to stop, and do a 'quick relax'. If you accompany it with a quick image, like imagining that you will do whatever you are about to do perfectly (e.g picture that perfect dive before you do it), even better.

Problem resolution: When you need to resolve a problem, rather than rushing in to deal with it urgently, and therefore relying on your habitual and goal directed mode of approach, stop first and relax. This gives you a chance to open up to a more free-flowing and possibly novel approach or set of approaches. Part of this is letting go of the need to solve the problem, or get the right answer. A relaxed, noncritical free-associating mode yields more fish in your net: you can then select the best solution.

Working with others: When working with others, whether you are a therapist working with a client, or one of a group of colleagues at a team meeting, or a member of any other working partnership, take a moment for both or all of you to relax into yourselves before you try to do any serious work. If things are getting heated or tense or stuck in some way, simply stop and do it again.

I remember the community meeting at the Skyros Centre, our personal development centre in Greece, when we had a real problem because a staff member had dropped out due to illness, and all her group members wanted to crowd into the course being run by one of the other staff members, who refused to have them all. For a while, the problem seemed insoluble. Then I asked everyone to stop, relax, and meditate on it. When we all spoke again, a compromise emerged as if by magic and everyone went away feeling listened to, cared for and proud of having done their best.

Deepening your focus: Use the counting down that deepens relaxation (step 5) to deepen your focus on whatever you are about to do. The best way to do this is to give instructions specific to that task. For example when I'm writing I might say to myself: 'I'm going to count down from ten to one, and with each number I'll feel twice as relaxed, twice as able to focus, twice as able to write beautifully and well.' On the other hand, when I'm problem solving I suggest that with each number I'll be more and more able to define and solve my present problem.

Play and daydreaming: Use your relaxing for play as well as for work. A few moments of relaxation plus appropriate countdowns and a great image does as much good for sex as it does for project planning.

And remember, too, that although imagework is different from daydreaming, there is no need to throw daydreaming out the window. Having satisfying day-dreams can sometimes be excellent for relaxing, and can have a healing quality too. In fact, when you consciously choose to daydream as a means of living better rather than of escaping from life, you are really doing a kind of imagework.

So do use some relaxation time to fantasise about having whatever it is you want in life, whether it be a good holiday or a wonderful love life or a star role opposite your favourite film idol. A great experience is a great experience, whether it 'really' happened or not, and wonderful memories do not have to be made up only of real events. Making up 'escapist' fantasies only becomes problematic if you deceive yourself with them. Otherwise, it just adds to the pleasure of life.

As my old friend Naomi used to say when I would interrupt her anecdotes to correct the facts: It doesn't matter whether it's true: it's a good story.

IN CONCLUSION

Nothing works all the time, nothing works for everyone, it's easier to relax deeply when everyone is doing it in a group than by yourself, and when you most need it your favourite method may fail you. I hope that has cheered you up.

What I'm really trying to say is that you need to be as creative and flexible and persevering in your approach to relaxation as to life in general. And it is important to remember that the more you practise relaxing when you don't desperately need it, the easier it will be to slip into that mode when you do.

All cautions aside, relaxing is such a pure pleasure in its own right, without even taking account of its manifold benefits, that it would be a shame not to welcome it with open arms into your life.

6

THE IMAGE AS LIFE METAPHOR

Who am I?

After taking the step of committing herself to being a full time writer, Evelyn found herself unable to write. She felt horribly stuck and wondered if she'd made a big mistake. When I gave her an earlier version of this chapter to read, she decided to try out the 'Image as Metaphor' exercise on her own, and see if she could get some insight into her situation.

An image emerged of a large amphibious creature rather like a sea serpent, with a black shiny skin, confined in a very small wooden box. When she looked down on the box from above she discovered that its top was made of very flimsy plywood slats. She suddenly realised that the creature could easily shatter these. She suggested to the serpent that it could break out of the box, but it continued to huddle fearfully inside.

As she stepped into the image and 'became' the creature, she found that she felt totally vulnerable because of her soft skin and was terrified of leaving the box. Switching roles, and becoming the 'guide', Evelyn asked the serpent: 'If you *could* get out, how would it be?' She then became the creature again, and in seconds she burst out of the top of the box, rearing up many feet into the air, and became a multicoloured, powerful hissing serpent. She felt absolutely wonderful.

Evelyn saw immediately that her block was due to her fear

of exposing her sensitive self to the public eye with her writing. She also realised that she had the potential to be far more powerful and colourful and, indeed, to make a real impact. She now felt confident, rather than fearful and compressed, and was able quite literally to launch herself out.

Within a few days, Evelyn sent her first article to a newspaper. They liked it so much that they asked if they could put her name on their list of freelance writers. The next time I saw her, I noticed that even her clothes were more colourful.

In this chapter we will explore how we can use imagery in this receptive way to get messages from our unconscious so that we can know who we really are, and what is going on for us, and act out of a sense of inner clarity. The technique introduced here can be used to understand clearly and deal more effectively with any situation or problem, whether it be our general life situation, problematic work relationships, or a marketing campaign. In order to act rather than react, we need to be able to pause, understand ourselves as well as the inner structure of the situation we are in, and determine the simplest and most appropriate way to move forward. This is what using an image as metaphor enables us to do.

IMAGING A PROBLEM

This first and most basic use of imagery involves inviting an image to emerge in response to a question, and then working with the image. As in the case of Evelyn's serpent, the images that come in this way have the powerful ability to sum up with a telling metaphor the basic structure of whatever it is you are asking about. The metaphor tends to be so accurate that the more you explore it, the more it can be seen to correspond on every level and in every detail not only with the specific problem but even with your life as a whole. The implicit becomes suddenly explicit, the complexities of the problem become streamlined into a simple structure, the history of the situation becomes obvious, and suddenly a resolution emerges where it seemed impossible before.

During one imagework session, Ken, the father of a girl in her early twenties who was having problems finding a career, wondered how he could help her. How much should he run around to get information for her? Should he push her? Should he just let her get on with it? What is the role of a good father? He had arranged to have dinner with her that evening and was tense and confused about what to do when he met her.

An image emerged of a cross. Ken was distressed: he associated the cross with his pattern of having a sacrificial sense of responsibility toward the people in his life, and he hadn't realised that this was what he was unwittingly doing once again. He didn't want to play this role with his daughter. What could he do to change this? He 'became' the cross, and suddenly found himself burning. He realised that he was no longer a cross, but a beacon burning high on a hill. This idea worried him at first, yet it felt warm and wonderful. He realised that he had become a fixed point to which people came for light and warmth.

Ken saw immediately that transforming his sense of burdened responsibility to one of open and receptive warmth and understanding was the key not only to dealing with his daughter, but with his relationships more generally. He went out to meet his daughter looking forward with pleasure to a warm and light filled evening.

Since the image also represents an internal thought form or program, as you work through the image you often find that you have directly shifted your previous state of body, mind, and spirit. One imagework student, Anne, had a tense jaw, and invited an image associated with it; a tied knot emerged. As she worked with the knot and managed to unravel it, she discovered to her surprise that her jaw had loosened along with the knot. This is why one of the more powerful methods of quick relaxation (see chapter 5, A Quick Relax, no. 4) is to allow an image to emerge of your tension, and then transform the image. The tension goes right along with it.

Furthermore, you can extend your understanding and clarity about present, past, and future by consciously mapping the image back onto your lives and seeing the parallels. Thus Anne, by understanding how the knot got tied, what it took to unravel it, and what would happen to the piece of rope when it was no longer a knot, could draw some far-reaching conclusions about her general life pattern and possibilities.

THE POETIC IMAGINATION

What sort of images come up for people? Any and every image is possible, for we are all natural poets, and the strangest images are often the most straightforward to understand. I remember one professor who came away from an imagework session with computer programmers so amazed at the poetic quality of the images that emerged naturally from these super-rational mathematical students that he felt as if he'd just attended a seance.

Some typical images that come to mind are: a rock nestling under a cliff, worn away by waves, dreaming of eternity; a sunflower, face lifted up to the sun, its stalk aching because it needs support; a bird, with its wing damaged, unable to find a place to shelter and heal; an aspidistra in a plant pot that is much too small, thinking that if she lets her leaves go brown she might get some attention and get her pot changed; a tiger in a cage, remembering the way it used to be in Africa, yet convincing himself that it's okay and safe in here and where would he go anyway?

The images usually have an intuitive meaning both to the person whose image it is, and to others who hear it. If you are working in a group, other people can join in and ask questions, or send wishes: 'Rock – I wish you the pleasure of children playing on you and admiring you.' 'Sunflower – my stalk aches too. Perhaps we could join forces and support each other.' 'Bird – I wish you other birds to hover round you and heal you.' 'Aspidistra – try another way to get a new pot than by getting ill.' 'Tiger, why not try the cage door – you can always go back in the cage if you want to.'

THE LOGIC OF THE IMAGINATION

The images have their own inner logic, which may not be the logic of everyday reality. It is crucial to sense what the image-being – which is what I call the personified animal, plant or object that emerges as the image – wants to do, no matter how much this may conflict with biological facts or rationality. I remember the joy we all had in an imagery session when a 'pig' decided it wanted to stop wallowing and start to fly – and did.

The image-being does always know best what its next step should be. There was the time I was on my last day of holiday and felt unsettled and didn't know why. I got an image of a boat near the shore, neither in the water nor out, feeling stuck. Understanding now that my unsettled feeling must have to do with the fact that it was my last day and I didn't know how to deal with this, I thought I'd better push the boat back on the shore. But although I tried and tried to do this the boat kept slipping back into the water. So I decided to go the other way, and push the boat out to sea – and that felt absolutely right.

I came to the conclusion that although it was my last day on holiday I needed to go all out and get the most out of it rather than simply close down as I tend to do near the end of an experience. The highlight of my holiday was the visit to a little village church which I made that day only because I could see in front of my eyes that boat in the middle of the sea feeling wonderful.

Image as Metaphor: The Structure of the Exercise

How do we get these images? Eventually you will simply ask for an image, and almost like flicking on a television set, there it will be. But at first, it may seem a bit daunting. It's probably easiest to begin by working with someone, or putting the exercises on tape. But if you work by yourself and simply shift seats so that you are the guide asking the questions in one seat, and the image-being in the other, you will feel almost as if you are two separate people in one.

As always, you need to remember the principles of image-work of chapter 4, and then begin by clearing a space (see chapter 4) and relaxing (see chapter 5). If you are working alone, put a cushion or chair opposite you to serve as the chair of the image-being: this is where the image will 'appear', and where you will sit to become the image. You return to your original seat always when you are asking guiding questions. Many people prefer to keep their eyes closed when they are the image-being, because this enhances the experience for them. Find out what is most comfortable for you.

The basic structure of the exercise is as follows: You encourage an image to emerge, and study it from a number of perspectives. You then enter into the image, becoming the image-being, and deepen the exploration. Then you look back, and get a sense of what led up to the present situation, and look forward to find out what is the next step for you, and try out this next step. You then appreciate both your conscious and your unconscious selves for their joint effort. Now you take time to think about the image and map it back onto your life and consider what the implications are for the future, and then emerge from your relaxed state. Thus, the steps are:

Preparation: Clearing a space and relaxing
1   Inviting an image
2   Studying the image
3   Becoming the image: deepening and exploring
4   Getting a sense of the history
5   Getting a sense of the possibilities
6   Appreciating and emerging
7   Reflecting
8   Looking forward
9   Emerging

In other words, you allow an image to emerge and tell its story, beginning with the present, then going to the past, like a flashback, and then the future, and eventually you draw conclusions more directly about your life. The preliminary question asked in the exercise below is a general one: 'Who are you and what do you need to know at this moment in your life?' Later you can vary this to ask specific questions about specific problems.

You may wish to have some paper and felt-tip pens, crayons, or paint ready, either for creating an image to begin with, just in case thinking of one proves difficult, or for drawing the image afterwards.

The exercise form given below is rather long, and may seem daunting. This is mainly because it is full of alternatives and explanations to cover every eventuality that might come up for a novice imageworker. A short form of this process is given at the end, which is particularly useful when you have only a few moments and need to quickly understand something or someone, or to make an instant decision.

To keep you company in this process, I will work along with you, inviting an image to arise and following all the steps with you. You'll find a summary of my experience in Appendix Two. I promise that I am not going to cheat and find an image that I know sounds good, but rather literally will follow along right now as I am writing this, doing the exercise with you. So remember: don't look for an image that *you* think is a good one; the first image that comes to mind is the best one for you at this moment.

I remember Michael who asked for an image to help him decide whether to reveal an important secret in his life. He got an image of a factory. What did this have to do with his question, he wondered. He went into the factory where he saw tins coming off a production line. Even more disappointed with the image, he was about to reject it when he noticed that they were tins of baked beans. Suddenly, one of the tins exploded, the beans shooting out every which way. Then the message appeared in the air: 'Spill the beans.'

IMAGE AS METAPHOR: BASIC EXERCISE

(Please note: The instructions are in the form appropriate for guiding yourself through the exercise. If you are guiding a partner, change the pronouns as in: 'I'd like *you* to allow an image to emerge' rather than 'I'd like to allow an image to emerge').

Preparation: Clearing a Space and Relaxing

1 *Inviting the image*: Suggest this:

Basic instruction: 'I'd like to allow an image to emerge of an animal, a plant or an object that somehow represents who I am or what I need to know at this moment in my life; the first image that comes to mind, whether as a word, a picture, a sound, or a fleeting sense. This image is now sitting in the chair opposite.'

Thanking the unconscious: When the image emerges, say: 'Thank you unconscious. I appreciate the gift.'

In case nothing happens: If nothing comes to mind at all, try the following alternatives in turn until one does:

a 'Unconscious, I thank you for your efforts to protect me, but I would like to explore these images. Please help me to do so in a safe and natural way. I ask you to allow an image to emerge . . . (continue as in basic instruction)'.

b 'I now imagine that my unconscious is like a wonderful rich sea full of treasures, and floating up right now out of this sea is an image that represents who I am or what I need to know at this moment in my life. This being is now sitting opposite.'

c 'Looking back over the past day or two, remembering all the things I have seen, I notice one memory image that seems to draw my attention. This image is now in the chair opposite me.'

d Take felt-tip pens and paper and suggest: 'I would like to allow an image to emerge on this paper of an animal, a plant, or an object, etc. (as above)'. Then just choose colours and put the pens to paper and draw without thinking. Get to know the image on paper and then imagine it sitting in the chair opposite.

e Take the 'nothingness' or the 'blankness' of not having an image to be your image and explore that.

Comment: I hope you haven't already forgotten to take the first image that comes to mind, not the first one that you like. And don't worry if you can't see it vividly – just let it fill out in time.

2 *Studying the image*: Allow the image to become clearer. What does it look like? What colour is it? Does it make a sound? Does it have a smell? Does it move? How? What is its relationship to the environment?

Imagine that your mind or spirit goes up and out of an imaginary hole in the top of your head, and hovers above and around the image, looking at it from above, from behind, and from the sides, and even from underneath. In other words, get to know it from as many perspectives as possible. What more do you notice from each perspective?

Comment: Remember that the image as you perceive it does not have to conform to any known scientific principles. In the world of the imagination, anything is possible.

3 *Becoming the image: deepening and exploring*: Step into the image. This means in this case getting up and sitting on the seat where you saw the image. (If this is not convenient, just step into the image in your mind). You are now this image-being. Feel this absolutely, concretely, first: feel the ground under your feet (if you are an animal) or around your roots (if you are a plant) or the wind against your wings (if you are a bird). What do you notice?

Now, returning to the seat of the guide, get to

know the image-being as deeply as you can, in a kind of intimate exploratory interview. The following are some good questions to ask. You can also ask or say anything that feels right to you as you sensitively tune into the image-being. If you are working on your own, remember to switch seats when you alternate between being the guide who asks, and the image-being who answers the questions.

Some exploratory interview questions:
　'Tell me about yourself.'
　'What is the essence of being you?' – the sunflowerness of the sunflower, or the tigerness of the tiger, or the boatness of the boat, or whatever the image-being is.
　'Where are you? What can you see around you – what can you hear? smell? taste? feel? sense intuitively?'
　'How does it feel to be you right now, physically, emotionally, or spiritually? What is the best thing about your life, and what is the worst of it? What do you hope for and what do you fear?'
　'How do you feel about your situation? Do you feel at home in the world around you or in conflict with it? Is there a problem that needs solving? Do you feel stuck at all?'
　'Who else is there with you in the situation? How do you relate to them? If there is no one, how do you feel about that?'
　'How do you move? What sounds do you make?' (at this point, if you are able to, do get up and move as this image-being, and

make the sounds of this being).

'What else do you notice about being you, this image-being, at this moment in your life?'

Comment: As the image-being, take a moment before answering to sink into being the image, and to sense the answer the image-being would give, rather than the one that you, the human adult, would give.

Remember also that all these questions always refer to the image-being, not the adult human. So when the question is about 'this moment in your life' for example, this is not the life of a person, but the life of a big red bus, or rainbow, or cloud, or aspidistra, or whatever it is you are being at that moment.

As the guide, don't forget that the questions above are sample questions. As you feel sensitively in tune with the image-being, other questions will occur to you and it is fine to ask them. Just get used to thinking that you are having an intimate conversation, not with a person but with an image-being.

Once you are used to working with imagery, you won't really need to keep shifting seats, but will be able simply to step into the image in your imagination, and then alternately guide yourself and answer the questions without confusion. This makes it easier to do your imagework in a public place without embarrassing yourself. But actually moving physically does seem to have a powerful enhancing effect.

---

4 *Getting a sense of the history*: Ask the image-being about the background of the present situation. 'What led up to your present situation? Was there a time when things were different? When? How were they different? How and when did the change take place?'

Comment: Every situation has a history, and by understanding the history you can make better sense of the present and future.

It is useful to be very precise about how long ago the change happened as this often yields important clues. A month ago? Six years ago? When I was small? Don't forget that the questions are still not addressed to you as the adult human, but you as the image-being.

5 *Getting a sense of the possibilities*: Ask any of the following questions, some of which are different ways of saying the same thing, until you get a sense of what the next step for the image-being is.

Future possibility questions: 'What's next? What do you need to do to feel better, or to make your life more complete, or simply to move forward? What seems right? What should happen? How would it be or feel to be completely okay? If you could wave a magic wand over your life, how would you like it to be?'

Carry through: As you imagine this next step – do it, and enjoy it.

If the image-being is happy as it is, don't push change onto it, though you may comment about your perception of the situation if it doesn't feel right to you.

If you get stuck: If there is a sense of stuckness, or the image-being cannot find out what to do or dare to do it, try one or all of these: 'What's stopping you from moving forward? What do you fear will happen?'

'What feels good or useful about even the seemingly negative aspects of the way you are now? Is there any other way to accomplish the same result that is more pleasant?'

'I recognise you don't want to or can't see how to move forward. But if you *could* move forward, what would it be like? If you *were* to change, what sort of change would it be?'

'Let your mind or spirit float up and take a perspective from above looking down, surveying the scene. What can you see that would be useful for this image-being? If you could whisper something from above to the image-being, what would that be?'

'It is now x time later (x time is five minutes, an hour, a day, a year, or whatever period is appropriate) and you feel good about your life. What is happening now? What did you do?'

Carry through: With all these questions, as soon as the next step does become clear, follow through by suggesting 'Do it, and enjoy it'. And you can continue to ask 'What's next?' until there's a natural resting point.

Comment: This is a crucial stage in the exploration, for we can sense what choices we have available and try them out in total safety.

When we are stuck, and can't seem to get anywhere, the first step is to find out what is stopping us rather than trying to move forward against internal opposition (which is a bit like trying to move your car with the hand brake on). It is important to see, also, the positive functions of the present attitude, which probably have something to do with protection. Once you understand the function, you can help the image-being find a healthier way to accomplish the same thing.

Sometimes if we are really so frightened of change we can't even imagine it, we need to be 'tricked' into a moment of experiencing the new. For this purpose 'I know you don't want to do x, but if you did, how would it be?' is quite miraculous. It enables us to imagine freely without all the fears that attend change since we are stating clearly that we don't intend to do it. Of course, once we have imagined the change, we may find that it is so nice that we do want to change. Sometimes, by imagining it we have already changed.

Recently, one of my students had an image-being, a little rabbit, who was absolutely refusing under any circumstances to accept love into her life – saying she knew it was good for her but she simply would not take the risk. I acknowledged to her that she need not do so, but how would it be if she did? I can still see before my eyes that look on her face of pure joy when she allowed herself to imagine how it would be, and the relaxation in her whole being a few moments later when she admitted that for the first time she felt there was now some hope.

When it simply seems difficult to find out what to do next, then shifting perspectives often helps: hence the suggestion that you shift up and look down. ('Oh yes, the motor of the boat is broken, but from above I can see that the boat is so close to shore that you could row there.') Or that you shift forward in time and look back ('It's half an hour later and I can see that what I did was to stop struggling in the quicksand and call for help and that someone did come to help me.')

---

6 *Appreciating and emerging*: Tune back into the original image. What is happening now? Is there a change? How do you feel about the future?

Thank your conscious and unconscious selves for their teamwork.

Review the pictures and feelings you have just

been through, and notice the best picture/feeling in all that. Allow yourself to feel/be that again, and to notice exactly what it is like, both physically and emotionally, so that you can recognise that state of mind and body in future. You can if you wish create a 'cue' to bring this feeling back more easily. Do this by seeing the picture, stepping into it, letting yourself feel it again, and, at the moment it all comes back to you in full strength, touching two fingers together or touching part of your body that you associate with that feeling. This is now a cue that will help to bring the feeling back. Test it immediately after you emerge to see how it works.

Comment: Whenever you have done any imagework, it is always crucial to return full circle to the original image and see what changes have taken place. If there are no changes at all, it may well be that the work has not yet gone deep enough or resolved itself. Going back to the beginning helps you both to evaluate and to appreciate the steps you have taken.

The major work with this image has now been done. The process you have been through is a transformative one in and of itself, in that you have begun to transform the deep symbols that program your life. You have also, just by going through this process, become more at home with your unconscious.

---

7 *Reflecting*: Using your conscious resources: Spend a few moments now reflecting on what you have just been through, and also keep the image in the back of your mind over the next few days and continue this process. Here are some possible questions:

'What did that image mean to me? How does it

reflect my life as it is and has been? What do I feel good about as I look at this clarification of my underlying program? What do I feel uneasy about? How does this image fit in with previous images I have had of myself?'

'What are the feelings associated with the starting image? Are they familiar? When do I feel them? How old was I when I first felt that way? How would it be different to feel the way the changed image-being feels?'

'If I map this image back onto my life, like laying a diagram on a piece of tracing paper over the reality of my life, what correspondences can I find, in the past, present, and possible future referred to?' (Be specific here; there is likely to be a one-to-one correspondence between all the aspects of your image and the nature of your life. For example, if as the image-being your life situation changed five months ago, or six years ago, this may well be an accurate description of a real change in your own life at that time).

If you really cannot understand what the image means, try talking to your unconscious and saying: 'Unconscious, can you give me another image that will help me to understand the image I have just had? I'd like to allow an image to emerge that will illuminate my previous image.'

Comment: While until now you have been encouraging your unconscious assumptions and images to come forth and reveal themselves, reflecting involves utilising your conscious resources more fully to round off the work and to take the insights you have already begun to gain a step or two further. It also gets you into the habit of taking seriously, in your conscious everyday life, the messages that come in such a strange form from an inner dimension that we usually ignore. In this way, you can multiply the benefits of the imagery work. This, then, is the time to use your conscious mind to make sense of, and make use of, the intuitive work you have just done.

8 *Looking forward*: Now is the time to think about what this all means in practice. Ask yourself some of the following questions:

'What are the practical implications? What does it really mean to make this change – what do I need to do practically in order to take my next step?'

'If I were the transformed image-being (the one who has already taken the next step or made the change) how would I deal differently with this problem and with life in general? How would I get up in the morning, eat breakfast, go to work, and so on – i.e. what would a day in my life be like if I had this new image in the background? How does that compare with my present life?'

'What could stop me, or how might I stop myself from making the change? What frightens me about it? How do I usually sabotage myself?'

Comment: This is the time to begin to make some conscious choices about how to integrate these new understandings into your life.

9 *Emerging*: When you are ready to emerge from this deeply relaxed state, suggest the following: 'I'm going to count up from one to five and when I

say five, I will open my eyes, feeling relaxed and alert, feeling better than before, as if I've had a long refreshing sleep, and bringing back with me the best feelings, pictures, and insights from my explorations. One, two – coming up to the surface, eyelids lightening; three – alert but still relaxed; four, five – eyes open.'

Comment: Because this deeply relaxed state is also a highly focused one, it is best to begin your reflecting and looking forward before emerging from it. If the image has been an important one, you will certainly want to continue your reflecting and planning after you emerge and over the next few days and weeks.

Later: At various moments during the next few days or weeks, simply notice if you get the same feeling as the one you had as the image-being at the very beginning of the process. Then, if it is not what you want, just wonder how you might experience things differently if you were the image-being at its best, after it had taken the step it needed to take. Or ask the changed image-being for advice: 'What do you think I should do now?' Or, if you created a cue for yourself, use it to bring back the good feeling, and then decide what to do.

Every now and then, also, just tune into the image-being and see what state it is in: is the rabbit feeling friendly, or running around in a fright, or hiding in a corner? This is a good indication of your present state of mind.

Painting the image: Another very good thing to do is to sit down with paint, crayons, or felt-tip pens, and draw your image. When you've done so, it is a good idea to imagine that you are the painting (as you imagined that you were the image-being) and say: 'I am this painting. This is how it is to be me,' and explore further. It would be helpful if you had a place that you could leave your painting out for a few days, so that you can, as the feeling takes you, add to it or change it.

Comment: As soon as you have a clear image of a positive way of being, you have a resource you can use. A clear positive image is implicitly a plan or pattern of being and acting. You can say: 'If I were this image-being, e.g. this motorised snail, or this free-flying bird, or this friendly rabbit, how would I deal with this situation?' Or else you can see these image-beings as advisors and ask them what to do.

Because every image is really a resource and advisor, you will find before long that you have so many potential members of your internal board of expert consultants that you will wonder how you can afford to keep them all on your payroll!

Do get into the habit also of tuning back into images you have created already just for a moment to check your state of being. I, for example, over a period of time, kept tuning into a boat that seemed to represent my state of energy in relation to my work. When it was out at sea I knew I was in the middle of life working with my full energy. When the boat was a mess I knew that my disorder or chaos had reached too high a level and I needed to stop and do some internal clearing and ordering. If I was sailing against the current, I guessed I might be doing something that would be counter-productive. When it was upside down on the shore I gave up whatever work I was doing and had a rest.

IMAGE AS METAPHOR: QUICK METHOD

If you have only a few moments, try this brief format (which is really a quick summary of the process above):

1 *Invite the image*: Tell yourself 'I'd like to allow an image to emerge of an animal, a plant or an object that somehow represents who I am or what I need to know at this moment in my life, the first image that comes to mind.'

2 *Study the image*: Observe the image and its relationship to its situation, and then look from above, the sides, and below. What do you notice?

3 *Become the image*: Step into the image. Ask yourself: 'What is the essence of being me at this moment? What is going on for me? What is the best aspect of it? The worst of it?'

4 *Get a sense of the history*: Ask yourself: 'Has it always been this way? If not, how and when was it different, and how and when did it change?'

107

5 *Get a sense of the possibilities*: Ask yourself: 'What's next? What's the way forward?'

6 *Appreciate and reflect*: Appreciate the joint effort of your conscious and unconscious selves, and reflect on the meaning.

7 *Look forward*: Consider how you can make use of your image or the understanding you have gained from it in future.

APPLICATIONS

The unconscious body: A very powerful way of using this exercise is for understanding and changing a feeling in your body, whether it be a headache, or a vague discomfort in the pit of your stomach, or an anxiety feeling. After relaxing, tune into any body feeling that you want to understand or change, and ask for a name or an image. Then put it in the chair opposite you, and continue just as you did above, getting a sense of the feeling, deepening and exploring, finding the next step, appreciating, reflecting, looking forward, and emerging.

During the 'appreciating' stage, though, it is important to check back to the body feeling you began with, rather than just to the original image, and see how you are feeling now. If the feeling hasn't changed at all, you probably haven't quite reached the heart of the problem.

Problem solving: More generally, this exercise is a versatile one, and can be used to make sense of any situation or problem. The only thing you need to do is to vary the first question, and the unconscious, like a computer, will select an appropriate image.

For example, one I use when I am working as a consultant for professional development rather than personal growth is 'I'd like you to allow an image to emerge of your work and your relation to your work at this moment in your life.'

Counselling: When I am working with people in any kind of counselling or psychotherapy role, I often just stop them after the first description of what is going on and say 'Take a moment now, and see what image emerges'. And off we go. Imagework students tell me that they have learned to do this in everyday conversations with friends, and therefore feel much more able to be genuinely helpful. When a friend has a problem they just ask what image comes up, instead of feeling called upon to give advice that they suspect will never be followed.

Another technique I use in counselling is to say to myself: 'I'd like to allow an image to emerge of an animal, a plant, or an object, that somehow represents the person I am counselling and their problem at this moment in their lives'. I then get a sense of the meaning of the image, and offer it to the client: 'This image has come up for me – does it mean anything to you?' In my experience the image has an immediate and powerful significance to the other person in 99 out of 100 cases, and often represents the turning point of the counselling session.

Understanding and evaluating others: Similarly, if I am interviewing someone, and want to get a quick sense of what my intuition is telling me, I say to myself 'I'd like to allow an image to emerge of an animal, a plant, or an object, that represents this person sitting opposite me.' If I don't have time to go into the image and understand it while the interview is going on, I spend a few moments exploring the image afterwards. It gives me the benefit of being able to use my intuitive understanding along with my conscious appraisal to make decisions.

VARIATIONS

There are some other ways to get images that you may find useful. You can either get a quick sense of their meaning, or work on them in much the same way as above.

Asking the unconscious: Speak directly to your unconscious and say: 'Unconscious, please give me an image that will help me to understand this problem. Unconscious, how would it be best for me to go forward? Please give me an image.'

Magic Screen: Imagine that you are sitting in your own private cinema, with a magic screen in front of you. Ask for an image to appear on the screen that describes your present situation. After seeing that one, ask for one that describes what you could do to shift the situation.

Tell a story: Tell yourself a story that begins: 'Once upon a time there was . . . ' (either: a little boy, a little girl, or an animal, a plant, or an object). Follow the story through, saying what the characters are thinking and feeling, and doing, what led up to the present events, and how the story ends. You may continue then and say: 'And then what happens? And what happens five years later?'

Images tell the story: Consider three or four aspects of a problem that you have, or a project that you are planning, and allow an image to emerge for each. Watch them combining and recombining, follow any story line that emerges, observe them from all perspectives, talk to each of them, and then make sense of the story, mapping it back to the original problem. For an example see Appendix One: The dog, the carrot, the samovar, and the fishing boat.

Standard images: Any image becomes yours as you explore it, so starting from a standard image can yield important insights too. Trees and rosebushes are classic standard images: become a tree or rosebush, and find out about yourself. I like using the image of being a city: What do you look like? What kind of buildings do you have? train station? university? shops? monuments? banks? transport? government? back streets? slums? and so on. This can yield wonderful insights.

IN CONCLUSION

Doing this exercise may not have been easy this first time. So now, do congratulate yourself, not because you made a brilliant discovery (even if you did), but simply because you took the time, and risk, to begin a process that most people shy away from all their lives. While the results may not show at once, and your development is likely to be a gradual process, with lots of enthusiastic starts and depressing defeats, one day you will turn around and say to yourself, 'You really have changed, haven't you.'

One of the changes you may find is to do with your values. Inherent in beginning to work with imagery is the understanding that your internal world is of value: that you care not only about external events but about your internal integrity, sense of meaning, or feeling of rightness, and you are willing to devote some attention to it. For many people, this is a crucial shift. Of course, you will without doubt also find that external events work better because you have paid attention to reviewing and revising your internal plans of action. Indeed, if they didn't, this work would become a form of escapist daydreaming – relaxing enough, but deprived of its practical power.

It is worth mentioning that although I do emphasise stepping into the image in your mind or even changing seats, it is possible, if you wish, just to observe the image and talk to it rather than become it. This is particularly useful if you are doing this imagework in a public place, and are afraid that even if you don't change seats, you will reveal yourself by your gestures or facial expressions to be a playful monkey when you are trying to comport yourself as a successful executive.

When I have time to work deeply, I still prefer not only to step into the image but also to shift places, particularly if I feel stuck. I have even developed a style of changing seats in public places that doesn't look too bizarre. Or so I believe.

Using images to sense your next step, definitely does not mean forcing yourself to change or telling yourself you should be different, or hitting yourself on the head with any of the insights you have gained. It means clarifying your patterns, and waiting for yourself to unfold naturally, because as your images change, you will slowly but surely change too.

It is, of course, often absolutely necessary to use your will and determination to carry your plans through, but this should not feel like a constant painful inner struggle but rather like a difficult but necessary path that you are determined to follow and, in a sense, are happy to follow. Being able to use your will effectively is in fact a part of the natural unfolding process.

If you find you are not making any changes, it is worth exploring what is stopping you, imagining concretely how it would be to have made this change, or sensing whether you need a slightly different image so that you can feel comfortable. But expend the effort on creating a clearer, and more appropriate pattern. It is never useful to whip yourself to fit into shape, no matter how good a shape it seems to be.

Do also enjoy and appreciate the images you get, and don't get discouraged or angry when nothing seems to be working. This too is part of your relationship with your unconscious, and reminds you that you, as your conscious verbal self, are not totally in control. You can ask for a gift from the unconscious – or, to be more precise, from the image making domain between your conscious and your unconscious – but you shouldn't demand or expect it.

It reminds me of how I used to feel when my children were

toddlers and I'd come home from work with a present for them. I so much loved the look on their face when they were delighted and surprised by the little gift I had taken the trouble to choose; and perhaps it was this look that motivated me to choose another some other day. But when I walked in and they demanded 'What did you bring me?', the pleasure died, and I immediately thought they were spoiled brats and that I shouldn't bring them any more presents.

The unconscious may well be rather similar. When you are delighted and surprised by its gifts, it wants to give you more and more. But when you come to expect the gifts and are angry when you don't get them, you may go through a period that feels rather like 'no more presents for that spoiled brat.'

7

IMPROVING RELATIONSHIPS
Exploring the between

James, a 50-year-old university lecturer, could not forgive his uncle Ned for having failed him when he most needed him. James admired and had even modelled himself on Uncle Ned, whom he considered to have great intellectual and emotional power, but Ned always seemed to look upon James with a kind of patronising amusement. At a time when things were going badly wrong for him, James had approached Ned and sought his advice. His uncle was kind but unhelpful. Subsequently, whenever James sought his uncle's friendship, Ned seemed to spurn and even disapprove of him. James's life was full of failed relationships, and yet this one seemed to be the most painful of all. He couldn't find any way to deal with it or understand it.

One night, as James was listening to a Beethoven sonata, he began to weep uncontrollably. He was reminded of Ned, who often wept when he listened to music, and realised once again how hurt and despairing he still was at this failure to make contact with his uncle. The next day, during an imagework session on relationships, I suggested to James that an image emerge of someone with whom he had unfinished business. A thin, tall, emaciated, and severe Ned popped up opposite him, smiling at him with an ironic smile, puffing at his pipe.

James confronted Ned with his anger and resentment at

him. 'You are older and wiser than me', he said, 'You could make our relationship work. So much good could come from a relationship between us. We could have a deep meeting of minds. I desperately need you to guide me, to be what my father wasn't. I sent you a record once and you never acknowledged it. That has hurt me for years. Why do you do this to me? Why are you so dismissive?'

When James switched roles and became Ned, the answer came quickly. 'You have always wanted things I couldn't give you. I love you, but you have to solve your problems yourself. I didn't really like the record – so I didn't know what to say. Please understand that I have been so concerned with my own problems that all I might have done was to pile my problems onto you. You are much more successful than me. I am a failure: a wanderer, a hobo, an empty shell. Please don't model yourself on me, or expect anything of me. I would like to hug you, but I cannot help you.'

James then switched back to being himself. He was still angry, and still felt that uncle Ned could give more if he only wanted to. He voiced all his resentments, and made a demand that Ned write to him, or at least acknowledge the bond between them.

When he switched roles and became Ned, he told James that he was being manipulative – Ned was not prepared to give any more than he wished to. 'I'm too old to change. You must find your own way, and you must open your heart. I do feel my heart is more developed than yours, James. All I can promise is – my heart goes with you.'

Switching back to being himself again, James was reluctant to give up his anger and resentment. 'I understand it in my head. But it doesn't work to open my heart. It's not safe. I may open myself up and get rejected.'

Then he looked up at his image of Ned opposite and saw the caring look on his face. He found himself saying to Ned 'I wish you to be at peace. Perhaps *I* could have given *you* more.' He now saw that Ned was crying. James held Ned's hand, and promised to stop seeing him as a failed god, and expecting him to be what he was not. Ned was smiling peacefully now. James too had given up his pained look, and smiled shyly and lovingly at the group.

AS WITHIN, SO WITHOUT

In relationships, as in other areas of life, one could say 'As within, so without'; internal models of relationships that we may have formed very early can set the scene for unsatisfying adult relationships which we seem to be unable to transform. Of all the patterns we get locked into and have trouble getting out of, relationship patterns are among the most powerful and the most painful. Certainly more songs and novels have been written about them than about anything else.

Relationships are particularly confusing because they involve other people, and hence it is difficult to distinguish which bit has to do with the other person, and which bit has to do with oneself. So, since most of us have learned to control situations by blaming someone, we wonder who is to blame. Often we blame ourselves. But sometimes we rage at the other person. Or we blame our parents. Or we get depressed and hopeless, or just resigned. Or we get rid of the relationship and start a new one. And then, too often, though thankfully not always, our new ones turn out mysteriously like the old ones, even when we swear that this person seemed so different and we couldn't possibly have known . . . .

The enemy of stuck patterns is the light of consciousness and of communication: consciousness has to do with how we let ourselves know what is happening inside us, and communication is the way we let others know what is going on. The more accurate we can be to ourselves and to others about what is going on, the more likely we are to be able to recognise our patterns for what they are and shift them.

We have already begun to see how imagework can be used to increase our consciousness of our patterns. By allowing an image to emerge, we allow a metaphor for our life pattern to emerge, and we begin to face it, and in so doing to alter it. The

same is true in working with relationships: as we play out our patterns in our imagination, we can observe and recognise them more clearly.

In relationships, however, the focus expands to include communication: discovering how we can talk to others in a way that helps us to understand each other, reach each other, forgive each other, leave behind the past and move forward.

It is important not to forget that while there are two partners in an interaction, you are the only one you can influence directly, so why not start there? When working with couples, I have found the most powerful results happen when I say to each: 'Assume that the other person is never going to change. What can you do?'

I COULDN'T POSSIBLY SAY THAT

The basic process in exploring and transforming relationships through imagework is similar to the one we used in the last chapter. In just the same way, you need to summon the image, study it, deepen and explore, explore the past, move toward a resolution, appreciate, emerge, reflect and look forward. However, in this case rather than guiding an image – being, the emphasis is on communication with another person, so in this case you invite an image of a someone with whom you have 'unfinished business' or unresolved issues, and talk to him or her.

When you are doing this exercise, the experience may be so vivid that you will really feel the person is there. You may then feel like stopping the conversation because, as so many people have said to me over the years, 'I can't do that. I couldn't possibly say such angry things to my mother' or 'I wouldn't dare be so open with my boss.' or 'What's the point, since my father has been dead for years.'

If this happens, do remind yourself that the person you are talking to is not the real person, but that internal image of the person that lives inside you. It is not your mother, but the image of your mother; not your boss, but the authority figure within you. The internal image and relationship is the one that dominates your life, and must be addressed. This is often a far more crucial process than telling another person what they may be unable or unwilling to hear anyway.

So give yourself the prior assurance that the other person is not really in the room with you, and the revelations need go no further, so that you are free to be totally honest with yourself. Even if the person is alive and within reach, you need never reveal to him or her what you have learned, unless you so choose. Preparing whether, and what, you might actually say to the person comes at a later stage, and is much easier when you have been totally open in the first stage.

You may also wonder, when you are doing this exercise, how it is that you perceive things differently when you sit in the seat of the other person. Are you in some way really being the other person? Or is this just your fantasy about them? When you shift seats you are certainly contacting that 'everyday unconscious' of thoughts and feelings that you *almost* know but don't quite have access to. Thus James must have sensed unconsciously what Ned really felt, but he didn't consciously know it until he switched seats. By doing this exercise, then, you contact the best intuition you have about the other, which is probably far more developed than your conscious understanding.

Depending on your view about our ability to connect directly with other people's thoughts and feelings, it is not impossible that when we do this exercise we are also 'tuning in' to someone else, and learning something that we simply did not know. After all these years of working with images, I believe that this can and does happen, and this possibility is discussed further in chapter 16. On the other hand, many people find it makes more sense to see all the insights as aspects of our own resources and unconscious understandings. The insights are equally valid whichever way you look at it.

In any case, in so far as we are dealing with our own relationship problem, it doesn't always matter whether what we believe about the other is even true. It only matters that we believe it, and are affected by this belief. Indeed, on another level, this drama that we are playing out with another person can be considered to represent an internal drama or relationship between two aspects of ourselves. The part the other person plays can be considered an unexpressed aspect of ourselves that we do not acknowledge and therefore project upon and meet in others. When we work through this relationship, therefore, we are transforming an internal dynamic as much as, or even more than, an external one.

You can work on these internal dynamics directly in the two exercises: 'Parents Talking' and 'Inner Male and Female', listed under Variations. Once having played out the conversation between the mother and father in you, or the male and female in you, you may begin to notice the echoes of these inner conversations in your outer relationships.

COMMUNICATION PRINCIPLES

There are simple communication principles that, when followed, make conversation and ultimately relationships work better. These rules help to unravel which feelings belong to you and which belong to the other person. They assist you in confronting the ambivalence inherent in relationships and breaking the taboos and collusions in your communication patterns. They are also designed to help you to be assertive in the best possible sense of the word, which means being able to be clear about your own wishes and point of view and yet still continue to hear and understand the conflicting wishes and point of view of the other. They are ultimately ways to encourage your creativity in dealing with and transforming your relationships.

A summary of seven important communication principles is given in Appendix ~~Two~~ THREE. I suggest that you consult the appendix and use these principles as guidelines in the image-work exercise below. If you find that you want to use them in your everyday life too, the rewards will be even more far reaching. But remember not to use these as mechanical rules: take seriously the meaning and purpose of the principles, and see if you can change your attitudes rather than just your language.

In my view, one of the most crucial attitudes to adopt in trying to transform relationships is hope – the belief that things can be different. Most of our everyday rules of communication are designed to maintain the status quo of relationships – not to rock the boat. They are based on a static concept of ourselves and of others: this is how I am, and this is how you are, and all we can do is get by without creating too many conflicts.

In fact, if we take the view that we all act as we do because of our images and our view of the world, then it is up to each of us to be willing to listen to the image or view that leads the other person to act as he or she does, to think about how that relates to our own images and views, and to consider whether we can help to create a shared view that makes our relationship work better.

This hopefulness and willingness to consider the other's view of the world needs to be expressed in the way you communicate with the other person. Thus, rather than thinking, or saying 'You are a cruel person', you need to consider the alternative approach: 'When you act that way, it feels as if you are being cruel to me and I get very hurt. What is going on in you, or what is it about the way you see me, that leads you to act that way? How can we change this?' Communicating with this attitude has the added advantage that the other person is less likely to feel attacked, and the problem becomes a joint one to work on together. This means that you are both more likely to find a creative solution.

In other words, take a dynamic approach that assumes that we cannot ever be sure what a person *is* in a fixed and permanent sense. What people do is an expression not of their 'essence' but of a view of the world which may be open to change – especially if we ourselves are willing to listen to their view, be clear about our own, and build a bridge between us.

TRANSFORMING RELATIONSHIPS: STRUCTURE OF THE EXERCISE

The structure of this 'Transforming Relationships' exercise is as follows: you allow to emerge opposite you an image of someone with whom you have a relationship problem or to whom you would like to relate better, notice how they look and feel to you and then begin to say what you feel towards the person. You then become the other person and respond and then switch back and forth between you, each saying what you need to say. You may also occasionally switch to a third position, the position of an observer or counsellor, so that you can look at what is going on in the relationship as a whole. You explore possibilities, become clearer about each other's view, negotiate new ways of relating where possible, until there is a feeling that you have shifted something. You then check back to see if there has been a change in the image, thank your conscious and unconscious for the work, reflect on its meaning, and consider how you will act in future, and emerge.

The format then is:

Preparation: Clearing a space and relaxing
1   Summoning the image
2   Studying the image
3   Talking to the person
4   Switching roles and becoming the other person
5   Continuing the conversation
6   Becoming the wise observer
7   Moving toward resolution
8   Appreciating, reflecting, looking forward, and emerging.

TRANSFORMING RELATIONSHIPS: BASIC EXERCISE

Preparation: Clearing a space and relaxing: As always, you need to prepare a quiet place and time, where you won't be distracted. Choose a comfortable seat or cushion for yourself, and place another one opposite you. If this exercise is done seriously, it may bring up lots of deep feelings, and you would probably benefit a great deal from having someone you trust with you who helps you through the exercises, so that you can really relax and deeply experience your feelings. A brief relaxation exercise is also very important.

1   *Inviting an image*: You may have someone particular in mind whom you want to talk to, or you may wish to allow your unconscious to let you know which relationship is unresolved and needs

your attention. Two alternative wordings, there-fore, are:

a *Specific person*: Allow to emerge on the seat or cushion opposite you an image of x. The person may initially emerge as a picture, a voice, a sensa-tion, or in any other way. Allow the image to clarify.

b *Unfinished business*: Allow to emerge on the seat or cushion opposite you an image of someone with whom you have unfinished business – unresolved or uncomfortable issues, problems or feelings. This can be someone in your life now, or someone who used to be important to you. The person may or may not still be alive. Allow yourself to see and acknowledge the very first person that comes to mind, whether as a name, a visual image, a voice, or in any other way.

When the image emerges, in any form say: 'Thank you unconscious. I appreciate the gift.'

If nothing happens try saying to your unconscious: 'Unconscious, thank you for your effort to protect me. But I would like to explore this relationship. Please help me to do this in a safe and natural way. Please allow an image to emerge now.'

If still nothing happens, simply proceed as if the person were sitting opposite you, and know that the image will clarify as the work continues.

2 *Studying the image*: Look at the person sitting opposite you, and try to see him or her as vividly and concretely as possible, almost as if they were in the same room with you. What are they wearing? What is the expression on their face?

What impression do they send out? How do they make you feel? You might also like to allow your spirit to go up above, around, underneath, and inside them, looking at them from every perspective possible so as to get a further understanding of them.

3 *Talking to the person*: Talk to the person opposite you, whom we can call Other, about all the feelings you have. Tell Other about your good feelings and your bad feelings. Most important, say whatever you haven't ever said to Other in real life, and even what you haven't yet dared to admit to yourself. Tell Other what you want. End by asking whatever question or questions you would like answered.

Comment: When you ask a question, it should be a real question that you sincerely want an answer to like 'What is the real reason you reject me when I'm needy?' and not 'How could you possibly be so mean to me?' which is really a hidden accusation.

---

4 *Switch roles and become the other person*: Now switch roles and sit in Other's seat. Take a moment to sink into being Other, just as in chapter 6 you sank into being the image. Sit like the person, and sense what it would really be like to be the other person, and see how the world looks from their point of view — and of course, most particularly, how you, whom we will now call Self, look from their point of view.

What did Self just say to you and ask you? Be as

accurate as you can. How does Self look or seem to you. How do you feel about what he/she has said? What is your response? End by saying what you want, and asking whatever you want to ask.

Comment: In most interactions we only see our own point of view. This is an opportunity to see the world from the point of view of another, and yet know you will be able to return back to your own seat and your own perspective again.

It is most important when you switch roles to really get into being Other – not to caricature, or just become a slightly filled out version of how you see the person anyway. If there are no surprises, and you are just saying and feeling what you would have expected the other to say and feel, you are probably not getting into the other person's skin. On the other hand, if you do allow yourself to really be Other on a deep level, you will be astounded at the way you can answer questions and explain things that you simply did not know you knew as Self.

5 *Continue the conversation*: Keep talking to each other and switching roles when it feels right. This is the time to clarify what you feel at present, and to try and move on to a better place in your relationship.

Comment: Remember that as long as this person is part of your inner world, it is not good for you to have this disturbance and discomfort between the two of you, which is necessarily also a disturbance and discomfort within you. So aim to find a better working relationship with Other, no matter how angry and resentful or hopeless you feel, because the bad feelings are in you, and hurting you, rather than the other at whom they are aimed.

6 *Become the wise observer*: Put a cushion or chair on the side and imagine that someone who is wise and loving, knows you both well, and cares about you is sitting on that chair. This person also happens to be the best relationship counsellor in the world. When you're ready, switch to this third position, be this wise counsellor, and look at and review the interaction that has just been going on. What can you see? What is the nature of this relationship? How are these two people colluding with each other? How would you advise them?

Comment: Having already expanded our consciousness to the point that we can see the point of view of another, we are now getting a sense of what is going on in the interaction between these two people. This third position of wise counsellor is sometimes the most useful position of all.

---

7 *Move toward some resolution*: Continue the conversation until you are clearer about each other's point of view, and feel you have reached as far as you can go in making your relationship work better. You should feel some sense of relief, or resolution; that the relationship no longer feels so stuck, though it may still be painful. The goal is not perfection, but rather a sense of having made some kind of shift, which may well be only the first of many such shifts. Thank each other for having taken the time to listen and really engage in this team effort, and say goodbye for now.

8 *Appreciate, reflect, look forward and emerge*: Conjure up the image of Other: how do they look

now? How do you feel about them now? Notice any shifts and congratulate your conscious and unconscious selves for that very difficult work you have just engaged in. Both before emerging, and over the next few days, reflect on what has just happened to you and what you have learned. Now is the time also to think about the implications: what practical steps do you want to take; what real conversations do you feel it is appropriate to have?

VARIATIONS: EXPANDING POSSIBILITIES

Working on relationships always challenges our own limits. Experiment with the following variations as a means of expanding your personal possibilities for understanding and enhancing the relationship on which you are working, as well as all the others in your life. Remember, as always, to return to the original images and examine your feelings about Other, and to say anything new that feels right to say to them.

1   *Taking back your projections*: As long as you have unfinished business with another person, some of your energy is invested in the other person rather than being available to you. This makes you feel weak and at their mercy, and makes you project onto them powers and attributes that may have more to do with you than with them. If you can pull this energy back you feel both stronger in yourself, and more able to see the person clearly as a separate individual.

Try this: Imagine that your energy is coming out of the top of your head, rather like strands of spaghetti (or, if you prefer, rays of light or energy) and is stuck in the other person. Feel, see, and sense this. Now imagine pulling back the strands of spaghetti (or rays of light or energy) out of the person, and into a hole in the top of

128

your head, and let the strands (or rays) sink into you. Notice any difference in the way you feel, and in the way the other looks, and whether there is anything different that you could say now.

If you feel there are strands (or rays) coming out of your heart or belly into the other, you can try pulling those back too. See how this feels.

Note that this exercise is also useful when your energy is trapped in something rather than someone – your work, or your money problems, or your fame; if you are obsessed with anything or anyone, this is a good time to spend a moment doing this exercise.

2 *If I loved me*: How would this and other relationships work if you could hold on to a feeling of loving and appreciating yourself? Having a stable positive sense of yourself, rather than needing others to give this to you, is another way to take back your projections and see the other person clearly.

Think of a time you've felt really confident about yourself and really appreciated and loved yourself. Then step into the picture, and breathe as that person does. Or spend a moment appreciating yourself now, and really feel that self love. Or, if these first two are difficult: try *'If* I really appreciated and loved myself, how would it be?'* – and sense how this would feel.

As you feel the feeling of love and appreciation for yourself, touch together your thumb and forefinger, thus creating an association cue with these feelings. Now, carry on the conversation with Other, or talk to anyone else you have difficulty with, but keep holding onto the feeling that you love and appreciate yourself in a way that doesn't depend on this other person. If the feeling seems to be evaporating, just touch your thumb and forefinger together again, and remind yourself 'If I loved and appreciated myself, how would I respond?' Notice how this conversation is different from your original one.

129

3 *Beyond the personal self*: Relax fully into yourself, feeling at home and at peace. Look at the person opposite you, and try to reach beyond their present personal self to get a sense of how they would be if they were fully evolved, fully themselves, fully in tune with the universe, or however you might describe it.

Now, have a conversation with the other person's 'higher' or more evolved self. It is best to talk now about the Other as 'he' or 'she' so as to distinguish between the everyday person and this more idealised highly evolved aspect.

Switch roles, and enter into that more evolved consciousness and look at yourself from that point of view. How do you appear to the more evolved Other? How would you look if you were your own evolved Self? Let the two evolved selves talk about the two personal beings who are engaged in this unfinished business.

4 *Ideal and disastrous dialogues*: Imagine that this relationship is an ideal one. How would your dialogue go? Go ahead and have the conversation. Now imagine that this relationship is the most awful and disastrous relationship in the world. How would your dialogue go? Go ahead with this conversation.

These conversations will give you a clear idea about your hopes and fears, and will often specify exactly what change you are wanting. Compare them with the original conversation, and find out what you can learn.

Try this too: Replace the image of Other with the image of an aspect of you, perhaps the good parent or the good friend within you. Switch roles, be this aspect of you, and try saying to yourself those ideal words that you wanted Other to say. Switch back. How did that feel? Is that how you usually talk to yourself? Or are those disastrous dialogues more similar to your internal conversations?

Consider the possibility that from now on whenever

you want something from someone else, you think first of how you could give it yourself. You want someone to tell you how beautiful you are? Tell yourself you are beautiful. You want someone to stop criticising? Stop criticising yourself first. Give yourself that ideal relationship for just a few days and see how this goes. Charity begins at home, as they say.

5 *Parents talking*: Imagine that your mother is sitting on one of the chairs, and your father on the other, and they are talking about their feelings toward each other. Switching between the seats to play each one in turn, begin by having them talk to each other as they normally do, or did. Then allow them to tell each other what they have never told each other, and to see if they can work through their relationship and resolve some old difficulties. Then take the position of the wise observer, and look at the interaction. Help these two people to see what is going on between them and to make peace. What do these dialogues remind you of in your own life? Can you change your outer relationships in much the same way as you resolved the difficulties between your inner mother and father?

6 *Your inner male and female*: Jung points out that the relationship we have with the opposite sex is intimately connected with the opposite sex being within us. Allow to emerge on the cushion opposite you the male in you (your male aspect, your male history) if you are a female; or the female in you (your female aspect, your female history) if you are a male. How does he/she look? Ask his/her name. Talk to him/her. Say how you feel, etc. Switch roles and be him/her. How does Self look? Continue the conversation and work toward resolution. You may wish to end by inviting the opposite sex-being to become integrated with you by hugging them and allowing them to melt into your heart. Then reflect on that relationship. How is it similar to your relationships with the opposite sex? What are the implications?

131

7   *Preparatory conversation*: This time, rather than conversing with your inner image of the other, imagine that the other is really in the room with you, and you are role-playing the conversation in advance to iron out the snags. Find out what you want to say to the other in real life, and switch roles to find the response. Carry through until you feel clear about what is appropriate to say, and how.

APPLICATIONS:
REAL LIFE QUICK EXERCISES

The skills you have just learned can also be used when you are out in the hurly burly of relationships. The difference is that rather than actually switching seats, you need to imagine that your consciousness goes out of the top of your head and changes seats for you, so to speak.

Try any of the following quick exercises in the middle of a conversation, or when observing someone. One to five are based on the exercises above, and six to ten are based on the communication rules in Appendix Three.

1   Imagine that your mind or spirit or consciousness goes out of the top of your head and goes into the top of the head of another person. How does it feel to be that person? How do you sense they see you? (Note: Do practise this first when you are just watching people in a bus station, café, or restaurant; it's good also to try this with a friend and check out how accurate you can both be).

2   Imagine your consciousness goes out of the top of your head, and goes into the wise observer role. How does your interaction look from that point of view? Then continue the conversation.

3   Pull back your projections (See exercise variation 1). Then continue the conversation.

4 Say to yourself, 'If I loved myself and appreciated myself now, what would I say?' (See variation 2). And then continue the conversation.

5 Spend a moment seeing the person as their higher or more evolved self. (See variation 3). Then continue the conversation.

6 When you have strong feelings that seem a bit extreme for the circumstances, stop a minute and ask yourself: 'What's the feeling behind the feeling?' For example, perhaps behind the fury there is hurt. Or perhaps behind the hurt there is fury. If so, say so.

7 Use only 'I' messages: Say how you *feel*, not what the other person *is*.

8 Listen accurately and empathise with the point of view of the other and then be clear about your own.

9 Negotiate clearly: be prepared to say what you want and what you are happy to offer.

10 Find out what you have in common with the other, and then consider your differences as variations on a theme.

When you've done any of these little exercises, notice whether you interrupted one of your normal patterns and interacted or perceived the other a bit differently. If so: wonderful.

IN CONCLUSION

Relationships are so important and so difficult, that you owe yourself further congratulations for having tackled this chapter. Remember that divine virtue of forgiveness: forgiving both yourself and the other person for not having the perfect relationship, or being the perfect lover/friend/spouse/parent/child. And don't expect to have solved it all now. If you have shifted a bit, have a different feeling inside you about the other or about yourself, or simply find yourself more ready to smile at the world, then that's great. The more you work on improving your consciousness and your communication, the better things will get, both inside you and between you and other people.

8

RESENTMENTS, REJECTIONS, AND MOURNING
Saying goodbye

When my father died recently, I intuitively knew the moment of his death, and felt I was with him, although he was thousands of miles away. As I tried to stay in touch with him after his death, these very real images of his experience came to me, as if from another dimension:

I saw him walking alone on his pathway. It seemed incredibly painful. This pain was the pain of trans-formation – of having, so to speak, to change all one's molecules into a different state of being, and of facing an unknown path ahead alone. I felt I needed to focus with him on this painful path he was on.

I then saw him trudging along with a sack on his back. The sack was full of the memories and feelings that tied him to life, and though it was very heavy, he didn't want to let go of it. He put it down for a moment, and then picked it up again. He then trudged up a hill with it, exhausted.

Finally he put the sack down and started to sift through it. It transpired that it was full of all his resentments and bitterness and 'if only' feelings about life – all the things he wasn't happy about. The happy memories were not in there at all. What he had to do was to go through them all, and say about each of them, 'So be it'. When he had finally done that, he was finished with the sack.

He then started walking towards the light, and four angels came to greet him. Always a modest man, he could hardly believe it. 'This feels like heaven. Why are they doing all this for me?' he seemed to be marvelling. I laughed, and whispered to him, 'This *is* heaven.' Soon after, surrounded by the angels massaging him with light and love, we said goodbye to each other, and there were no more images.

This story may or may not be a literally true picture of life immediately after death. But it is certainly a deep metaphor for the path of transformation involved in saying goodbye: a process that is necessarily painful and yet can ultimately release us into the light of a new stage in our lives.

GOODBYES IN ALL SHAPES AND SIZES

This chapter is about saying goodbye to people, and even to things, that we are tied to in a way that is no longer appropriate. When someone has died, or we have parted from them for any other reason, we need to let go and say goodbye. When we carry resentful feelings towards someone and cannot relinquish this negative connection, we also need to let go. And, where possible, we need to learn to say a full goodbye before we part from someone or something that has been an important part of our life.

Life is full of goodbyes. Some are lightly spoken, as we rush excitedly toward a new phase or a new adventure. Others make us feel that we are losing a part of our self that we can never regain. Some are full mutual farewells, and others are rather like the sound of one hand clapping in the wilderness. Some feel like inevitable steps toward growth, and others we experience resentfully as slaps in the face. And again, some partings are drawn out for years, seemingly not resolvable, while others are like amputations that leave us no time to adjust. Whatever way they present themselves to us, good-byes always carry within them the whiff of death and the promise of rebirth.

The sad fact is that many people never get to the stage of rebirth because the goodbyes have not been fully dealt with, and the other person, or that aspect of themselves, has not been fully released. Many people carry within them wounds that have never healed properly, and this is probably one of the major causes of physical illness as well as emotional unhappiness.

Turning the Corner

Transformation is painful, and we have many ways to avoid pain. Furthermore, while we are in the midst of it, it may feel as if there is no future beyond, and that by saying goodbye we are somehow once again killing that which is already dead, or destroying that which we still hope will return to us. It is only when we have taken a risk and stepped forward that we are able to turn the corner and see what is ahead.

I remember Joanne, who had had two still-born babies years ago, to whom she had never said goodbye. She always had an empty bloated feeling in her stomach, which made her uncomfortable, and yet strangely also comforted her. When I encouraged her to imagine the babies and talk to them, she talked of her love for them, and the pain of losing them, and admitted how desperately guilty she felt because somehow she felt responsible.

When she had finished, I suggested that she say Goodbye. She refused, because if she said goodbye she would be 'killing' them again; she wanted to carry them with her always. But just as Joanne said 'No, I won't say goodbye', she gasped and said 'Oh, they've just gone.' They had done it for her. It was as if by acknowledging and facing her feelings, she had unconsciously given them permission to go. The bloated feeling in her belly went too, and she felt, for the first time in years, light and free to start life afresh.

The paradox is that it is not the loving feelings that tie us most to past relationships, but the more negative difficult ones. It was not so much Joanne's love, but her guilt, that made it impossible for her to say goodbye. Similarly, my father's sack was not full of his loving memories, because he could still enjoy these even if he was no longer tied to the people. It was his resentments and 'if only' feelings that bound him to life, and until he sifted through these and made his peace with them he seemed doomed to trudge on exhausted and alone.

We can say goodbye to people and to relationships and still love them freely. It is unresolved and unresolvable feelings that keep us tied to them. This is as true for the people that choose to end a relationship, as for those who have been left.

If we feel angry, resentful, and bitter, we are still demanding something from the other person in our minds, asking them to be different or to have been different, and hence we feel we cannot go away unless we get it. When we feel guilty and angry at ourselves, even if it is because we never expressed our love enough, or because we caused so much pain when we said goodbye, we are still demanding from ourselves that we should be different or should have been different, and so we cannot let go.

Similarly, if we cannot make sense of what has happened or don't even know what has happened, we are left with questions and doubts that we cannot put to rest, and are thus deprived of the certainty that makes resolution possible. People whose loved ones have disappeared without explaining or saying goodbye, or have been 'disappeared' by governments with no news of their fate being received, or indeed have died in disasters in which their body has never been recovered, have incredible difficulty going through a normal mourning process and saying goodbye.

It is these unresolved feelings that are also most poisonous for our insides, both physically and emotionally. It is only when we face the feelings and the doubts openly, and are able to say 'So be it', that we can forgive others and ourselves, say goodbye, and move forward into the light.

A Good Death

The problem is probably not so much that we are cowards and want to avoid pain, but that we have never been taught how and why to say a full and proper goodbye. Thus, when Adrian's father died suddenly in a distant country to which he could not travel even for the funeral, he felt unable to find a way of dealing with his feelings of sudden loss and change, nor with the unfinished business which could now never be finished.

He thought of anthropologist Colin Turnbull's accounts of the Mbuti pygmies, who understood that when someone died, people had to let go of him or her completely in order for it to be a 'good death', which would enable them to get on with their lives. He knew that he too needed to go through a similar process to let go of his father. But how? He was in Atsitsa, our holistic health centre in Greece, just a few days after his father's funeral, and decided to attend my imagework session on 'saying goodbye'. He wrote this account of his experience:

There were about eight of us there, as I recall, in the relative cool of the evening, high up on a hill overlooking a darkening Aegean sea and a brightening western horizon. I shall never forget it. We sat in a circle. At first I just felt embarrassed. The therapist asked us to visualise the person we wanted to let go of or say goodbye to. We did, in silence with our eyes shut as we focused. Then she asked us to describe the person aloud and then to address him or her. 'Tell him or her what you want to say'.

To my surprise I found quite quickly that instead of expressing grief, sadness or regret to my dead father, I was expressing anger. I berated him for things he had done or not done to me and my sister; I shouted at him for not having stood up to our strong-willed mother when necessary, and for patronising my sister and me so cruelly instead of fostering our independence. Did he not realise how unconfident and dependent this had left my sister, and how furiously and dangerously rebellious it had left me? Did he have no idea of the implications for our lives that flowed from this? I told him about all that and (quite unfairly) blamed him for it all.

. . . Then the facilitator made us all change places with the imagined person we had been addressing, by shifting to the centre of the circle and facing out towards where we had been sitting. We had now to be that person and answer back to our real selves. The shift was quite difficult for me and caught me unawares. But it was decisive. I found myself sitting as my father often had, with his shoulders hunched and his head forward. Ringing in the great and echoing internal chamber of this imaginary dialogue with my dead father were the last words I had just barked at him: 'Don't you know that it was no bloody good behaving like that?' I faced outwards to where I had visualised him sitting, and I found a voice within me, his, now answering back, as it were, and all he said, with his head down and his shoulder forward was: 'You're right, I know, I know'. And then the visualisation faded and the imagination closed down.

. . . (I then imagined) my father in a birch bark canoe, tethered to a rope that I was hanging on to from the jetty at the bend of a vast sweeping river. It seemed doubly appropriate in this case, for just as I was hanging on to him so too was he hanging on to me. Until I let the rope go neither he nor I could get on with what we had to do. We were interrupting each other's journeys. Though I don't believe in an afterlife, the image, the idea, and the ploy seemed to help in this process of parting. I imagined the canoe floating off down river while I walked away from the jetty and back to the activities of life. Unfinished business had been done. It made me feel much at ease.

. . . I began to realise then – and this bore in on me more fully as the days went by – that something in me had been settled. . . . He had, in this imaginary encounter, acknowledged that it had been wrong to behave as he did, and all that I had needed was that acknowledgment from him . . . . Instead of having a sense of inconsolable loss, of diminishment and despair, of unacknowledged anger and frustrated grief, I emerged feeling clearer and at much greater ease, appreciating in a more balanced way his good and long life, the happy times he had given us as children, his weaknesses and strengths, what he had done for us, and what we had meant to each other.

. . . The sky had become dark purple as dark Greek grapes, and the moon appeared over the shoulder of a hill. . . . The smell of dinner wafted up. I was ravenously hungry. It was time to eat: it was time to go on. Despite the distance between my father and me it had after all been a very good death.'[1]

Running Out of the Door

The best time to begin to say goodbye is, where possible, before you part. Much marriage guidance counselling is not about helping couples to stay together, but about helping them, if they wish to separate, to say a full goodbye.

But this is not always easy. Difficulties with saying goodbye can take more than one form. While some people hold on too long to relationships and feelings that they need to let go of, others do the opposite: they just run away for dear life. In escaping prematurely, not only do they leave an unresolved mess behind that is a hundred times harder to heal, because the loved ones left behind have no way of understanding what has happened, but they themselves never experience the full cycle of death and mourning that allows for a real rebirth, and they tend to go on repeating the same pattern again and again.

A client of mine, Ellen, left a ten-year-old marriage, found a new flat, and moved in, just days after she decided to end the relationship. She did not want to talk to her husband about it and felt she had nothing to say – it was over. She had gone dead sexually some years ago, following, as she realised now, an anger against him she had been unable to express. She had now gone dead emotionally, and that was that. Life beckoned, and she just wanted to run out of the door into the exciting fairground out there; if she stopped to say goodbye she might miss something. But this was not the first time she had done this, and she feared she would go on doing it all her life.

As we explored her feelings, she realised what was stopping her from saying goodbye properly: her greatest fear was that she might feel guilty, or he might convince her that she was being silly or wrong, and she might have to stay. This way, she didn't need to look at the guilt, or at the pain in his face, and she could feel free to do what she wanted and knew was right for her.

We then talked of the difference between feelings and decisions. Her initial vision and decision to leave the marriage was clear and firm. She needed to have enough faith in this to be able to stop for a while and tolerate the whole host of feelings associated with going, without feeling that they implied new decisions. As long as she really knew what was right for her in the long run, she didn't need to run out the door and grab it.

As Ellen learned to trust her intuition that she was doing the right thing by leaving, and her ability to choose to go freely despite the painful feelings on both sides, she was able to deal with the emotions involved in saying goodbye. First through imagework, and then in a joint session with her husband, she explored her feelings and he talked about his, and they said goodbye and wished each other well in their new lives.

The cycle had been broken, and she now felt more hopeful that in her next relationship she would express her feelings before she 'went dead', and say goodbye before she left – if indeed she had to go at all.

Other Attachments

Saying goodbye is not always to people. You sometimes need to say goodbye to a home, or a neighbourhood, or a period in your life. Bernard, one of my imagework students, was having trouble finding a new house, and began to sense that it was because he couldn't say goodbye to his former home.

Walking in the park, worried about his inability to move house, he sat down on a park bench and invited an image of a guide to help him with his problem. In his imagination, a small dancing figure appeared in the distance. As it got nearer, a quick tap dance and a line from one of his songs revealed him to be Fred Astaire. Fred began to sing lines from two of his songs, one of which was 'Won't you change partners and dance with me?' and the other was 'After you, who, could be my sky of blue? After you, who, could be my love?'

Fred Astaire explained to Bernard that leaving his home and finding a new one was like leaving a woman and starting a new relationship. To let go it was necessary to say goodbye to the female spirit of the house. He suggested summoning up the spirit of the house and dancing with her, singing his song, thanking her for being around such a long time, and saying farewell. Bernard did this in his imagination right then and there. After this joyful experience of saying goodbye something shifted in him, and he was freer to look with an open mind at houses, and to decide upon a new house that fitted the new Bernard.

Can There Be Life After death?

When we are deeply involved with someone, whether the feelings are positive or negative, it is as if our selves or spirits or thoughtforms or lives are joined together in some way, so that letting go seems to be letting go of part of ourselves.

If the other person has actually died, there is often a temptation to follow after the other to join one's 'other half', and indeed many people *do* die soon after their long-term spouses have died. If there is no death involved, we often stay totally involved with the other, even years after we have not seen them, just so as not to have to separate. We do not want either of us to have a life after that death.

This is why it is so important in the ritual of saying goodbye to recognise, as Adrian did with his father, that we need to cut the ties that bind us to the other, and let the other go, knowing that they can have an existence apart from us, and we from them. This doesn't mean that we cannot love each other or be there for each other any more on some level, but only that the binding tie has to go, and we both have to be free in our relation to each other, while we continue on our respective paths.

It is harder to understand what it means to let someone go on their path when a death is involved, especially if you don't believe in life after death. Many people do believe that the spirits of people who have died sometimes need to feel that their loved ones have accepted their death in order for them to continue on their way. But whether or not you believe this is so, it does seem certain that people who are about to die sometimes linger on until they feel that their unfinished business is resolved and their loved ones have given them permission to go. There also seems to be a deep psychic necessity within us to set the other person free after their death before we can go on with our own lives, even if this only means giving them permission in our minds to 'rest in peace'.

Setting someone else free in your mind is also crucial when you are carrying resentful feelings. There is nothing like feeling unfairly treated for keeping you tied to someone who has wronged you until and unless they have either acknowledged their fault or been punished for their wrong doing. Sometimes at the back of this is the fear that if you let go of your resentment, you are acknowledging that perhaps they were right and you were wrong. Thus when you carry resentments, you are unable to forgive either yourself or the other and say 'So be it', and the wound continues to fester.

I remember Alice, for example, who was full of resentment against her parents for what they had done to her. Despite her many problems she refused to get any kind of counselling or therapy – it was their fault, and so they should pay for it. If they refused, too bad. She wasn't going to let them off the hook.

Bernie Siegel, a holistic surgeon who believes that holding on to resentments is a major contributing factor to cancer, tells a little fable about introducing God to his sickest patient, a woman with cancer whose husband had run off with another woman. God promised that he could ensure that she would get well. 'All you have to do is love, accept, forgive, and choose to be happy'. The woman looked God in the eye and said 'Have you met my husband yet?'[2]

Resentment does not in fact punish the other at all, but only ourselves, since it is our own life that it poisons, and our own physical and emotional health that is being threatened. Being right is just as bad for us as being wrong, as long as we cannot be at peace.

It is therefore crucial not only to express your resentful feelings to the other, whether in reality or through image-work, but also to cut the ties of resentment and retribution, and let the person off the hook. This means acknowledging that other people have a right to an existence of their own despite their failure to meet your expectations – and so do you.

If you can imagine good things happening to that resented person and come to feel okay about it, and imagine yourself happy even if they haven't done what you want, you have not only set them but also set yourself free. You may also have reminded yourself that none of us are here to live up to the expectations of others. Perhaps you have a right to be less perfect too.

The People Who Have Chosen to Befriend Me

When we feel angry at, or resentful of others, or guilty and unforgiving of ourselves, we need also to re-examine our original expectations and models. We all have built-in models of how mothers, fathers, sisters, brothers, friends, lovers, colleagues, and all the other people we relate to in life should be, and what they should offer us and we them. Few people meet these ideal expectations – nor perhaps would it be a good idea if they did – and therefore there is an awful lot of room for anger, resentment, and refusal to forgive others and ourselves in every relationship.

I remember the afternoon some years ago when my father

was still alive, and I was absolutely furious at him. I went for a long walk to deal with my anger, resentment, and hate. Finally, after a long conversation with him in my imagination, I was able to see that the biggest problem was that he didn't fit my model of how a 'father' should be. Suddenly I found myself saying to him in my mind 'I will stop expecting you to be father to me. Thank you for being one of the people that has chosen to befriend me on this life's path.' My love for him, and my acknowledgment of his love for me, flowed back and I felt at peace.

Since then, when I am in trouble because of my expectations of others or of myself, I try to let go of the 'role' expectations, and acknowledge what we have freely given each other as people that have chosen to befriend each other on our life paths. Almost magically the resentment and guilt melt away, and the love surges in to take their place.

SAYING GOODBYE: THE STRUCTURE OF THE EXERCISE

The following 'Saying Goodbye' exercise is useful in any situation where you feel that you are too tied up with someone, and need to say goodbye. This may be because they have died and you have not let them go, or because they have rejected you, or you them, and you have not got over it, or because you feel angry and resentful at them, or guilty towards them, and you keep going over and over in your mind how it should have been. It can also be adapted to say goodbye to things, places, or life stages.

After allowing the image to emerge of the person to whom you need to say goodbye, it is good to begin with a 'life review' of the relationship. It is often said that when someone is about to die, they see their lives flashing before their eyes. In the same way, before saying goodbye, we can review the pictures that represent the relationship, including both the happy scenes and the painful ones, and thus see the life of the relationship flashing before us.

147

It is then important to talk to the person and share all the feelings you have, both positive and negative, both rational and irrational. The communication principles of Appendix Three may be useful here. This is a moment of truth that we need to respect deeply and may involve a struggle to reach. We all carry a lot of clichés in our minds, and these tend to get activated when we lose a person whether through death, or rejection, or in any other way. It is important to go below this level to what I call the 'death truth', the truth that you would face if your life depended on knowing it, or perhaps the truth that you would face if you knew you were about to die.

It may be, for example, that you have to face the fact that the person was a burden to you, or you to them. Or that you had lots of petty feelings of jealousy, resentment, and annoyance that you are ashamed of. Or indeed that on some level you are happy they are gone. This 'death truth' is always less sentimental than we would like, but when we face it, we feel a great relief.

Once your relationship has been worked through, and you feel ready to say goodbye, it is time to cut the tie between you, using an appropriate image. Then, having done so, allow yourself to imagine the other having an existence that is full of happiness and good things, although you are not there, and yourself equally having a life full of happiness and good things without them. This step is particularly important in the case of resentments, when it is so hard to accept that a person who has wronged you should still have a good life. It may in fact not be possible to do so at first; but working on it for as long as it takes you to reach the point that it feels comfortable is itself a healing process. In the case of death, you may imagine the other having an after-death existence of any sort you believe in, including simply resting in peace. You conclude as usual by appreciating, reflecting, looking forward, and emerging.

Thus the format is:

Preparation: Clearing the space, relaxing
1   Inviting the image

2 Life review of the relationship
3 Talking to each other
4 Moving toward resolution
5 Saying goodbye and cutting the tie
6 Wishing each other well
7 Appreciating, reflecting, looking forward, and emerging

SAYING GOODBYE: BASIC EXERCISE

Preparation: Clearing the space, relaxing (Note: The exercise is phrased as one of saying goodbye to a person; if it is a place, a life stage, or anything else that you need to say goodbye to, just allow an image to emerge for that, and follow the general structure, adapting the language where appropriate.) Do remind yourself of the communication principles of Appendix Three before beginning.

1 *Inviting the image*: Allow an image to emerge of someone sitting opposite you that you need to say goodbye to. See them clearly. What are they wearing? How are they sitting? What is the expression on their face?

2 *Life review of the relationship*: Relax, and allow to flit before your eyes all the pictures that come to you of your relationship with this person. They may be enjoyable or painful. If they are enjoyable, step inside the picture and relive them. If painful, you may wish to stay outside and look at them calmly. Acknowledge with these pictures all the facets of the relationship that you have had with this person.

3 *Talking to each other*: Now talk to the person

149

opposite you and share everything you feel – the good things that you appreciate them for, and the negative things you resent them for. Don't worry if it sounds irrational. Just let the feelings come out.

The feelings are likely to include: *anger* – about events in your life together, and at their leaving you or otherwise hurting you even if it wasn't their fault; *resentment* – about the unfairness built into your relationship or into the parting; *guilt* – that you didn't do things differently or better so that the relationship could have been happier, or didn't do enough to save their life; *fear* – of the future; *pain* – about your loss, and about what they are going through or have lost; *love* – for them and for the life you had together; *longing* – for it all to be different, or for the person to come back; and *relief* – that it is all over. The important thing is to be honest and not sentimental about all these complicated and ambivalent feelings.

Then switch roles and sit in the seat of the other. What do you notice? How do you feel as this person, and how does Self (the original you) look to you? Did you hear what he or she said? What is your response?

4 *Moving toward resolution*: Continue the dialogue until you feel that you have reached some sense of completion. In the case of a recent painful separation or death this can take days or weeks or even months of conversations. Take as long as you need.

It may be useful, if you feel that you are finding it hard to let go of your expectations of the other, to try saying to them 'Thank you for being one of the people who has chosen to befriend me on my life path.' See how it feels.

5 *Saying goodbye and cutting the tie*: When you are ready, say 'Goodbye.' Feel the depth of that goodbye. Be aware that this doesn't mean that you cannot love or relate to the person, but that they are no longer involved with you directly in the kind of relationship you have had with them. It is now time to cut the tie. Two images you can use are:
a   Imagine that the person's spirit is a balloon, whose string you need to cut so that they can float freely away, always able to return to you, but never again tied.
b   Imagine that the person is a boat, tied by a rope or streamers to the shore where you are standing. Cut the tie or the streamers, and let the boat float out to sea or down the river.
   Or choose any other image that feels right to you that involves cutting a tie.

6 *Wishing each other well*: Allow yourself to imagine the other person going on without you. If they are still alive, imagine good things happening to them – whatever it is that they would consider good. This is particularly important if you have been angry or resentful, but may require a lot of painful practice before you can do it comfortably. If the person is now dead, imagine them going onto whatever your picture of death is. Also imagine yourself having good things happen to you, despite the fact that this person is, for better or for worse, no longer part of your life.

7 *Appreciating, reflecting, looking forward, and*

151

emerging: When you are ready, appreciate your conscious and unconscious for having gone through this very painful and releasing process. Reflect on its meaning to you, both before emerging and over the next days and weeks and sense how your life can be different now that you have said goodbye.

IN CONCLUSION

Once you have said goodbye to someone, remember that you don't need to feel they have gone away for good, but only that you are no longer tied to each other. You can still go back and talk to them anytime, and use them as a helpful presence in your life, whether in real terms, if they are live and available, or in a feeling sense if they have died or are not accessible. Your paths have now diverged, and they are not there for you in your everyday life, but your caring for each other can be forever.

9

USING THE PAST CREATIVELY

The child in me

The past is here and now. It lives within us, not only in the form of memories, but in the form of images and attitudes that can serve both to block us and to enrich us. Like a living organism, it can grow and transform.

For example, Lenny, a graphic designer in his sixties who was a participant at one of our holiday centres in Greece, always seemed to find it so hard to be real with me, although I could see he was really trying to reach out. I wondered how he had become quite that frightened of people. In an imagework session on 'The child in me,' he invited an image of a child with his name to emerge in the chair opposite him. The child that popped up was a terrified child who was beaten regularly by his father.

Lenny began to talk to this child and comfort him, and promised to be his friend and protector. After lunch, he went to the beach, taking the child with him in his imagination, and they made little sandcastles together. He felt the mixed pleasure and pain of both child and adult as they played together for the first time. The next day when Lenny came to the group, he began to talk about his experiences, and cried and cried with relief. He told us how that morning for the first time in his adult life he had woken up without morning terrors.

Ginny, a young college student of mine in her final year, wanted to take a counselling course but was terrified of groups, and had hitherto avoided them whenever she could. As we looked at the problem, a memory emerged of being in the school playground and being taunted by the other girls and boys, who made fun of her family and of her messy way of dressing. She turned around and ran away, feeling totally humiliated.

Ginny's pain showed in her face as she relived this episode. I encouraged the adult in her to go into that traumatic situation with the child. The adult Ginny imagined holding little Ginny's hand and loving her. As the adult, Ginny told the child that she needed to stand up to the children rather than run away because one couldn't avoid unpleasant situations forever.

Little Ginny, feeling bolder now because she had the adult Ginny to help and advise her, imagined going back to the playground. When the children began to taunt her, she shouted at them, telling them that they were stupid and cowards, and that they should pick on someone their own size. She then walked away proudly, and started to play with another friend in the playground. Big Ginny applauded her from the sidelines. When little Ginny finished playing, big Ginny walked her home from school, hand in hand, and promised to be there for her when she needed her.

Ginny emerged from this imagework experience with a new sense of confidence and pride. The next group meeting she had to face was still scary, but no longer terrifying, and she was surprised to find herself enjoying the challenge.

CAN WE CHANGE THE PAST?

In the world of the imagination, past, present and future can co-exist simultaneously because of that special quality that images have of presenting all experiences as totally present. This is why it is possible through imagework for the adult to bring the child into the present, and make friends with him or her, as Lenny did, or for the adult to step back into the past and help the child to make different choices, as Ginny did.

It seems a strange concept to try and change the past. We normally think of our memories as facts that shouldn't be tampered with. For example, perhaps you remember being hurt as a child and you believe that this memory explains why you don't trust people now. This may be so, but the reverse is also true: you don't trust people, and you explain this by this memory of being hurt as a child.

If we think of all the millions of moments that constitute our past, and recognise how few of them we consciously remember, and furthermore, how many of those memories may not be absolute recordings of fact but rather one story of what happened, we begin to see that somewhere in us we are already selecting and transforming our memories without realising it. Memories are not simply an objective record of the past; like any historical record, they are part of a particular approach to history. They can be seen as the personal mythology that accounts for our present life.

Think back to your own earliest memories. Could they be seen to sum up something about your own personal mythology regarding yourself? If we want to change our personal mythology, we need to go back into the old records and find new ways to make sense of them, so as to bring a new set of lessons into the present and future.

Past, present, and future are, in fact, continually in the process of reconstructing themselves in the light of each other. When my past is full of memories of being a victim, my present and future look full of suspicious traps that I must be careful not to fall into. When I feel depressed in the present, all I can remember about my past is a series of miserable experiences, and my future looks hopeless. When I have a sense of positive purpose about the future, the self same history may seem like a series of steps leading inescapably to that purpose, and the present will look delightful. In those wonderful moments of finding a 'truth that sets us free', past, present, and future transform themselves together, for they are all part of a total life meaning.

If our memories are as much an expression of our view of the world as the cause, then how do the experiences of childhood directly affect adults? At the most fundamental level, the past affects us through our images of the world, and our relationship to the world. In other words, the experiences we had as children, and how we interpreted those experiences, and how we reacted to those interpretations, led to an attitude, an expectation, a belief, an image, a certainty, of how life is and how we can deal with it. The experiences may even be totally forgotten, or their importance minimised, but these inner programs live on.

As adult and child work together through imagework, although the past does not change, the attitudes and images left over from that past can and do. Lenny and Ginny could not alter the facts of their lives, but they could change their present programs based on this past. In a sense, it is the past within us that we are changing, not the objective past. It is thus possible to begin to understand and heal the personal history that lives on in our bodies, in our unconscious images, and in our habitual behaviour patterns, and gain real choice in our present and future as adults.

ALL OUR EARLIER SELVES – AND THE FUTURE ONES TOO

The past that unfolds through imagework is often, as in the instances described above, a painful one, and full of outdated assumptions and decisions. But this is by no means always the case. For example, if you are anxious and frightened at present, you may get an image of a child going through a similarly frightening and anxious period, and you as an adult will need to comfort and support the child. On the other hand, the child that emerges might be one who is feeling carefree and excited, in which case you may find the child bringing you some joy and freedom from fear.

Furthermore, whether sad or joyful, the child that emerges always has some very lovely qualities that we as adults may have left behind, or may only sporadically make use of. One way to think of it is that we have living within us all our earlier selves – and, as we will see in later chapters, our future selves too – and these selves need to work and play together if we are to fulfil our potential to be resourceful and wholly alive adults.

The one-year-old and the fifteen-year-old within me, for example, have different strengths and gifts, as well as different vulnerabilities. The one-year-old has an innocence and curiosity and energy and total acceptance of the world as it is and of herself as she is. She is also completely at the mercy of the people around her. The fifteen-year-old has a lovely gauche quality and a budding interest in males and in sexuality and a real uncompromising commitment to finding out exactly what the nature of the world is and what everything means. She is also socially quite terrified, can never figure out what the rules of a situation are, and feels she is always doing the wrong thing and dressed the wrong way – which she is.

Normally, we switch between one age and another unconsciously. I may wake up in the morning feeling like that little one-year-old, sit down at my desk and become a competent adult, and later in the evening when I consider whether to go to a party, the adolescent in me may emerge feeling so shy and frightened that I decide to stay home. By being able to get in touch with my various selves of different ages, and set up communication lines between them, we can share rather than alternate. As an adult, I can draw on their resources, and, in turn, offer them the strengths I have acquired over the years.

For example, after a few occasions when I stayed home from parties following a great struggle and then was sorry, I became aware that it is not all of me that doesn't want to go to the party: the fifteen-year-old is excited but frightened, while the adult thinks the party might be nice but is not sure whether it is worth getting dressed up for when one could have a nice quiet read in bed. The next time a party invitation came up, I reassured the fifteen-year-old that I, the adult, would tell her what to wear, take her along and introduce her to people, and generally make sure she had nothing to be afraid of, but that I would appreciate sharing in that pleasure and excitement about parties that I seem to have lost. We went to the party 'together' and had a wonderful time.

Beginning to befriend these early selves also has the added bonus that we can experience a lovely caring family growing within us. I know that when I first made it a practice to carry on conversations with the child in me, I felt that I would never be truly alone again. And this was so.

TALKING TO THE CHILD IN ME, and RECREATING A HEALTHFUL PAST: THE STRUCTURE OF THE EXERCISES

This chapter has two basic exercises: in the first, 'Talking to the child in me,' you bring the child into the present, as Lenny did, while in the second, 'Recreating a healthful past', you go back into a past situation, as Ginny did.

The first exercise is an opportunity to make friends with the child within. Before beginning, do refer to Appendix Three to remind yourself of the principles of effective communication. Then invite an image of the child to emerge, talk to the child, and work through your relationship. A basic assumption in this process is that although you may have your difficulties with each other, you do both have to live in the same body, so you might as well get along better than you do. You may need to negotiate how you can each meet your separate needs in a democratic way. After thanking the child, plan to go on with this conversation and make it a regular part of your now expanding secret life. Think also about how you can create a life style that suits both of you.

The child that emerges may be a child of any age, and each time you do this exercise a different child may emerge. This is because the memory that is selected of the child is the one that has some relevance to the situation and the feelings that you are involved in today.

Thus the basic format is:

Preparation: Clearing a space and relaxing
1   Inviting the image
2   Talking to the child
3   Moving towards resolution
4   Appreciating, reflecting, looking forward, and emerging.

In the second exercise, 'Recreating a healthful past', you allow an image to emerge of an event in the past and then help the child to get through it in a different way. The easiest way to do this is to go back into the past as the adult, and by loving, talking to, aiding, suppporting, and generally advising the child, encourage the child to redo the scene for a last time in such a way that the child emerges feeling enriched rather than damaged.

The child can then be encouraged to relive other similar episodes that come to mind, always with the aid and support of this new adult friend. The final step is to appreciate the new learnings, think about how they apply to your life as you live it now and as you would like to live it, and turn to the future, and imagine how you will confront a similar situation with a new attitude.

In brief, then, the format here is:

Preparation: Clearing a space, relaxing
1   Inviting the image
2   Studying the image
3   Reliving the event and other similar episodes
4   Appreciating, reflecting, looking forward, and emerging.

TALKING TO THE CHILD: BASIC EXERCISE

Preparation: Clearing a space: relaxing

Do also read or reread the communication principles in Appendix Three.

1   *Inviting the image*: Allow to emerge on the cushion opposite you a child with your name. What is the child wearing? What is he or she doing? What is going on for him or her internally? What is the expression on his or her face?

2 *Talking to the child*: Talk to the child, and tell the child how you feel toward him or her. Then switch seats, and become the child. How does it feel to be you? Did you hear what the adult said to you? How do you feel about it? Tell the adult, and when you're ready switch back and continue the conversation.

3 *Moving towards resolution*: Begin to be really open and clear with each other, and to work through any difficulties that arise. It is often useful to think of negotiating since you may well both have different needs and yet you live in the same body. Find out how you block each other now, but also what you can offer each other in future, or do already offer each other. Continue until you feel a sense of resolution or peace between you.

4 *Appreciating, reflecting, looking forward, and emerging*: Thank the child for being so open with you. Check how the child looks and feels now. This is a good indication as to whether a shift has taken place. You may wish to hold the child, and let him or her melt within you. Feel the energy this releases.

Both before and after emerging, reflect upon the significance of this encounter and look forward and see how you can live or act or feel differently now that you are aware of the child's and the adult's needs and strengths. Be as specific as possible.

Be prepared to make it a practice to ask the child every now and then: 'What do you think of this plan?' and to take the child's response seriously. It should be possible to negotiate agreements that meet the needs of both. If you are blocked when you are trying to sit down at your desk to work, it may be because while you as adult want to work, the child wants to play, and there is a deadlock between you. As adult you may say to the child: 'Since you want to play and I need to work, if you help me work steadily for an hour, I am willing to go out and play after that'. Make a date also to meet the child regularly and talk with him or her: and make sure you keep your date. As you know, children expect promises to be kept.

RECREATING A HEALTHFUL PAST: BASIC EXERCISE

Preparation: Clearing a space, relaxing

1 *Inviting the image*: There are a number of ways of inviting a past event to emerge that is relevant to you at this moment. Here are a few you can try: a *The feeling of the past*: Notice what you are feeling at this moment: this may be an emotion, or even a vague body feeling. Focus on it; be at the centre of the feeling. Or think of a problem that you are having, and picture yourself in the middle of it, and discover the feeling associated with it. Again, focus on, or be at, the centre of that feeling.

Ask yourself either: 'How old do I feel?' or 'When was the first time I remember feeling this way?' Whatever the answer is, follow up with being that age, or re-experiencing that episode. Thus, if you say 'I feel very young – about three' follow up by saying 'I am three-years-old and what is happening to me? Who is around me?' and relive the episode.

b *The time tunnel*: Imagine that as you are

walking along in a wood, feeling the leaves crackling under your feet, you come across a tunnel that seems to go down, down, down, into the ground. This is a time tunnel. At the top of the tunnel your present age is marked. Step into the tunnel and then begin to climb down year by year, the ages marked on the side as you go down, until you find yourself stopping at an age in which something happened which remained unfinished and is still affecting you today. Notice what age you stop at naturally (don't force it). Then continue 'I am x years old. What am I wearing? Who is around me? What is happening?' and relive the scene.

c *Empty picture frame*: Hanging on the wall is a picture in a frame. The picture represents a scene that you played a part in at some time in the past which is relevant to your experiences or problems today. What is the scene? Relive it.

d *Childhood places*: Go back to the house you lived in as a child. As the child, go into your bedroom and explore it, noticing how you feel. Look at yourself in the mirror. What are you wearing? What is the look on your face or the message conveyed in your body? You may also want to go for a walk, perhaps to school, or to other places you remember. What is the dominant feeling?

e *Recovering positive experiences*: Allow yourself to remember a time as a child when you felt really good about yourself in a way that didn't have anything to do with pleasing other people, or when you felt you learned something really positive. Go back and relive that experience.

f *Journey back to the beginning*: (This needs

more time than the others.) Allow your spirit to go out of your body and move above you so that you can watch yourself from above. Observe yourself going through the last day or two, then the last week, then the last six months, then the last five years. What do you notice in each time period? What are you doing, how are you living, who is around you? Now go back to your teens and ask the same questions. Now the first five years of your life. Now travel back to the time of your birth. Relive it. Now you are in the womb. What is this like? Now go back to the moment of conception. What is this moment like? Allow a word or an image to emerge that represents your essence at that moment. Now begin to go forward again, noticing how your essence is expressed or hindered, until you reach the present day.

Comment: Some of the experiences you go through using any of these methods may be painful or even traumatic. It is perfectly acceptable and may even be advisable to move out of your body and look down from above yourself on traumatic experiences, rather than staying inside. This can save you a lot of pain, and may prevent you from blocking off experiences that are just too hard to relive directly.

---

2 *Studying the image*: Explore the scene further. (If you have done the Journey back to the Beginning, choose one scene that comes to mind.) Allow your spirit to move out from your body, and look down on the scene from above, from below, from the different sides. What do you notice? Enter into the various other people in the scene. How do they

see it? Try to find out as much as you can about those aspects of the situation that the child did not and could not understand at that time.

3 *Reliving the event and other similar episodes*: Now, as the adult, you go back into the past and join the child. What can you say or do that can help the child? This may be a hug, or an explanation that the child needs, or advice, or whatever feels right. Reassure the child that he or she is no longer alone.

Encourage the child to relive the scene in a new way that represents a model for dealing with situations like these and that leaves the child feeling good. This involves not only supporting the child, but also helping the child to see how he or she dealt with the situation, and to suggest other resources, other attitudes, or other interpretations, that would enable the child to deal with the situation in a new way. Sometimes the resources or attitudes the child needs are ones that the child already has in other circumstances, or they may be ones that the adult has developed since, and can offer the child.

Go forward into the future and notice any similar situations you have gone through. In each case, redo the situation along the same lines as the original one, always with the help and support of the adult.

Comment: Steps 3 and 4 are less obviously appropriate if your original experience was that reached through 1e, 'Recovering a positive past experience.' It may still be that even in these cases there is more to learn and an even richer way to deal with the situation than was obvious then.

---

5 *Appreciating, reflecting, looking forward, and emerging*: Thank the child for going through this episode one last time, and promise him or her that you will be there in future. Hug the child. You may wish to let the child melt into you, feeling the energy released within you.

Both before and after emerging, reflect on the meaning of what has gone on. Look forward to the next situation that is similar to those you have just experienced. How will you recognise it (by a look on someone's face, or the feeling in your stomach, or whatever)? How can you live it through along the model you have now set up? Be as specific as possible.

APPLICATIONS

These exercises, while they refer to the child, can also apply to any past experience, even if you were already an adult. They can even be used to look at something that happened just yesterday. It may then seem odd for the 'adult' to be intervening in what happened recently. But you will find that the adult in you is that mature part of you that doesn't always come into play in the middle of stressful situations, even though you and all the other protagonists in that drama look like adults.

IN CONCLUSION

Some of our deepest pessimism comes from the assumption that the future must resemble the past. The past has created footprints in the snow, and we follow on in those footprints, because it seems the natural thing to do. This can be very frustrating and painful when we realise that the footprints are not really leading where we wish to go.

But we *can* learn to roam around in the hunting ground of

the past, opening it up to the light of the present day, and creating a new set of footprints that result from real co-operation between all the ages that dwell within us (including, as we will later see, our future selves). A real sense of hope and creativity about life, and one that is based on a respect for past, present, and future, can emerge from this co-operation.

It is not always necessary to go into the past to shift our attitudes, as all the other chapters in this book make clear. But images of early experiences and early family relationships do reveal a kind of mythic structure within which we may still be operating, and remind us of the patterns we tend to fall into particularly when stressed. These patterns may well change naturally through a new relationship, a crisis, or any event that is so extreme that it jolts us and dislodges us out of our habitual structures. By exploring and transforming our images from the past, however, we can choose to change the patterns ourselves rather than wait for life to be our teacher.

Remember always to appreciate the child for doing his or her best in a difficult world. When you think of what difficulties the child survived and dealt with, despite limited knowledge and experience, heightened vulnerability, and often too little love and support, you will be impressed by the resilience that eventually made it possible for you as adult to function as well as you do today.

Be grateful also for those special qualities that the younger you had but which the adult you may have felt forced to leave behind because of the demands of the world or of your inner expectations. What you have once had is not lost, but only put away in a cupboard that you have neglected to open recently. Now that you are beginning to open your cupboards, you will find all kinds of treasures falling out.

Don't forget also to appreciate yourself as an adult for all that you have gained over the years and for your ability to offer to, and receive from the child, an understanding and love and wisdom that is profoundly creative for both of you . You may even find yourself patting yourself admiringly on the shoulder and saying those familiar words: 'My, how you've grown!'

10

SENSING LIFE CHOICES, MAKING LIFE DECISIONS

Where am I going?

During an imagework session on life choices a few years ago, I suggested that group members picture themselves walking down the road of their lives, where they would reach a crossroads, and could try out the various paths into the future. Polly had a powerful experience, which she wrote to me about recently:

'At the crossroads, I chose first a lovely grassy green lane – banked high with blackberries. This was my ideal image of the life I was hoping to lead in the country. At the end of the lane was me – a Mrs Applecheeks – wearing an apron, hands on hips, hair in a bun, and ample bosom – standing in front of a larder piled high with shelf upon shelf of blackberry jam. I thought – ugh – and went back to the crossroads.

Now I went on the 'not so inviting' path – gravel and puddles. I walked up the path, splashing in the puddles, and at the end was a large building with people moving around, inside and out of doors. I wanted to be one of them.

When you suggested that it was five years on, I found myself sitting inside on a rocking chair, oldish,

holding hands with a man – grey haired – also in a rocking chair. We were in the middle of the building, with people moving in and out around us – right in the middle of the action.

Today – I lose count of how many years on from that choice of a path, perhaps three years on – I actually live in a house up a gravel drive – full of puddles. At the other end of a long gravel road – also full of puddles – are my farm buildings. Together with an expanding group of interested people, I am working towards developing this into a retreat and a healing centre. An architect friend is drawing the plans for my house in a barn down there. As the barns and the land adjoining are mine, I do sit in the centre of it. We all have a long way to go before I'm in my rocking chair. Meanwhile, I'm having an amazing time living through my own 'vision'.'

Nowhere does imagery seem to be so magical a tool as when we are sensing goals and making choices. While by now you may be used to the fact that you can bring the past into the present and work with it, it is harder to believe that you can bring the future into the present and learn from it. Yet this is so.

This doesn't mean that the images you come up with will always be as photographically accurate as Polly's were, though this does happen surprisingly often. What is more usual is that you can sense the major direction or nature of what you want, rather than an accurate and detailed 'prophetic' picture.

Often the clue that the future you are sensing is the right one for you is that combination of surprise that indicates that your conscious mind had not yet worked this one out, and a deep inner recognition which betrays the fact that on some level you have always known this to be true.

Helen's picture of the future, which was very different indeed from Polly's, came to her with the same shock of surprise and recognition. She wrote to me later: 'You invited me to stand five years into the future and to visualise myself in detail. Not easy, but I eventually formed the picture and, with it, came a deep inward smile of contentment. I was doing absolutely, totally, utterly, nothing.

'I have now applied for early retirement and expect to leave my job at the end of April. I know that there are possibilities of freelance work, but I've made no specific arrangements. I just want to *be* for a while.'

Life goals and life choices are weighty words, but when the future calls us, and we want to know what it is saying, and how we will get there, it may not tell us about creating an amazing project, nor about helping all the world's unfortunates. It may just gently remind us that for a while we need to do nothing.

MODERN DAY PROPHETS?

Do we all have the gift of prophecy? Or do we create that future because we have seen the image? And is the future fixed and fated? Or do we have some choice in the matter? These questions come up again and again when we look at the future through imagework.

Because imagework, like dreams, opens a window into various levels of our unconscious intuition, it may well be that some of our pictures of the future really *are* the result of transcending time and space and seeing the future, or rather one or more of our possible futures. Even if this is so, the future is still our choice: Polly found two futures, and the one that really happened to her would have been pretty unlikely had she not made a conscious choice to follow a less inviting path at that crucial moment in her life.

But in any case, the 'crystal ball gazing' aspect of imagework, exciting as it may seem, is a very minor part of what we are doing when we tune into the future. Just as only a minute percentage of dreams tell of the future rather than of our own wishes and fears about the future, so it is with imagework.

In the main, we are simply doing what we do all the time when we set goals and make plans – we are building up pictures of what we expect from the world, and then making the kind of choices that fit into and bring about those pictures. The difference is that we are able to do it far more effectively because we are making use of the powerful partnership we have created between our conscious self and our unconscious intuitive wisdom.

SETTING GOALS AND SENSING GOALS

Usually, we work out our life choices and set our goals by figuratively drawing a line forward from our present conscious expectations into the future that these would create. Often our conscious self is, unbeknownst to itself, influenced by unexamined unconscious fantasies, or by other people's expectations which we have swallowed over the years. For Polly, an idyllic country life full of blackberries represented perfection – until she tried it. Luckily, having done that in her imagination, she didn't need to spend years of her life pursuing a false dream.

At other times our conscious self draws up one plan, and our unconscious self has quite different intentions. These are the times when we find that we keep creating sensible lists of what we are going to do today, or lovely plans for what we will do tomorrow or next week or next year, or fantasies about the perfect life, and yet we never seem to do anything to make this future happen.

By trusting our intuitive ability to project ourselves into the future and test whether it feels good, we can *sense* the appropriate way forward, rather than *setting* the goal that looks right from where we are standing. In this way it becomes possible to find a way of life that fits us, rather than fitting ourselves into a model that we think, or others think, we should have. It is then not so surprising if this future that is really ours does come about, and, even more important, brings us the contentment we expect it will.

TAKING THE FEAR OUT OF HOPE

Creating a picture of the future serves another important function – reducing anxiety. In any creative movement between the present and the future, there is always the anxiety that we will fail to create what we intend. A small amount of anxiety is useful: the sympathetic nervous system prepares us for action, and we have that wonderful surge that creative people rely on to get things done. But too much anxiety can incapacitate us, to the extent that we don't dare go for what we want, or we go for it with such tension that we set ourselves up for trouble.

But, to quote an old cliché: seeing is believing. Once we have seen the future, it is easy to believe that it will be, and that all we have to do is get there. It is almost as if we have a vivid memory of having achieved this goal before, and this keeps us hopeful when the going gets rough.

I remember how it was when we were setting up Atsitsa,

our second centre in Greece. The summer brochure had to go out before Christmas, when the centre didn't yet exist. We did have the place, and knew what we wanted to create, but the house and grounds were still a building site, and more important, there was no staff. That January, I 'tuned into' the future using imagework, and found myself picturing a time six weeks from then, with most of the staff team already chosen. I breathed a sigh of relief, and went on confidently to do what I needed to do to create a staff team.

Six weeks later, I did indeed have most of my staff. I cannot say whether this would have happened anyway – did I see an image from the future, or did I create this future out of the image? What I do know is that without that image at the back of my mind, I would have been operating under the strain of an enormous amount of anxiety, fear, and doubt. Instead, the process was more like getting ready to go out in the morning – the question is what you will wear, not whether you will be able to get dressed at all.

Another crucial feature of future sensing is the ability to look back and see how we got there. Thus when I visualised having my staff team chosen, I also looked back to see how I'd done it. In retrospect, the steps were obvious. Having seen them, I could now go ahead and do them. No problem.

If all this is beginning to sound too magical again, it isn't really. The understandings we gain access to through imagework are not picked out of a hat with no prior information or rational considerations. Because we are not looking into a crystal ball but rather just using our best potential, the future that we are able to discover depends as much on knowledge as on intuition. The imagework we do after we have taken the trouble to 'do our homework' is likely to be more defined, and more useful, than that which we are able to do without any relevant information. Imagework is always a partnership between the conscious and the unconscious, and between reason and imagination, and this partnership is its major strength.

A GOAL A DAY KEEPS THE FUTURE OKAY

This ability to project yourself into the future and look back to how you got there is not limited to long-term decisions and plans. It is just as useful when you want to plan, or make decisions about, the next half year, half day, or half hour.

I myself seldom walk into a new situation, and particularly one in which I have an important role to play, without stopping for a moment, and projecting myself forward into the future by saying to myself: 'It's the end of this event, and I feel good about it. What is the good feeling, and how did I get there?' This gives me a clear sense of what I really want and how to get it. In order to find out what path not to take, I sometimes also do the opposite: 'It's the end of this event and I feel awful about it. What is the awful feeling, and how did I achieve it?' By understanding what I really wish to accomplish, and what I need to avoid, I can walk into the situation with a clear focus, and go for what I want.

The results of this intuitive sensing of goals are always so different from my conscious beliefs about my goals that I am still constantly surprised. For example, a few months ago, I walked into an imagework training session with the conscious goal of teaching the students as much as possible. But when I tuned into the positive 'end of the session' image, what I found was: 'The good feeling is of warmth and closeness in the group, and that shared sense that we have been through a journey together and have positive wishes to send each other on our journeys. I accomplished this by relaxing, and caring about everyone, and encouraging them to care for each other.' The negative picture of the end of session was 'I feel rushed and hurried because I tried to do too much. Everyone looks strained and stressed, and I'm exhausted. I wonder why I bother to run these courses. I seem to have got to this point by thinking I needed to teach the students everything I know.'

Had I tried to follow my original conscious intention of teaching the students as much as possible, I would almost

175

certainly have ended up feeling bad rather than good about the session, and yet been unable to understand why. Instead, I chose to go directly for the goal of creating warmth and closeness. The students learned just as much as usual about imagework, but a lot more about human relationships, and we all ended up feeling refreshed, relaxed, and hopeful.

I often use the same process to make difficult decisions, whether small or large – I put myself forward to the time after the decision has been made to find out what I did decide. I also utilise it in groups, courses, or team meetings to create shared visions. Once everyone has projected themselves to the end of the session, and clarified what experience they really want, it is easy to create a shared plan for the group that will bring people together creatively and pleasurably.

WHY DO WE NEED TO BE GOING ANYWHERE?

Why is the future important anyway? Why not just live in the present? We do need to live in the present, but the present always emerges from the past and reaches toward the future, and it is this historical process that gives events their meaning. Actions of any kind have a purpose or intention, and clarifying our intentions is what sensing the future is all about. Even reaching to grab a luscious fruit is an activity in the present which derives its meaning from the felt desire of just a moment ago, and the intention to eat the fruit in the next moment.

Thus the point is not to live in or strive for the future, but rather to live in a present that makes sense to us. It does seem that the feeling that what we are doing has some kind of meaning or purpose is central to healthy and happy living.

Carl and Stephanie Simonton,[1] pioneers in the use of visualisation with cancer patients, discovered that those who showed an exceptionally good response to treatment all had one thing in common: they had strong reasons for wanting to live, could elaborate on these in a detailed way, and felt that

176

this strong commitment to the future was responsible for their good progress.

Conversely, depression, confusion, and illness are common effects of the feeling that we do not know what we want, cannot direct our lives effectively, and are unable to see a positive pathway into the future. At the heart of this feeling is often the inability to express creativity in our lives.

Creativity doesn't necessarily mean producing massive results, or being at the forefront of art, science, or mathematics. It means having the sense that you can always create or discover something which that gives you, and others, pleasure and meaning. What you create or discover could be an insight, or a lovely garden, or a sculpture, or a health centre, or a flower arrangement, or a happy family atmosphere, or a new approach to life, or a new way to love. As long as it emerges freely out of your inner well of life energy rather than being a response to expectations, and has a quality of freshness and vitality about it, it is creative and life-enhancing.

The exercises in this chapter are relevant to sensing any kind of long or short term goal, expressing any form of creativity, or making any choice or decision, whether it is to do with personal health, self esteem, relationships, work life, or anything else. You will find that the whole process can help you to uncover your real purposes in life, feel more hopeful about the future, give you a focus and direction for your energy, and get a sense of yourself as an active creative being in charge of your life.

LIFE PATHS: AND MY FUTURE SELF: THE STRUCTURE OF THE EXERCISE

The exercise that Polly did was based on working with the image of life as a path or road, with our choice points pictured as a crossroads or a fork in the road. The process begins, as usual, with clearing a space and relaxing, and then inviting an image of walking along the road of our lives and coming to a crossroads. Trying out the most attractive path first, you walk along and find out how it is to be on this path now, and five, ten, and fifteen years later. You are then able to try out all the other paths too – unlike in real life where opportunity is sometimes said to knock only once. It is also possible to rise above the scene, and get an aerial view of all the paths. Sometimes the most surprising insights emerge then – for example all the paths may end up in the same place after all. You can then return to the crossroads and decide which you like best. You conclude as usual by appreciating, reflecting and looking forward to the practical implications of your insights.

Thus the format is:

Preparation: clearing a space, relaxing
1   Inviting the image: a life path with a crossroads or fork
2   Trying out the paths
3   Taking an aerial view
4   Returning to the crossroads and making a choice
5   Appreciating, emerging, reflecting, and looking forward

The exercise in which Helen put herself forward into a future when she was doing nothing at all was part of a larger process called 'My future self' that involves directly projecting yourself into a future time when you feel good about what you have chosen. The time period selected depends on the kind of goals you want to look at or the choices and decisions involved.

Thus you may project yourself into being eighty years old to explore your life goals, or five years from now to explore your medium-term choices, or three to six months from now to explore your shorter-term plans and decisions. You may also project yourself to the end of the day, or the hour, or the session, or the interview. Once having done this, you can look back and see what choices you made and what attitude you took in order to get to this point.

When looking at life goals, there are three major areas that are important to consider; relationships with others, work or creativity, and your personal relationship to yourself. I also like to add the aspect of life itself – how we feel about the way our fate has come forward to meet us.

It is worth having a look not only at the future that you would feel good about, so as to see what path you want to follow, but also at the future that you would feel awful about, so as to clarify where danger lies. Sometimes people find it quite difficult to imagine a positive future; in this case it is best to begin with the negative future, and then move on to the positive one.

In fact, I originally introduced the notion of looking at the negative future when I was working with a man who felt too hopeless to be able to find any positive pictures at all. Once he had looked at and understood the negative future he was set on having, he found it possible, and a great relief, to picture a future he might actually enjoy, and which seemed to be within his reach.

The format then is:

Preparation: Clearing a space and relaxing
1   Inviting my positive future self
2   Exploring the image
3   My interpersonal, creative, and personal choices – and life itself
4   My negative future self
5   Appreciating, reflecting, looking forward, and emerging.

LIFE PATHS: BASIC EXERCISE

Preparation: Clearing a space, relaxing

1   *Inviting the image*: Imagine yourself on a road, the road of your life. What sort of road is it? What is the scenery like? What are you wearing? How does it feel to walk on this road?

Now you come to a crossroads or a fork in the road. Can you see what the signs say? What do the different paths or roads look like from here? Which seems most inviting?

2 *Exploring paths*: Go down the road or path which seems most inviting. What does it look like? How does it feel? What happens to you on this road?

It's five years from now. What is happening now? How do you feel? What is life like for you?

It's another five years on (ten years from today). Now what is your life like? How do you feel about it?

It's ten more years on (twenty years from today). Now how is it for you?

Having looked at this path in detail, return to the crossroads and try out the other ones in exactly the same way.

3 *An aerial view*: Allow your mind or spirit to rise above your body and float high enough above the roads so you can see the whole pattern. What do you notice?

4 *Returning to the crossroads and making a choice*: Now go back to the crossroads. Which choice now seems to be the 'path with heart' – the one that feels good to you, that is most in line with who you are and what you want in life?

5 *Appreciating, reflecting, looking forward, and emerging*: Appreciate your unconscious for the help it has given you, and your conscious for daring to look at these difficult issues clearly. Both before and after emerging, ask yourself: What do

the different roads mean to you? What implications does this experience have? What choices
do you need to make in the near future so that you
follow a path you can feel good about? Be as
specific as possible.

MY FUTURE SELF: BASIC EXERCISE

This exercise can be used with respect to any time
period in the future at all. I suggest that you start
by imagining your eighty-year-old self, so as to get
a sense of your long-term goals. Then choose
whatever shorter time period or periods feel most
relevant to you. Simply keep repeating the same
exercise, but with a different initial instruction.
Note that it is easier – and very essential – to be
more specific about your choices the shorter the
time period it is.

Preparation: Clearing a space and relaxing.

1 *Inviting my future self*: Decide on the time
period that you want to explore and then suggest
to yourself one of the following:
a I'm on a space ship going off the face of the
earth. I return to earth at *x* time in the future (give
the number of years or months forward, or the
date) when I am eighty-years-old/ten years older/
five years older/six months older (choose the
appropriate period) and happy about my life.
b I am tuning into the dimension in which past,
present, and future are one, and I am now eighty-
years-old/ten years older/five years older/six
months older (again, choose an appropriate
period) and happy about my life.

c It is now *x* years/months/days/hours (as appropriate) from now, and it is the end of this period in my life/course/session/interview/day (or whatever) and I feel really delighted with how it's been and what I've chosen.

Comment: If you are projecting yourself many years forward, it is easiest to imagine yourself on a space ship actually going off earth and then coming back again. For shorter time periods, or once you are used to the exercise, this is not so necessary, and you can just project yourself to the time you want by giving yourself a suggestion.

---

2 *Exploring the image*: Begin by making the image of your future self really vivid and concrete, particularly if it is a long time period forward. Ask yourself some of these questions, adapting the language if it is not appropriate for the time period you are envisaging:

'What am I wearing? What do I have on my feet? What can I see around me? How do I feel in my body, mind, and spirit?'

'What is the good feeling I have? What was the most important thing I did or experienced to reach this good feeling? What really has made life or this time period or event worthwhile? Looking back at the younger me at the beginning of this period, what do I notice? What do I want to whisper that would make life easier for him or her?'

(If you are the eighty-year-old: 'How do I feel about being eighty years old? When I look forward to death, how do I feel about it? What would I tell the younger me about being old?')

182

3 *My interpersonal, creative, and personal choices – and life itself*: Having established a clear image, start to explore the following specific areas. In each case, begin with the initial specific questions listed under that heading, and then go on to follow the same general process:

a *Interpersonal*: How have my social relationships been – family, partners, friends, colleagues, acquaintances, etc.? (Go on to the general questions).

b *Creativity or work*: What did I accomplish or create and how did I go about that process? What was work like? How did it fit into other aspects of my life? (Go on to the general questions).

c *Personal*: This has to do with the part of my life that concerns only myself. How was I in my relationship to my self, to my body, mind and spirit? How was my self esteem? How did I take care of myself? (Go on to the general questions).

d *Life itself*: How do I feel about the way life has treated me? What did I learn over all those years about life itself, about the turns of the wheel of fate? (Go on to the general questions).

General questions for areas a–d: What do I feel best about? What did I learn the hard way? What was most difficult to deal with? What still seems unresolved? What could I tell the younger me that would help them?

Do say it, being absolutely specific. Does the younger you understand? If not, make sure he or she does.

4. *Negative future self*: Now try: 'It's *x* time from now/I am *x* years or months older/It's the end of this event or period (whichever is appropriate) and

183

I feel absolutely terrible. What is the terrible feeling? What is the most important thing I did to make that happen? Reviewing my interpersonal, creative, and personal life, as well as life itself, where did I go wrong? What could I tell the younger me that will help him or her not to end up like me?'

5 *Appreciate, reflect, look forward, and emerge*: Thank the future you for his or her help, and ask him or her to serve as an advisor for you when you need him or her. Both before and after emerging, reflect on what this has all meant, and what the implications are. How will you specifically and practically carry through these understandings?

QUICK VISIONING

A brief format, particularly useful for short-term goals and decisions, or if you are doing this exercise regularly, is simply:

1 *It's x* time from now (or: It's the end of this event) and I feel good about it. What is the good feeling? What did I do to bring that about?
2 It's *x* time from now (or: It's the end of this event) and I feel awful about it. What is the awful feeling? What did I do to bring it about?

APPLICATIONS

Group work: At the beginning of a group session of any sort (whether it is a course, a committee meeting, or a staff meeting), it is always useful to go around and ask people what their expectations are. Instead of, or in addition to, the usual expectation statements, try getting people to put themselves forward to the end of the meeting feeling good about it – or awful – and see what they feel good or bad about and how they got there. This lets the group members know what they, and everyone else, is wanting on a deep level, and helps the group to create a satisfying shared vision. At the end of the session, spend a moment discovering how similar or different the feelings are from what everyone imagined. What can you learn from that?

Everyday activities: Discovering your intentions by sensing the future should not be limited to major life choices. Every day we engage in myriad activities that we could do better if we were clear about our intentions. So whether you are preparing to clean the house, write a lecture, do your gardening, go on holiday, or go out on a date, do take a moment to stop, put yourself forward to the end of that task or event, sense your positive future, and look back and see how you got there. If you have time, check also into that negative future to make sure that this is not the one you are about to trip yourself into unwittingly.

Inner consultant: Your future self who feels good about his or her choices is a wonderful consultant. Now you have not only all your younger selves to share resources with, but all your older selves too. Do make use of this wonderful resource of having a wiser, older you to help you on your way.

IN CONCLUSION

Knowing where you want to go in life, whether in the short term or the long term, is more than half the battle. The next chapter is about making sure you get there, if it doesn't just all seem to fall into place. Don't see these exercises as one-off events. If you make it a practice to keep tuning into your future self at every choice point, and at the beginning of every day, and to consult with your future self or selves as to the next step, you will really begin to understand what it means to be able to rely on your own personal vision.

===== 11 =====

CARRYING THROUGH LIFE CHANGES, DOING THINGS BETTER

How do I make sure I get there?

Sitting at a *taverna* table in the Greek village of Skyros, I was chatting with my friend Isaac about writing this book, 'You must give some evidence that people do make life changes as a result of these techniques,' he said. Hardly had he finished his sentence, when a woman walked toward me and said hello. 'You don't remember me', she said, 'but my name is Lydia. You came over last summer to the Skyros Centre when I was there and did a session on life changes with the whole community. You asked what change we wanted to make, and I found myself saying "I want to let go of financial security in my life." Then I said to myself "But that's ridiculous." But I did that life change exercise, and do you know that, sceptical as I was, during this past year I have given up my job as a headmistress, have now been travelling for a few months and thinking about what work I will do, and *I am completely without financial security and loving it.*'

I have met Lydia again recently and discovered that now, a year later, she is thrilled with her new life. And money has turned out not to be a problem – it just seems to flow in as she needs it.

We've all thought about things we wanted to do, changes we wanted to make, dreams we wanted to fulfil, and yet have not quite been able to take the first step, nor even really believed we would ever do it. What seems like inertia keeps us going in the same direction we always have taken – better the devil we know than all the angels we don't know. Every now and then, however, there is a catalyst – something happens, and suddenly we find we are able to do it. We have been given a push in the right direction. Through imagework, it is possible to give ourselves that push.

Our unconscious self protects us by being conservative. It won't make changes easily by itself, and usually waits for conscious insights and experiences to filter through to it. A single traumatic incident, or a series of more gradual learning experiences, may lead the unconscious to make a U turn. The unconscious self also doesn't much like it if our conscious self decides to make major changes without consultation. So we may consciously make decisions, write lists, or plan change, and then find that we are unconsciously sabotaging everything.

However, if we enlist the unconscious and say 'Here's a new idea – can you work on it with me and be my consultant?', we suddenly have its willing support. Using the resources of both conscious rationality and unconscious intuition, we can create a new picture or pattern, supply appropriate supports for the change, and sketch out the steps to get there. When the picture is clear enough, inertia can take over again, but this time it is rolling us merrily along to fill in the gaps and make it all happen. The secret is prior consultation, and good teamwork.

WHAT'S WRONG WITH THE GOOD OLD WAYS?

It is rather like new management taking over a company and wanting to make big changes. Directives get sent down, but nothing really happens. Paperwork gets lost, small confusions are created, and the company basically operates as it always has. The staff are used to the old ways which have always worked well enough, and are, perhaps very rightly, suspicious of the new management – 'How can they possibly know what's good for our company?'

But then the new boss holds a meeting and tells the staff: 'I'm delighted to be joining this team, and I want to talk to you about this company we are all committed to. I think it's a great company as it is, and a great staff, but some change might make it even better. This is my image of how the company could be, and some ideas about how to make it happen. What do you all suggest? And what do you think is the best way to make these changes? How can we work together to make this company greater?' Suddenly there is a magical shift in the atmosphere. Ideas fly around, enthusiasm abounds, and changes that are decided upon are quickly and effectively carried through.

THE NEW ME

A major link between the present and the future that needs to emerge from the consultation between the conscious and the unconscious is the creation of a new self image that is acceptable to both. If we are not to take a terrifying and dangerous leap in the dark, we need to have an image of ourselves as we will be after we have taken the leap. If we can see that we are still intact, still likeable, and better off than before, the leap becomes a challenge rather than a risk.

The exercises in chapter 10, which were about discovering what sort of future we wanted, already supplied that missing link. When we sense the future, we are creating pictures of how we will be after making a change, and this is often sufficient to tip us into a new reality and to engage inertia on our side.

But not always. When we need to make a major shift in attitude but find it difficult to make because of ambivalence, fear, confusion, or desperation, or when we wish to make a major improvement in a complex skill, we often need a bit more help to make change effortless and natural. This chapter's exercise is therefore designed to help carry through the changes we already know we want, but are having some trouble with. This includes improving skills we already have, or doing those things we intend to do and yet can't seem to get around to or face, whether they involve an attitude change, a new project, a diet, or a difficult phone call.

HOW I COULD BE

Imagework always starts with the image of who or where you are now. Before you can change, you need to be able not only to understand your present pattern, but also to accept the person you are now. When we are angry, contemptuous, or impatient with someone, this does not encourage change – the person is more likely to freeze, get angry, or otherwise find it impossible to make any move. The same is true of your attitude to yourself – it is only when you see that the person that you are now is making the best choice he or she is able to at this moment, and you send him or her your sympathy and support, that you can hope to encourage yourself to make new and better choices in future.

The next step is to invite an image to emerge of the new you that you will be after you've made the life change. We often find it difficult to change because we simply have no picture of being that changed person which we can associate with ourselves. Other people may be non-smokers, assertive, confident, organised or able to set up a centre or write a book, but not me. Through visualising and entering the image, it is possible not only to fill in the picture and put our face and body to it, but to figure how it feels, how we would operate, and what changes we would need to get there. You don't know how to get organised: allow a picture to emerge of yourself as organised, and find out what you do. *You* may not know, but the organised you does.

It is then also possible to look back and see how you got from where you were to where you are now. This is the power of harnessing hindsight for the purposes of foresight that we talked about in the previous chapter.

190

Ella, for example, wanted to start a new community arts centre in the north of England where she lived, but she didn't have the money to do so, and wasn't sure where to get it. When she created a picture of herself having achieved her goal, and looked back to see how she'd managed it, she discovered that the first step had been to get the people together, and the ideas clear, and the money came later. She was relieved, and felt that she now knew how to make a start on her project.

Sometimes it is not the absence of a picture that is the problem but a negative one. When you ask for an image of yourself after having made the change, you may find that the new person whose image emerges is just not to your liking. This should not discourage you, because it simply lets you know why you've been having such a hard time making the change.

Alan, who was a rather unconventional journalist, told me that he desperately wanted and needed to become more efficient, but couldn't. When I asked him what this efficient person would be like, he didn't know. He certainly knew all about the precise nature of his inefficiency. His picture of his present self was so much clearer than that of his future self it was simply easier to stay within it.

I therefore helped him to allow an image to emerge of how he would be if he were efficient. But when he did so, Alan just recoiled in horror. The new Alan he was imagining was a cold, uncreative, soulless automaton. No wonder Alan's plans to change never worked. It was only when he began to work on evolving an image of a wacky, creative, but clear and effective man that he could begin to shift. And the more he worked on imagining this the more he naturally found himself changing without trying. He literally became what he imagined.

Once you can get a picture of the new you that you can feel both clear and good about, change can be astonishingly quick, as Helga, a member of a week long imagework course, once demonstrated. Helga is German, and her English was not good enough to participate in the group directly. She sat next

191

to a German friend who translated for her what was going on, and also translated what Helga wanted to say back to the group. This was a cumbersome procedure, and slowed the group down a bit, but Helga was very committed to the group, and it did work. At the end of the week, we did the Life Change exercise, and Helga imagined herself as having made the life change of becoming more confident and assertive.

I can still picture that dramatic moment when, as she stepped into the image of herself as she would be after she make the life change, she began to tell us what was happening – and English, rather than German, came out of her mouth. We all stared at her in dumb amazement. She explained 'I feel so confident now – I don't mind speaking in English and making mistakes.'

DOING THINGS BETTER

No matter how good you are at doing something, there is always someone who can do it better. Don't get discouraged – use that person as a teacher.

'Experts' – people who you believe are further on along the road that you seek to follow – can be wonderful sources of inner guidance. The expert may be a swimming champion if you want to improve your swimming, or a mythical monarch, if you want to become more proud and regal, or a dog, if you want to learn to be frisky and wag your tail at the world.

By allowing an image to emerge of an expert, asking for advice, and then stepping into their shoes and 'being' that person, you've created a template for your body, mind, and spirit that helps you to operate better naturally. And in fact, any image you use that gets you to operate better in your imagination will work. Once you've created such an image, then it is often useful to practise the skill or attitude in your imagination, until you feel totally confident. And each time you are about to do something, or even when you are about to have a practice session in real life – a piano or a swimming lesson for example – just pause, and relive that image of yourself doing it perfectly. The difference in your performance can be quite amazing.

When I wish to demonstrate to a group of imagework students the power of the imagination to improve a skill, I start by asking them to bend down and touch their toes. I then conduct a brief guided fantasy in which they imagine their bodies to be made of rubber and totally elastic, and they take great leaps and do backward somersaults over high fences. Having done this, I ask people to bend down again. Most people find that they naturally bend between two and six inches lower than before. Try it.

Besides finding an inner expert, do also introduce an inner friend or supporter who wants you to succeed and will encourage you even when your own enthusiasm flags.

Teams always do better when they have fans cheering for them on the sidelines.

Some people like to introduce an inner innocent, ignorant, slow or naïve person to whom they have to explain everything. In this way, they become the experts themselves, and find that they miraculously know the answers.

I CAN'T AND I WON'T

Our attitudes to getting what we want or doing what we intend are also pretty crucial. Imagine that you got up in the morning and said to yourself: 'I've got to clean my teeth; I'll just die if I don't clean my teeth.' If you're anything like me, you might find that you trip on the way to the bathroom, break the toothpaste tube when you grab it, hunt around for the toothbrush unable to see it anywhere, and then start getting furious that you're expected to conform in this ridiculous way to your mother's warnings about tooth decay, march out of the bathroom, and feel bad the rest of the day that you didn't clean your teeth.

When we have to do something, and try super hard to do it, not only does the tension make us less effective, but there is an equal and opposite inner force that comes into action to say that we can't and we won't. This process creates the ambivalence that keeps us from reaching the goals that seem most desperately important.

The other pole of this attitude is the 'give up while you're ahead' approach of deciding that you probably won't succeed at what you want, so why try at all? 'No use planning to clean my teeth every day to begin with – I'm not that sort of person anyway.' And the hidden thought is also that at least if you haven't tried, you haven't shown yourself up as being incapable of achieving it, and can always nourish the possibility that someday you will decide to try and then of course you will succeed – maybe.

Some people go the 'I've got to' route, and fall all over themselves trying, and others go the 'Why try and fail' route, and fall all over themselves not trying. Most people alternate between the two. In one case we engage our wilfulness, and in the other we demonstrate our weak-willedness. Neither approach is conducive to doing or getting what we want.

The approach that does seem to work is taking an attitude that engages your will rather than wilfulness. This attitude has two facets which may at first seem slightly contradictory – 'intending' and 'releasing'. This means that on the one hand you fully intend to reach the goal, and on the other, are willing to let go of the belief that it is totally in your power to do so, and of the conviction that you *must* do so.

'Intending' involves believing that whatever it is you are aiming for can and will happen, and also being willing to put all your undivided and unambivalent energy behind bringing it about. You need therefore, if at all possible, to work through and resolve any ambivalence or anxiety and to become totally clear about your intentions. If you feel that you don't have a right to have what you want, or believe that it is impossible to achieve it, or think that there will be negative side effects that may outweigh the advantages, your intentions and efforts will be confused and counterproductive. I find that for me it is particularly helpful to feel not so much that I have a right to have it, but that *it is right for me* to have it; this means in my case understanding that when things go well for me, I feel better about myself, function better in the world, and take care of others better.

To fully intend the goal, it helps also to visualise it happening, and in this way get that feeling described in chapter 10 that in some sense if has already happened – it exists in potential and you have experienced it in your imagination – so that it only needs to be made real. All these facets of 'intending' will maximise your chances of success.

To really 'release', on the other hand, you must first remind yourself that you are not omnipotent, and that the goals you seek to achieve are never totally in your hands. In that sense you need to release the actual success of the task into the lap of whatever you believe is beyond your conscious self – God, the spirits, your unconscious, fate, the luck of the draw – or however you see the factors that limit your omnipotence. You are like a farmer who tills the field, sows the seeds, and does everything he or she can to have a good crop, but cannot control the weather which has the potential to bring all the efforts to nought. Once you have done, or decided to do, whatever you can, only trust and acceptance can bring the peace of mind you need.

Secondly, you need to be aware that in the unlikely event that you don't get what you want, no matter how important it may seem, it is not the end of the world. You will be able to say to yourself 'What's next?' and perhaps even recognise that it is time to change directions. In fact, it may be that not getting what you want in this instance – as you probably have already discovered at important times in the past – will open up a new possibility that you cannot foresee now.

The image we use for this process of intending and releasing is putting the picture of having achieved your goal in a bubble or balloon, intending in your mind for it to be, and then releasing it by sending the bubble or balloon off out of sight, and into the dimension of potentials waiting to be actualised.

Many people use a similar process in order to ask for events to happen or things to come to them that are not solely dependent on their own efforts – a parking space opening up, for example – and believe that the image creates an energy focus that can make real events happen in the world. Some claim that this method of putting whatever you want in a bubble, asking for it to be, and then releasing it works wonders for them. Try it. But do remember, as emphasised in chapter 10, that it is important to take time to sense whether what you are asking is right for you, rather than trying to have every wish of your conscious self come literally true, even should this be possible.

My ten-year-old daughter Chloe says that putting what she wants in a bubble does work well for her, but only when she is wishing for something that is good for other people as well as herself, and when she is wanting it 'for its own sake' rather than so that she can please other people. That makes a lot of sense to me.

MY CONFIDENT SELF – WHERE ARE YOU?

When the change you want to carry through is a major and difficult one, even contemplating change can be too scary to face. In this case you can always try the salami approach – just keep slicing off only as much as you can chew. As you work your way through the problem in your imagination, the changes themselves should follow naturally.

Norma, a young student of mine, gave me my best lesson in the salami process. She was so terrified of speaking in seminars that she was unable to attend if there was any chance that she might be called upon. She would spend hours writing a paper to present at her seminar, and then be unable to show up. She came to me to ask for help, worried that her college career would be damaged.

We began by having Norma imagine that she was sitting in a private cinema, and allowing an image to emerge first of her fearful self, and then of herself as she would be after she was totally free to speak in a seminar. Imagining herself as she was, terrified and unable to speak, was painful, but not difficult to do. But Norma was totally unable even to conjure up an image of herself speaking in a seminar.

We therefore worked on this step by step over a period of weeks. First she imagined a friend of hers on the screen talking confidently. After about a week of practising this imagework on her own, Norma was able to imagine herself on the screen. But when I asked her to step into the picture and feel the feelings, she froze. Again, after a week of practice on her own, she dared to step into the image, but only for a moment. As she continued her practice, her tolerance for being this person who was confident about speaking in class increased, until finally, weeks later, she was able to finish the exercise: she could step into the image and imagine spending a day as this confident person.

While this imagework was going on, she found herself little by little taking steps in her life that she would never have thought possible, and doing it naturally, always surprising herself with her own bravery. The steps in real life followed behind, but in the same direction as the steps she took on the screen. I remember Norma's delight at her first step – she found herself telling a joke to a group of friends in a pub. Later she blurted out a few words in a seminar when she passionately disagreed with someone's argument. Eventually, seminars no longer held any fear for her and her college life was transformed. When I talked to her a few years later, she told me that she still talked to the confident girl on the screen, and got help and support from her when things became difficult.

All this happened not as part of therapy or counselling, but by spending a few moments a week with her, and giving her homework to practise. I have in fact found the Life Change exercise particularly useful with people who know nothing about therapy but want to make specific practical changes in their lives, and are willing to practise on their own.

I recall an African student, Joe, whose English was poor, and who had almost no background in any of the subjects he was studying. He was having a desperately difficult time, and indeed, most of his lecturers were sure he would fail. But he was determined to succeed, because he wanted to go back to his country and make a contribution there and needed a college degree to do so. Having gained his trust, I convinced him that he needed not only to study, but also to keep practising the Life Change imagework exercise, and in this way work on strengthening a new image of himself as a confident man who was able, despite difficulties, to master the material in his courses.

Some weeks later, he proudly told me the story of how he sat down to a statistics exam, did his imagework exercise briefly, and then confidently wrote the exam. His lecturer was totally bewildered when he read the exam and asked 'How did you manage this?' At the end of the year, Joe came and thanked me, and told me that he had been awarded the prize for the student who had made the best academic progress that year. He promised to go on doing his imagework, and he also went on to succeed in getting a very good degree – despite the fact that I was still almost the only one on the staff who believed he'd make it.

LIFE CHANGE: THE STRUCTURE OF THE EXERCISE

After deciding what change you want to make, or project you want to complete, or skill you want to improve, the first step in the Life Change exercise is to tap into your present self image to see your picture of yourself. The imagework way to do this is simply to imagine a screen and allow an image to emerge of you as you are now before you've made the life change. This tends to be a caricature, which emphasises the difficulties you are having now. It is then important to understand what choices the person on the screen is making, to appreciate and support him or her in their efforts to deal with the obstacle course of life, and to let them know that you want to help them to make some more comfortable choices.

The next step is to let go of that image, moving it into the past, and allow an image to emerge of how you will be when you have been successful at making a change. As usual, you observe the image, enter into it, and explore it so that you become clear how it would be to be this person. You also look back and see how you got to this position – what was the shift or the step that allowed you to move from being the person you saw on the other screen to the person you are now. It is also helpful to call in 'advisors' who can support and counsel: one person who will cheer you on, and another who is an expert or at least further along in this area than you are. You may also like a 'naïve' whom *you* can teach and guide.

When the new image of yourself is clear, and you return to your observer role, it is time to engage the attitude necessary for success – putting the image in a bubble or balloon, intending for it to be, and also releasing it, sending the balloon out of sight, and acknowledging that it is not totally up to you, and that whether you reach it or not, you will still survive and flourish. You end as usual by appreciating, reflecting, looking forward, and emerging.

The format is:

Preparation: Clearing a space, relaxing
1   Inviting the image of a private cinema
2   An image of yourself as you are now
3   An image of yourself as you will be after you've made the change
4   Experts, helpers, and naïves
5   Looking back
6   Intending and releasing
7   Appreciating, reflecting, looking forward, and emerging

LIFE CHANGE – BASIC EXERCISE

Decide what life change, or goal, or project or skill improvement you want. Then begin by:

Preparation: Clearing a space, relaxing

1   *Inviting the image of a cinema*: Imagine that you are in your own private cinema. You're sitting in the middle of the cinema, and up ahead is a screen.

2   *Yourself as you are now*: Allow a picture of yourself to emerge on the screen as you are now, before you've achieved this goal. What is the picture? How does this person operate? Now describe what he or she is doing: not as an aberration or an act of stupidity, but as the positive, though

limiting, choice he or she is making at present. Why or how do they make this choice and what are the benefits and the disadvantages?

How do you feel about the person? Allow yourself to accept and support this person, even if you are not in favour of the choice he or she is making, and recognise that this is the best choice they are able to make at present, until they become able, with your help, to make a better one. Then let the picture move off the screen to the left, into the past. This is how you just were, but no longer are.

3 *Yourself as you will be*: Now allow a picture of yourself to emerge as you will be, after you have achieved your goal or made this life change. Look at this new picture. How is it different from the old one? Now, in your imagination, walk up to the screen and step into the picture. What does it feel like to be this person? How is it different from the other person you were? Really become clear exactly how you operate and what it is that makes this way of operating so successful. Spend a day as this person noticing all the details of how you live, including how, or whether, you get up in the morning, brush your teeth, eat your breakfast, go to work, spend leisure time, and go to bed at night.

Comment: If you don't like the person on the screen, or can't tolerate the anxiety of being that person, or don't get any image at all, don't despair: this just tells you why it's all been so difficult to do. Play around in your mind with the image of yourself until you find one that is comfortable: think of other people who do it well, or of how you could make that change and still be likeable, or just wonder: if I could make that change in a way I could feel good about it, how would it be?

Then go back and invite an image again. You may want to try out only moments of being that person if it is very threatening, until you feel more comfortable. Should the screen be totally empty, you can still step into it – you will probably find that a feeling emerges even though the picture wasn't there.

---

4 *Experts, helpers, and naïves*: Still living as that person, imagine that you now have with you two helpers, who may be real or imaginary people: one is someone who supports you and cheers you on, and one is someone who is an expert at what you are doing and can advise you. Who are they? Ask them whatever you like and see what they say. Step into their image and be them, to find out about the experience of operating expertly, and of loving and supporting this person that you are. Be aware that you can call on them whenever you need them in future. You might also imagine having a 'naïve' whom *you* reach and support.

5 *Looking back*: Look back and see what led up to this point. What steps did you take? Look at the person you were before: how did you get from there to here – what shift did you make that made this possible?
6 *Intending and releasing*: Now step out of the picture and go back to your seat. Look at that person on the screen, and recognise that this is really you as you could be and will be. Make a real decision that this goal is: *a*) possible, *b*) desirable, and *c*) one that you have a right to have or is right for you to have, and *d*) that you will put your energy and intentions behind becoming that person.

On the other hand, be aware that you don't *have*

to achieve it. Since none of us have complete control over the world or over ourselves, it is just possible that it won't happen. In that unlikely event, you will still survive, and say 'What's next?' In terms of the image, put the image on the screen into a bubble or balloon, and say to yourself 'I fully intend for this to happen, and I release it,' and send the bubble or balloon off, allowing it to disappear from sight. It has now gone into the dimension of potentials that are about to be actualised. Some people like the idea of saying 'I *ask* and intend for this to be, and I release it.' This emphasises a receptive quality right from the beginning. You may wish to add also 'And it is so' – it exists already in that dimension of potentials.

7 *Appreciating, reflecting, looking forward, and emerging*: Appreciate your conscious and unconscious selves for that consultation. Before and after emerging, reflect on the concrete implications of what you learned, and look forward to see what you intend to do in a practical sense to make your vision come true. If the goal seems difficult, or just needs more practice, spend a few moments every day practising being that person you will be after you've made this life change. And before you enter into a situation in which you could use that skill, or before you practise in real life, focus for a moment on being that person once again.

If and when it does come true, don't forget to appreciate again – a pat on the back for you, your unconscious self, and the universe is never misplaced.

QUICK APPLICATIONS

1   When you want to make a change and are not sure how, or just feel bad about how you handled a situation, just spend a moment getting an image of yourself on the screen as you are now, and then one as you will be after you have learned to do it better or have made the change. Looking at the difference will clarify to you exactly what the nature of your present attitude is, and what change you need to make.

2   When you want to do something – even write a letter or make a phone call – that is weighing on you and goes round and round in your mind, just allow an image of yourself doing it to emerge on the screen, put the image in the bubble, and intend and release. This reduces anxiety, and gets it out of your mind and into the realm of potentials waiting to be actualised. This technique is useful whether you want to do the thing now or later. Thus if you just want to get out of bed, create a pleasant image of yourself up and about and doing something enjoyable, intend and release it, and then wait till you get out of bed naturally. Similarly if you need to make a phone call in the evening, do the same, and then notice that when evening comes you gravitate to the phone to get that call out of the way.

3   If you want something to happen for you which is not all up to you – whether it is a 159 bus, a business opportunity, or a new lover – try spending a moment imagining that happening, putting it in a bubble, asking and intending it to be, and releasing it. If it works at greater than chance level, why not? It also makes us feel more hopeful about life, especially if we remember the importance of *sensing* the right goal rather then just *setting* it, and releasing rather than *having* to have it.

IN CONCLUSION

The secret of imagework is to let your images take the strain – work on the images and struggle with the images until you get them right, but don't struggle in real life to *make* them happen. Intending is a clear direction and a determination, and releasing is a receptive letting things be. If you find instead that you feel a sense of confusion, or painful struggle, or burden, or worry, or any other uncomfortable feeling after you have worked on or set yourself a goal, then you need to reconsider both your goal, and your attitude to it. You may have set up a goal that is too demanding at present, or one that you haven't worked through your ambivalence about. And you may well have forgotten also to trust yourself and 'release'. Remember that a goal, or an intention to create change, is there to add to your life and make you feel better, not to give you one more 'should' with which to lash yourself with.

Make sure that the goals you choose to work on are balanced – that they include some to do with fun and play, and some to do with relationships, and some to do with your personal self-care and self-esteem, as well as some to do with work.

Dare to reach for goals that seem ideal but improbable – but don't feel you have to get there. Pointing to the moon may be the nearest we get to it, but even that can be deeply inspiring.

PART THREE

Expanding the Practice of Imagework

12

HEALTH AND ILLNESS
The angels of illness bring messages

When I suggested to Bryan that he use imagework to help with his problem of getting frequent disabling flu and colds, he was pretty sceptical. Imagework was fine for insight into his emotions, or for helping him find his direction in life, but physical symptoms were best left to science and a visit to his doctor. However, he was tired of having flu at least two and usually three times a winter, his fever so high that he normally lost a week or two of work each time, and neither science nor the doctor seemed to have come up with any solutions. He would have a go.

He decided to ask for a message from the 'angels of illness', his internal health counsellors. An image emerged of a brilliant blue sea, with an ancient Greek boat being rowed by several oarsmen sweating with exhaustion. Unable to make sense of this, he asked 'What does this mean?' The answer came: Orestes. He still couldn't make a connection. Then he saw the name Orestes broken up in large letters in the sky to O-REST-EASE. The message came through to him that he was the ancient Greek boat and its oarsmen, and was using all his energy all the time to row the boat. He got an image of the wind blowing, and the sails billowing, and the oarsmen taking a rest. He didn't have to use so much energy all the time, and could take his rest and ease when appropriate and let the sails do the work. In this way he would be less vulnerable to colds and flu.

This message apparently affected Bryan on a very deep level. To his amazement, he didn't have a single cold or flu for three full years, and only one slight cold the year after.

How is this possible? After all, Bryan didn't even consciously do anything. Like a dream that keeps returning because we haven't understood the message it is bringing us, so Bryan's flu and colds were a repeating message from his unconscious body that he didn't know how to listen to. And just as when we have understood the dream, we are no longer visited by it, so it was with Bryan's illness. Once the message became conscious through his image, the unconscious body's message was no longer unconscious, and the illness did not need to return.

ILLNESS AS RELATIONSHIP

Illness can be thought of as the organism's attempt to deal with a wrong relationship or disharmony within us or between ourselves and the world. Sometimes, and particularly when it is a minor illness, it can be thought of as a kind of protection – like a circuit breaker that cuts out before the whole system blows.

Our total organism includes mind, body, spirit, and emotion, functioning as part of the physical world and the social world. The disharmony may therefore be on any one, or more than one, of these levels. Thus, we may be filled with toxins from the food we eat and the air we breathe that we have no protection against, or we may be physically overtired and therefore more prone to illness, or may have reached a sticking point in our lives that we cannot resolve, or be full of repressed resentment that we are unable to let go of, or have a depressed immune system due to the death of a spouse or loss of a job, or be struggling so hard to meet social expectations that we have no energy left over with which to take care of ourselves or to fight illness.

Any time the balance and flow within ourselves and between ourselves and the world is disturbed for internal or external reasons, and particularly when our physical, emotional, and spiritual energy is being overtaxed, we are more prone to illness. This is particularly so when we do not consciously feel the feelings or recognise the process we are going through, so that illness is indeed the only means of expression left to our organism.

As emphasised in chapter 3, taking responsibility does not mean blaming ourselves. The disharmony within us is not only not 'our fault', but it often does not even originate with us. We are physically vulnerable to accidents, infections, malnutrition, toxins, and hereditary weaknesses that we are personally not responsible for, many of which result also from political, social, and commercial practices to which we may be totally opposed. We are also vulnerable to stressful life events that we have no control over, like bereavement, relocation, or job loss; our emotional reactions to these can directly impair our immune systems and thus make us more susceptible to illness.[1]

However, our immune system is far more at risk if we are unable to express our feelings or work through what has happened to us. Lack of love, loss of meaning, suppressed rage, and the inability to find a way through conflicts and problems are the ground upon which illness flourishes. One research study of men between the ages of twenty-one and forty-six indicated that those who were content with their lives had *one tenth* the rate of serious illness and death suffered by those who were most dissatisfied, even when the effects of alcohol, tobacco, obesity, and ancestral longevity were statistically eliminated.[2]

To describe it in terms of images: a deeply held image that you are a heavily laden donkey that is loved as long as it works hard – and the heavier the burdens, the more it will be appreciated – can lead you to illness. The illness is not a conscious choice, but rather your organism's reponse to the fact that it is not free to live in such a way so as not to get ill; it may even be your organism's way of protecting itself against worse problems. The image itself is not your fault, but rather the best and most creative way you knew to deal with family and other situations in which you didn't seem able to get the love you wanted just for being you. It may well also be an image that was sanctioned and encouraged in your family and culture. Furthermore, you are not responsible for germs, nor for the competitive stress at your job, nor for the fact that in this society people tend to be so over-identified with their work that many die soon after they retire because they feel useless.

However, having acknowledged the powerful combined forces of both inner images and outer pressures, you are in a wonderful position to step back, re-evaluate your strategy, and try another path into the future. At this point, you begin to have a real choice. You may decide that rather than being a donkey you wish to try out being a peacock, or a cat. Or you may resolve that in future you will prescribe yourself a few health days to revitalise and enjoy yourself, so that you don't need to have so many illness days.

I am not saying that if only you have the right attitude or image you will never get ill, nor even that the right attitude or image will magically cure you. Such a belief cannot help but increase our tendencies both to omnipotence and to self blame. But I *would* say that if becoming or staying healthy is a priority for you, it is crucial to understand and be open to changing those aspects of your relationship with yourself and with the world that you *can* do something about. To put it another way, you need to find out where you are stuck, and to find a way to solve the problem and move forward that is healthier for you than illness. In this way, at least you give your organism a choice, and a fighting chance.

BODY, MIND AND SPIRIT

Being multilevel organisms, we can approach health and healing in many different ways. We can, in order to get well or stay well, decide to take up regular meditation and relaxation, and change our pattern of exercise, diet, and/or work. We may, in order to heal an illness, also take drugs, submit to surgery, and benefit from all the discoveries of modern science. All these are powerful aids to the healing process and none should be ignored as a possible avenue.

But at the root of all that we do is consciousness: the will to live and to grow, the understanding of what it means to be well and whether indeed we wish to be well, and our inner attraction to health enhancing or health endangering life choices. If, for example, illness is the most convenient answer to what seems an insoluble problem, healthy regimes will not be adhered to, and medical science will find itself battling ghosts in the dark.

GOOD GIRLS DIE YOUNG

Some years ago I was hospitalised due to intestinal haemor-rhaging. I worked a great deal with my inner images in order to understand the nature of the illness and get a sense of how to heal myself and how to prevent myself from being ill again. I found, for example, that when I tried to imagine myself well I could find no joy in it, as it just meant taking on too many responsibilities once again. I struggled my way through until I could get a sense of a life that was worth living. I came out of hospital much changed by the experience, more hopeful about life than I had been for a long time, healed but still weak.

A few months later I was still without energy, sleeping a few hours every day as if I had a flu that never got better. I went to see the consultant at the hospital who told me that there was nothing physically wrong, and that it had to do with my 'spirit' – a striking comment from someone who professed not even to believe that stress was related to illness. I went home and struggled again to go deeper and deeper into myself to understand what was preventing me from getting well.

Finally I got an image of a childhood 'heroine' from *Little Women*, a novel I had adored and read and reread as a child. My heroine was Beth, a little girl who was always sweet and good, and never wanted to do anything but stay with mummy and take care of her and who died before she reached her twentieth birthday. I began to understand that my internal image of being 'good' was that you worked so hard in the service of others that you got ill, and then you really deserved to get taken care of. And furthermore, good girls die young. To be healthy was in my unconscious view almost immoral; in fact, you couldn't be healthy and good.

Right then and there, I decided that if that was indeed my internal choice, then I'd rather be healthy than good. My energy returned as if by magic the next day, and I have never had a relapse, nor for that matter, suffered from any other serious illness. However, since then, whenever I have even the mildest flu, I consider that if all were well I would *be* well. I therefore take the opportunity to look at my life and see what changes I need to make to render illness unnecessary.

POSITIVELY HEALTHY

Health is not simply the absence of illness. This becomes patently obvious when you take a good look at the so-called healthy people all around you and notice how unhealthy and unhappy so many of them look. I can still hear a childhood friend of mine saying: 'My father dropped dead of a heart attack at the age of forty and he'd never had a day's illness in his life.' I was deeply shocked at this bolt from the blue, and felt with her the supreme unfairness of it all. Yet it may be that, not being truly healthy, my friend's father's downfall was precisely the fact that he was never ill – without the circuit breaker of illness, the whole system did suddenly blow.

What then is full health? Health at its best has a positive, aesthetic quality of its own. When we are really healthy, it is a pleasure to see us and be with us because a sense of renewal flows from us. We take care of our body, and our body takes care of us, so that we look and feel beautiful in a way that has nothing to do with age, weight, or conventional good looks. In a larger sense, we take care of our relationship to the world, so that we meet the world with healthy pleasure, and the world meets us with the same healthy pleasure.

Phrases like 'bursting with health' or 'glowing with health' are suggestive of this state of full health. They convey the sense of being in touch with our inner fountain of life energy, which flows unimpeded through us and out to the world, as well as receptive and open to the life-giving forces of nature and of people. In the unhealthy and difficult world we live in, being fully healthy is not very often a permanent state, but the more often we can be like that, the better our life will be.

RECEPTIVE AND ACTIVE IMAGEWORK

In using imagework to deal with health and illness, whether we are actually ill or are simply not flourishing, we need to be receptive to images about our deep mental and physical processes, and to practise images in an active way that will enhance our capacity to become and remain fully healthy.

On a receptive level, we need to open ourselves up to images that tell us what is going on both in our unconscious body and in our unconscious mind. As usual, we need to gain an understanding of our deep unconscious assumptions, and begin to re-examine them in the light of our adult conscious wisdom. But we can also get direct information about our physical welfare from imagery. Not only can the prognosis of illness be predicted from examining the images of ill people, but there are also thousands of documented examples of the unconscious body sending an image or a message through an internal counsellor that tells the sufferer what is wrong while the doctors are still puzzled.

For example, one little boy with a brain tumour thought to be incurable was, following the advice of a doctor who believed in the value of imagery, practising visualising shooting the brain tumour with little rockets. One day he announced that he had just taken a trip through his head in a rocket ship and couldn't find the cancer anywhere. To everyone's disbelief, he was absolutely right: the cancer was gone.[3] Jean Houston[4] pioneer in the field of mind expansion and the development of conscious creativity, tells the story of how, at the age of twenty-three, when she was seriously ill with what the doctor called influenza, a group of ladies in flowered hats visited her in her delirious imagination and told her to get her mother to get her the blood test that's given to alcoholics. Her mother complied and to her surprise, a raging case of hepatitis was revealed.

Inner images or internal counsellors can often also give us specific advice about how to heal ourselves, which may include diet, exercise, or even medication, as well as minor or major shifts in attitude. Time and again people have found the advice sent by the unconscious body remarkable accurate.

When I was in mourning after a death in the family, my own inner health consultant told me that while I needed to go through the mourning process, my physical health was suffering, and I had to cut out salt, sugar, caffeine, and alcohol, all of which were 'hyping' me up and bringing me down, and to take vitamins and Ginseng. If anyone else had given me a prescription like this, I would certainly have taken it – forgive the pun – 'with a pinch of salt'. But somehow the advice was so powerful, that I just found myself following it. Within a few days not only did my physical strength return, but my emotional balance also seemed to reassert itself.

To heal ourselves, we also need to get messages about what it would be like to be flourishing and healthy, and what we need to do in order to become so and stay so. As we do this, we often find out what is stopping us from wanting to be healthy, as well as gaining a model or pattern for being fully healthy which may be totally new to us.

More painful, but equally important, is the opposite exploration: how would it be to be fatally ill, die, be around for your funeral, be able to look at your life afresh, and then actually live to tell the tale. Confronting all this in your imagination may seem horrific, but when you return to everyday life, you may decide to make sure it doesn't happen to you in real life if you have a say in the matter. This is particularly crucial if you have any worries about your life style, or about the possibility of life threatening illnesses or accidents.

Receptive imagework may be sufficient to set us on our way. But it is also useful to actively practise images that will facilitate healing and healthy living. These images are new programs that provide a pattern of healing and health that our unconscious body can respond to and fit into, and that will also guide our conscious selves to make the kind of life choices that are really healthy. In any case, any kind of peaceful imagework is an opportunity for that daily relaxation that is so healthful for mind, body, and spirit.

Becoming Fully Healthy: The Structure of the Exercises

The process I suggest that you follow, rather than being steps in one exercise, is really a series of exercises that will enable you to explore in turn what is going on now, what you could learn from imagining that you are terminally ill, what is stopping you from being fully healthy, and how to create healing images. Each exercise should be preceded by clearing a space and relaxing, and concluded with appreciating, emerging, reflecting, and looking forward.

Preparation: Clearing a space, relaxing before each exercise.

1   What is my present state of health or illness, and what does this mean?

2   How would it be to be fatally ill, die, and then have another chance?

3   How would it be to be fully healthy?

4   Creating healing images

5   Appreciating, reflecting, looking forward, and emerging after each exercise.

BECOMING FULLY HEALTHY: BASIC SERIES OF EXERCISES

Preparation: Clearing a space, relaxing

1   *What is my present state of health or illness, and what does this mean?*: There are a number of ways to use imagery to understand our present state. Here are some:

a   *Image as metaphor*: Focus on anywhere in your body where there is an illness or a malfunctioning, or, if there is no particular problem, just on your general bodily state. Suggest to yourself: I would like to allow an image to emerge of an animal, a plant or an object that somehow represents my illness/state of health/liver/heart/stomach or whatever is not functioning normally (insert whichever is appropriate) at this moment in my life.

Once the image has emerged, work on it as outlined in chapter 5. Be open to the possibility that the image may have something to do with diagnosing or describing your physical state, as well as being at one and the same time a metaphor for your emotional and mental state.

b *The Houses of Health and Illness*: Allow an image of the House of Health to emerge. Study it from all sides, then enter it. What is it like? How do you feel here? In the House of Health you will meet one or more health consultants. Who are they? Talk to them and ask them their view of your present health/illness situation, and what you need to do about it. Ask them to be as specific as possible in terms of giving you a program for health that involves mind, body, and spirit.

You may also try allowing an image to emerge of the House of Illness and again, study it, enter it, and find the consultants. What do they have to tell you about your life and what you need to do about it? Again, get them to be specific.

c *The angels of illness* (for when you are ill): On a hilltop, just in view, two angels of illness are sitting and whispering about you. What are they saying? Ask them why the illness has come to visit you, and what message you need to learn from it so that you can live in such a way that you don't need to be ill. The answer may come in words or in an image. If you don't understand, keep asking them to help you understand.

d *Painting the image*: Take a paper and some felt tip pens, and draw a picture of your illness, or of your state of health. Work through the picture just as you did with the exercise 'Image as metaphor', see chapter 6. Begin by focusing on the picture as a whole as image, and then on the individual aspects of the picture. You can also have a conversation between the various parts of the picture.

2 *How would it be if I developed a fatal illness*? Imagine you have been told that you have a fatal illness and have only one week to live. What illness do you have? How do you feel about it? What happens during this week? Notice how you react to the doctors, to the people who visit you, and to all the people that have been significant in your life. Whom do you want to say goodbye to, and what do you want to say?

You die. What is this like? Your spirit floats up and you watch from above what is happening. How do people react? How do you feel about their reactions? You go to the funeral and listen to what they say. What does this feel like? What epitaph will they write on your tombstone? What would be more appropriate and would represent the real truth about your life? What do you wish they could write?

Now look back at your life and consider that if you had it all to live over again, how would you change your attitudes and/or choices? Most important – how could you make sure that this time you lived a long and happy life and died naturally at a ripe old age?

Now imagine that you awake with a start, and realise that all this has been a dream. Consider now what you need to do to make sure this nightmare doesn't need to become a reality.

3 *How would it be if I were fully healthy*? Allow an image to emerge of yourself as fully healthy.

220

What are you like? How do you feel, act, relate to the world? What makes it worthwhile getting out of bed in the morning? If you find it difficult to find a satisfactory, healthy life, take the time to keep working through the feelings until you can find a way to imagine a fully healthy life that is a pleasure to live.

Comment: You can also, if you wish, adapt the private cinema exercise in chapter 14 on Life Change, allowing an image to emerge first of yourself as you are, and then as you will be after you have become fully healthy.

4   *Healing Images*: Here are a few ideas:
a   If you have allowed an image to emerge of your illness or present body state, now allow an image to emerge of the healing process. This can be realistic or symbolic. You can imagine your white blood cells working and the toxins leaving your system naturally. Or you can inhale and see or feel your entire body fill with radiant light and love, and then as you exhale see and feel all the toxins leaving your body through your breath and through the pores of your skin. Or you can float in healing water, or be bathed in a fountain of healing light. It is important that the image seems to you to be more powerful than the image that signifies illness, and that it can work naturally to heal you, and to allow the toxins to leave your body. This may not be possible immediately, because your present images will express your present attitude, but more positive attitudes and images should emerge as you work in this way.

221

b Imagine that your body and spirit naturally emanate a glowing light that expresses, surrounds, and protects them. Sense that in some way this surrounding light has been infiltrated, torn through, or otherwise damaged. Heal the damage, and reinstate the naturally shining light of your inner being.

c Imagine a circle of people around you that love you. These may be living or dead, or even figures out of your imagework, as long as you feel that they really care about you. Ask them to send you a healing love and radiance from their heads and hearts. Accept this love and radiance and take it in fully. Once you feel you have fully accepted it, you can send your own healing love and radiance to all of them. You may wish to join them now in the healing circle.

d Taking the image of yourself as fully healthy in step 3 above, practise being that fully healthy person. Go through a day, or through a difficult task ahead as that healthy person. Be aware that this fully healthy person is the real you and that your responsibility is merely to allow this real you to emerge and blossom.

e If you have created a sanctuary or place of peace for yourself in the relaxation exercise of chapter 5, spend time in the sanctuary, enjoying the tranquillity and the sense of a right relationship with the universe that comes about there so naturally.

f Imagine surrounding yourself with the shape of a pyramid, and feel its healing and centring power.

Comment: Whether ill, ailing, or not fully healthy, do spend a few minutes daily practising healing images, or images of living in full health. This has the dual purpose of encouraging your unconscious mind and body to move into new and more healthful patterns, and of being a form of meditation or relaxation, which as we have seen in chapter 5 is a vital adjunct to health and healing. These exercises are also vital when you are feeling low, hurt, vulnerable, or generally in need of any kind of healing. If you ever sense that you have been damaged in some way, heal yourself first, and then go out in the world to do what needs doing to right the wrong. But even if you think you are okay, it is worth working with these exercises; sometimes we get so used to a low level of health that we don't realise anything is wrong and we need to be reminded of our full potential.

IN CONCLUSION

On some level all imagework exercises are relevant to attaining full health. When you let go of fears and fantasies, heal your relationships and say goodbye where appropriate, and find creativity and fulfilment, you are a lot more equipped to want to – and to make sure that you do – live a long, happy and healthy life. Conversely, working through the exercises on health should help you not only to be healthy but also to live more happily.

Thus, the following description by Jane, a young imagework student of mine who was writing not about health but about the general function of imagework in her life, sounds rather like the story of an inner journey toward health:

It is as though of all the seeds sown inside us particularly in the early years, some are bad seeds and make loud noises inside us, often getting louder as we grow older. Through imagework, by working back down to the roots and coming to terms with the reasons for the disturbance, it seems we are able to quieten that noise, leaving a sense of peace in that area. After working on a 'bad seed' successfully there is a great sense of release and a weight has lifted. Thus the more 'bad seeds' or disturbances are worked on, the quieter it becomes inside and the lighter the being.

Perhaps it is these loud seeds that cause illness, and the inner quiet and lightness of being is a way of describing health.

13

DREAMS AS TURNING POINTS

Last night I had the strangest dream

When we work with images, we bravely don our diving gear and dive as deep as we dare to find the treasures of the sea. Dreams, on the other hand, are great treasures that the sea throws up from its bed and deposits on our shores. Most people take a look at these odd specimens and throw them right back into the sea, wondering what it has to do with them. But now that you have done some imagework, and understand the power of the sea of the unconscious to affect our lives, you will doubtless be grateful for these unbidden gifts, and be prepared to take the time to figure out why they were given to you and what you can do with them.

A great advantage of working with dreams is that we know that they must be the 'real thing'; because they come to us unbidden, they are clearly messages from our deep unconscious, and not something we may have 'made up' with our conscious intelligence. But by the same token, they often seem more tantalisingly out of the reach of our understanding than do the images that we ourselves dive for and work with. While the images that emerge during the imagework usually have an intuitively obvious meaning to us, this is not always true of dreams.

There are many theories as to what dreams 'really are': they have been thought to be the result of faulty digestion, or the not-yet-dealt-with information from our personal mind computer, or the revelation of our deepest fears and wishes, or a device for problem solving, or a message from other people who may be living or dead, or an indication of the future. They may well express all of these possibilities, and many more.

FORETELLING THE FUTURE

For example, there is a great deal of evidence that dreams can sometimes tell the future. I have, over the years, asked many groups of ordinary college students about their dreams, and have discovered that in every group of ten to fifteen students there are always one or two who can report dreams that foretold a future event with a precision that could not have been due to chance alone.

One student, for example, who regularly went to work in a friend's car, had a dream in which she and her friend, on their way to work, had a minor collision with a lorry at a particular junction, and the lorry driver looked out and shouted at them. The dream worried her, and she told her friend about it, but they set out for work as usual. Not only did a collision with a lorry occur at the same junction as in the dream, but the lorry driver who looked out of his window also had the identical face and shouted the same words as the dream lorry driver.

The fact that some dreams tell the future doesn't mean that all, or even most dreams do. When you have a nightmare, for example, it is almost certainly an expression of your fears rather than a prediction of a real future disaster. People who have dreams that foretell the future tell me that these dreams have a special quality which is quite different from the more normal dreams. Generally, the future related dreams are more realistic, often portraying scenes which one is observing rather than participating in, and the dreamer tends to wake up with the strong feeling that they have actually been to a real place. They are, in a sense, more like visions than like dreams.

MULTIDIMENSIONAL DREAM REALITIES

It is probably best to think of dreams as a portal into that multidimensional world of our unconscious self which we discussed in chapter 3. They therefore give us access to the countless resources that most of us are out of contact with when we are focused upon the material and social reality of our everyday waking life.

Thus the message a dream is bringing us may be to do with illness or other problems of the unconscious body, taboo thoughts and feelings of the personal repressed unconscious, intuitive wisdom from the universal unconscious, or not-yet-accessed files of the everyday unconscious, or, indeed, all of these. This means that different dreams may need to be interpreted in very different ways, and also that most dreams can be understood on more than one level.

The focus of imagework generally is on using images to understand and transform our relationship to life, and this is also the approach taken to dreams in this chapter. Perhaps even more than other images, dreams are wonderful at presenting us with just that dilemma that we are on the verge of solving, or in need of solving, at that moment. In my experience, dreams that are worked on deeply are always turning points, and the more uncomfortable they are the more important they may be.

LOST IN A DREAM

Some months ago I dreamt that I was on a train and had to go to the loo (lavatory) on the train. I mistakenly thought that this meant that I needed to get off the train, go to the previous station, and get another train in order to continue my journey. I didn't know where I was, or what the name of the previous station was. I searched desperately for a London tube map and couldn't find one, and I felt a very deep confusion and frustration as the map kept eluding me.

227

Dreamworking

I woke up, feeling quite distressed, and wondered what the dream was all about. I decided to work with the various symbols of the dream, in much the same way as we did in chapter 5, 'becoming' each aspect of the dream, and speaking to my dream self.

The map told me that it was eluding me because I didn't need it – not only was I looking for the wrong map, because the London tube map was irrelevant for the train, but in any case I didn't need a map because I could trust my deeper self to know the way. The train told me that I had bought a ticket and knew where I was going. The loo told me that taking time out during the journey was fine, and it was not necessary to get off and return to a previous station. I just needed to relax and trust the train.

Armed with these reassurances from all sides, I re-entered the dream and continued it. I returned to the train and relaxed, and suddenly discovered that I knew my destination – I was going to a conference between the universe and the nations, where I was to represent the universe. I didn't need to find an official map to know where I was and where I was coming from. I had rather to use my energy to prepare myself for the tasks ahead.

This dream had a postscript, which underlined for me that amazing interweaving of the psychological unconscious with the real world and probably made me take the dream even more seriously. I was sitting on a train the next day thinking about the dream, and a woman came up to me and said she was on the wrong train and could I help her? When she told me where she needed to go, I suggested that she get off at the next station and change. 'But I don't have my tube map and I don't know where I am,' she told me in a confused manner. I stared at her, hardly able to believe that I wasn't hallucinating, and said slowly 'You don't need a tube map for the train.' It transpired that she thought she had to go back to the previous station, which just happens to be called Water*loo*, and thought she should get there by tube. I was able to tell her confidently that she didn't need a map, and that she didn't need to return to the previous station, because she would find that if she got off at the next station she could change trains and continue her journey. When we settled down to talking about where she was going, I found myself slightly relieved to find that it was a course and not a conference she was headed for.

Turning Points

My dream both signalled to me that I had already made a shift in my life, and also pointed to the next shift I needed to make. In previous dreams I had seen myself rush around, impelled by the need to meet the expectations of others. I could see that I had now moved on, and was 'on the train', on the verge of finding my own direction.

But I was still interrupting my flow by my doubts, rushing off my own track to seek official – and totally irrelevant – confirmation, and ending up confused and lost. It was crucial, I could now see, to stop doubting myself, and trust that the route I had chosen was the right one and would lead to where I needed to go. It was time now to shift to looking at my purposes, taking them seriously, and preparing myself for what lay ahead. The idea of representing the universe in a conference between the universe and the nations was a rather grandiose metaphor for what I needed to do in my own small way, and I was grateful for the clarity it offered me.

The dream, or the dreamwork that I did on it, was an important turning point for me in the development of my vision of where I was going in life, and of my will to plan and carry out effectively what feels right to me. More recently I have for the first time had dreams in which I myself am driving and this has reassured me that I have begun to take charge of my life. It is only a beginning, I must underline, because the rather frantic way I have been driving in the dreams gives me a good idea as to what I need to be working on next.

WHAT IF I HAVEN'T GOT ANY DREAMS?

Before outlining the dreamwork exercise we need to address two possible problems: 'What if I don't dream?' and 'What if I can't remember my dreams?'. The first can be disposed of quite quickly because everyone dreams a great deal. If you don't remember your dreams, it may be as Freud believed because you repress the memory, but there is not too much evidence of this, and it is more likely that it is because you go into a very deep sleep and by the time you emerge to the surface the dream is lost. This is why the dreams you have early in the morning after you have woken and then gone back into a light sleep are often the ones you remember. I have talked to hundreds to people about dreams, and of these one and only one person literally did not know what a dream was because he could not remember having had any. He happened to be a phenomenally deep sleeper.

The way we wake and move immediately after our dreams is also crucial to our ability to remember them. As Ernst Schachtel [1] has pointed out, while language and adult concepts are easily retained 'in our minds', dream experiences, like childhood memories, are probably related to or held in our bodies and our kinaesthetic experience. This is why when we move the dream often seems to disappear or dissolve. This is also why telling someone the dream immediately helps so much to preserve it – we are translating it into a verbal code that we can remember in our minds, so to speak, rather than our bodies. Leaping out of bed right after we wake and before putting our dreams into words is therefore definitely not conducive to remembering them.

Before you go to sleep, speak to your unconscious and tell it that you appreciate your dreams and you would like to remember them. Then, when you wake and open your eyes,

close them immediately. Lie there and tell yourself or someone else the dream by going back into the dream and reliving it. This is in any case the first stage of working on a dream. You will probably also find that this is an ideal time to continue and work on the dream if you don't have to jump out of bed immediately.

Actually recording the dream in some way as soon as you wake up, with your eyes still closed, is a great aid to remembering and preserving your dreams. So before you go to bed, do put a pad of paper and pen or a tape recorder right by your bed. When you wake up, try to reach gently and with your eyes closed for the pad or tape recorder, and record any dream fragment you can remember. Trying to keep your eyes closed when you wake up is difficult, but simply close them as soon as you notice that you've opened them. This technique works progressively, so don't give up if it doesn't seem to have much effect straight away. Over the days you will find yourself remembering more and more dreams, and feeling more and more in contact with the world of dreams.

You don't need to have a whole dream to work with, nor do you need a dream that you have just dreamt. Any dream or dream fragment that comes to mind can be explored. Dreams that repeat are particularly good, since these keep 'knocking at your door' trying to tell you something important that you won't listen to. In my experience, when people work on a dream that has come back more than once, the message is very powerful, and in all cases that I know of, that dream doesn't return. What often happens is that the next dream is an expression of a new stage in the person's evolution.

Do remember that disturbing dreams are not 'bad dreams', for they signal the next step. Pleasant dreams are powerful too, for they can represent a state that we need to appreciate, and, if we wish, we can always find room for further development.

Dreams as Turning Points: The Structure of the Exercise

In working on dreams as turning points, the approach I suggest is along the lines I used in the dream above. You enter into the dream again, sense the background feelings and relationships, and re-experience it. You then observe the dream from above and from the side, have conversations with the various aspects of the dream, and with the dream as a whole, so as to go more deeply into the meaning. All this you have already begun to be familiar with from your work with your images in chapter 5.

You then go back into the dream, integrate into yourself as dream self all you have learned from the various perspectives and beings of the dream, and live the dream through with a new approach. You continue the dream into the future. It is then important to map your understandings back onto your life, and consider how you need to use that personal quality or understanding in your life at this very time. The format of the exercise is, in brief:

Preparation: Clearing a space, relaxing
1 Entering the dream
2 Studying the dream
3 Becoming the images
4 Integrating the viewpoints
5 Reliving and continuing the dream successfully
6 Appreciating, reflecting, looking forward, and emerging.

If you are not actually in the dream as yourself, you may decide to identify another aspect of the dream as you, the dream self. If none of the dream symbols seems to represent you, or you feel that you have really been an observer, ignore any instructions that are not relevant. You can still enter the dream, study the dream, become the various images, continue the dream, and appreciate, reflect, look forward, and emerge.

DREAMS AS TURNING POINTS: BASIC EXERCISE

1 *Entering the dream*: What is the background emotional or sensory atmosphere of the dream? Can you give it a name? Is it familiar? Now enter the dream, and feel the atmosphere. Live through the dream from start to finish, or whatever you can remember of it. If you are working with a guide, tell the person your dream as if it is happening right now. Recognise the feelings, the relationships, the situation of the dreams. What is familiar about these?

2 *Studying the dream*: Imagine that the dream is on a stage. Allow your spirit to rise up from above

and look down upon the dream and the dream self. What do you notice? What is the dream self's approach to life? What approach or personal quality might help the dream self to live the dream more happily? If you could whisper anything to the dream self what would it be? Then try looking from the left, the right, behind, in front, underneath. From each perspective notice what comes to mind about the dream and the dream self. If you are able to, you might actually move around physically, with the dream 'in the middle' so that you can actually look at it from the various sides.

3 *Becoming the images*: What is the most striking aspect of the dream? This may be a person, or a scene, or a building, or an object, or an event. Now step into that image, either in your mind, or by picturing it on a chair opposite and switching seats. As this image, talk about yourself and your viewpoint, including your view of the dream self.

Then go on, and become each other important aspect in turn – what does each feel and see? What does each want to say to the dream self? Where appropriate, have conversations between the dream self and any of these aspects, or between the various aspects. Each aspect of the dream, whether it is a person, a chair, or a bouncy movement, has a message that you as dream self or as dreamer need to listen to.

Now talk to the dream as a whole: 'Dream, what do you want to tell me?' Become the dream and answer.

You might find it useful also to continue the dream – what would have happened next had you not woken up at that point?

4 *Integrating the viewpoints*: When you feel you have learned as much as you can from the various perspectives, it is time to reintegrate the under-standings back into your dream self as main actor. Go back into the dream as the central dream character. Look around at each of the characters and each of the perspectives and think about what each has told you. Consider also what you have learned from continuing the dream. What do you now understand about how you live in the dream world and how you might live? Ask your unconscious to take in and integrate these various understandings and perspectives. Take the time to let them sink in.

Try to formulate as clearly as possible in words what you have learned, and, where a dream wasn't totally satisfying, what new approach or attitude or personal quality you need in order to live this dream in such a way that you would feel really better at the end of it.

5 *Reliving and continuing the dream success-fully*: Now, unless the dream felt perfect as it was, try reliving the dream with this new approach or personal quality. If you find it too difficult to imagine acting differently, just say to yourself: if I *did* have that quality, or if I *were* like that, what would I do? If you get stuck anywhere, go out from the dream and reassess and figure out whether you need anything else in order to go forward. Do try to find a way to live the dream so that it feels good to you.

Continue the dream into the future now. What happens next? What do you do after that? How is this different from when you continued the dream before?

Now, check out the solution from the various perspectives you took before. What do the other beings think? What does this new dream look like from above, below, and the various sides. If there are any further shifts that seem appropriate, try them out.

6 *Appreciating, reflecting, looking forward, and emerging*: When you feel good about the dream, thank your unconscious for the dream gift, and your conscious self for working so hard. Ask your unconscious to integrate your new understandings, and to offer you a new dream in the near future that will represent your new state of development.

Before and after emerging, think about the application of your understandings to your life. Where in your life are you relating to the world as you did in the dream? How could you operate differently? Often there is a very specific area of life that needs your attention in just this way.

Do also write down your experience, paint the dream, dance the dream, or express it in some other medium. Every new mode of expression, like every new perspective, will offer you something that you will find useful.

APPLICATIONS

This technique can also be applied to a real life event that you went through but were unhappy about, particularly one that you recognise as fitting into one of your patterns. You found yourself once again rushing to catch a train for work, worried that you would be late, and not feeling prepared. Or there you were in a familiar situation of feeling furious at someone for letting you down, saying all the wrong things and feeling bad afterwards.

Whatever the scene is, treat it exactly like a dream. Go back into it and relive it, recognising the feelings. Look at the scene from all the perspectives. Become the various aspects and people in the situation and talk to yourself. Then go back into the situation in your mind, and reintegrate these understandings into yourself. When you are clear what personal attribute or attitude you could use to deal better with the situation, relive the scene. Really enjoy getting it as you want it and feeling good about how you handle it. Make a commitment to yourself in future that this new way of operating will at least be available to you as an alternative when you are in this situation.

IN CONCLUSION

One of the important aspects of this work is that we begin to create new models for how we could be. By studying the dream, or a real life event, from all these perspectives, the rule that is presently guiding our approach and behaviour becomes conscious and clear, and a new rule or pattern can emerge. Reliving the dream or real life experience not only clarifies the alternative model, but it also serves as a practice run. It's then a lot easier to step into this new way of operating automatically even when we are in a stressful situation and would normally be prone to falling back on our familiar ways.

Another benefit is the fact that we can end up feeling good even about the most negative experiences. Normally, when we have had a disturbing or confusing experience, whether in a dream or real life, we are left with a residue of discomfort or unease. And while we may in theory believe that the most negative experiences are positive challenges and lessons for us, if we are feeling damaged, a little homily to ourselves on how good it is to feel bad just adds insult to injury.

Yet by working on it in this way, and reliving the experience positively at the end, we not only seal off but actually transform the disturbing internal memory into a positive one. We end up with a good memory of having acted well, as well as a positive plan for the future. So now it is the turn of your unconscious to say 'Thank you' to your conscious self for this lovely gift.

== 14 ==

PRESENTING MYSELF TO OTHERS

If all the world's a stage, why can't I have a better part?

My friend Clare tells me that we all not only need to decide what roles we wish to play in life, but also to get our scripts, costume design, and stage setting right. As a true child of the sixties, I used to find this idea just slightly shocking. Why would you want to play a role if you can be yourself?

Slowly but surely, however, I have come to the conclusion that, at their best, the roles we play *are* ways of being ourselves. Just as our language structures how we think, so roles are the language of social relations that structure the way we present ourselves and relate to each other in social settings. If we wish to communicate with people outside our most intimate circle of friends, we need to speak this language fluently enough so that we can express our inner creativity through it. Otherwise we will be seen, and see ourselves, not as children of nature but as social illiterates.

Roles are really frameworks for relationships, and models for how we think of ourselves, present ourselves, and communicate with others. Some are professional, like the doctor – patient, or social worker–client one; some are personal, like the mother – child, or sister–brother, or friendship ones; and some are more idiosyncratic, like the 'charming rebel' or 'self-sacrificing angel', 'superior being' or 'caring doormat' ones. Every role can be interpreted in many ways, and it is the individual way we interpret it that becomes our 'trademark'. Whether we are or are not conscious of the roles we play, other people will be responding to them, and will play a part that is complementary to ours. If I play 'caring doormat', it is not surprising if someone else lovingly steps on me.

Since we are all social beings, we do need to acknowledge that beside just 'being', there is also 'seeming'. We are not pure spirits, but rather we have both inner experiences and an outer persona. If we don't define our own persona and take charge of how we 'seem', we are leaving it to others to define it for us, and to draw conclusions we don't like. And we will always be lamenting, 'Why don't people take me seriously/ love me/respect me/fancy me' – or whatever it is that we seek and cannot seem to achieve.

This doesn't mean that we should use roles as a mask that covers up a real self we believe is not good enough, any more than women should use make-up as a way of covering up a face they believe to be ugly. Your true self, like your natural face, is by definition acceptable and lovable, and the more it shines out, the more attractive you will be to people. Roles can be seen as the medium through which you can express your authentic self socially – and indeed, through which you can decorate and celebrate that inner self that you are proud of.

FROM ORPHAN TO FASHION LEADER

I used to be almost totally ignorant of the language of social roles, and, assuming that everyone else was 'being themselves' also, I believed everything everyone said. If I said, 'How are you?' and people said 'Fine', I believed they meant this literally – and wondered why everyone else's life seem to work so much better than mine. If when they told me about their holiday, they selected the best bits to entertain me with, I believed that this was the whole picture – and my holiday never seemed so good by comparison.

The same was true of clothing: I would see another woman dressed beautifully, and simply didn't understand how much work this took – I thought that she just did this naturally because she was that kind of woman. If I looked like a pathetic orphan, it must be because on some inner level I was one, and there was nothing I could do about that. But I never stopped being hurt when people said to me, in a tone of sympathetic respect combined with pity, that I obviously didn't care how I dressed.

I really didn't quite know that people considered it quite legitimate to present themselves at their best. So as my face came up against other people's masks, I always got a bump on the nose. I was convinced that I was intrinsically not as good as they were. To try harder in these areas was unacceptable – in fact I thought that it was my duty to reveal myself at my worst to make sure that if people liked me they were liking the 'real me.' I believed in the 'Yes–No' theory of personality – you either have it or you don't.

So for me, it was an amazing and liberating discovery to learn that the roles people played in life were just that – roles that they had fashioned, and that they valued. Similarly the clothes they wore had not just 'walked out of the wardrobe', as my friend Clare pointed out to me, but had been carefully chosen to fit in with how they saw themselves or wanted to present themselves. When I looked at people I assumed I saw their essence. Clare saw – and when it was good, she admired – their performance.

All these insights came to me very late in life indeed – in fact it was only four or five years ago that I really began to lose my 'social virginity', so to speak – and I needed to move quickly to make up for lost time. It suddenly occurred to me that for years I had been doing the hard bit – exploring my inner and authentic self. Since I couldn't look good unless I really felt good, I had had to do a lot of internal work just so as not to be constantly embarrassed. In fact, I am very grateful for this process, because had I known how to consciously present myself, I might have taken an easier, and less satisfying way. But now, having done all that, I figured out that the social role bit must be relatively easy, and that a little work would go a long way. And so it was.

I decided that I no longer wanted to be viewed, and view myself, as 'orphan', so I needed to stop dressing like one. I wanted to be a kind of 'fashionable individualist' – someone who obviously knew the fashion, but used it to express her own personality. I learned to observe what other women wore, now seeing it as a choice they made, and one that therefore I could make too. Did I like it? If I did, I could try it. So instead of being diminished each time I saw someone who looked attractively dressed, I was delighted – she was a source of new ideas, not a threat.

To look the way I wanted to, I also needed to lose weight. Here again, I found that I could convert envy into will. Sitting on a Greek island beach with lots of beautiful slender Scandinavian women, and feeling incredibly fat and unattractive, I was suddenly struck by this revelation: if I admired their slenderness, I didn't need to envy them – I could just decide to become like that. So I decided right then and there how many pounds I would lose each year for the next three years. And I did it. It was incredibly difficult, but not impossible. It just needed to be the most important thing in the world, and for a few months every year it was. I was totally determined not to feel bad about something that I had the power to change.

I also learned to use the intuition and the imagework that I had developed for deep psychological work to teach me how to lose weight and how to dress. I tuned into the picture of myself as I wanted to be, and found a slim and active woman. My image taught me that weight loss was not just a device to please others and look attractive, but was a way to feel physically better and indeed to be what I really was naturally. I then looked back and saw how I'd achieved it – by a diet of fruits and vegetables. And so it was to be – I only had to do it.

I taught myself to walk into a shop and use my intuition to go straight for the clothes and accessories that would suit me. And when I tried something on, my internal Egyptian queen guide would tell me what she thought. If she gave the thumbs down, even if I couldn't see why, I left it in the shop. If she said she would kill for it, I bought it. Luckily I found that her tastes – and mine – were individualistic rather than expensive.

242

Not too many months after all this metamorphosis began, a young beautifully dressed waitress asked what my job was, and told me she had assumed I owned a boutique, a student of mine asked me where I got such unusual clothes, a hairdresser took down the address of the shop where I bought my handbag, and a man I chatted to when I was travelling asked if I was in the fashion industry. Each of these encounters was more flattering to me than if I had been told I equalled Freud in my psychological brilliance. And so it always is when you master a new role that seemed outside your reach. Who wants to be Freud when you can be fashionable?

THE SOCIAL SELF

Most people will not be quite as dangerously naive as I was, but there are few who will not have felt inadequate in the face of someone who is more skilled at social role playing than they, and hence seems to be self-assured and confident. On the other hand, many face the opposite risk of having played too well and too long, and having lost their sense of inner direction. If you have started from the other pole of the inner/outer dilemma you may have always assumed that we need to play roles, and only much later in life have begun to discover how important it is to be authentic. Whichever way you come at it from, the puzzle is still the same: how can you be yourself, and still play a satisfying and appropriate part on the great stage of social life?

Ironically, the more we consciously learn to master social roles, not out of fear but out of choice, the easier it is to be ourselves for we are no longer intimidated by people who seem to upstage us. If we consider ourselves to be students, we can thank the people that seem more sophisticated than ourselves – they are our teachers, whether they know it or not. And once we are secure in a social role, we can be confident enough socially to choose how, when, and where to play it, or whether to play it at all.

Remember that no roles are impossible for you, though some may be difficult or ultimately unsatisfying. The fact that someone else plays a particular role better than you may only mean that it is one which comes easy to them, while some roles that you play with finesse would seem to them out of reach. It's really only a question of how much you want to play a role, and how hard you are willing to work for it. The harder a role is to learn, the more important it needs to be for you to take the trouble. But the choice is yours.

It is crucial also to realise that roles always include implicit social assumptions, because they express present day social attitudes and social institutions. If you want to play the *femme fatale*, this may mean 'dumb, helpless, beautiful woman' to you, so it's not surprising you've avoided the role until now. Being a 'confident and respected teacher' may be associated in your mind with authoritarianism or corporal punishment, and this may be why you decided to play 'weak nice guy', which you may not enjoy too much.

But roles are always open to new interpretations. Why give up an attractive role because you don't like the way it is conventionally played? It's up to you to redesign it so that it does reflect your view of how people should relate to each other. You might, for example, find the attractive, sexy *femme fatale* in you who is also intelligent, confident, and strong; or that strong, confident teacher who can listen to students but can also be assertive about his or her own needs and expectations.

Some of the roles you are in the habit of playing at present are probably not getting you what you want. This may include roles you play in the most intimate relationships – 'pathetic child' or 'cold diplomat' or 'lovable fool' or 'self-sacrificing angel' are some that are commonly played. Become aware which roles you are no longer happy with. Then, find the roles you are attracted to, and which are more likely to get you what you want. Once you have, it is important to enter into them and play them to the hilt your way – in other words the way that you enjoy and feel comfortable with.

As you become more comfortable with role playing, you will begin to get a sense that there isn't only one way of being 'really you' – but that the self inside has a thousand faces, and you have only come to know and show a few of them.

THAT GREEN-EYED GUIDE

Since it is not always easy to know what roles we really want to play, given all the social conditioning that directs us inexorably towards meeting expectations, the best clues in our armoury of emotions are defensiveness and envy.

Some things that other people say about us really make us feel awful, and want to defend ourselves, while others that are equally negative don't really bother us. What are the worst things people can say to you? The trick then is to consider: do I need to go on feeling awful about this, or is this something I can and want to do something about? If it is, you've got an excellent place to start learning some new skills.

As to envy – it was my friend Debby who revealed to me that envy is what you feel when you see someone doing or having something that you yourself could do or have, but don't allow yourself. If you harness that green-eyed guide to work for you, you can begin to play the roles you want in life. Just learn to say 'thank you' to your envy for pointing out what it is that you are wanting but unable to admit to yourself, and decide what you want to do about that.

When defensiveness and envy point to something, however, they only point in a rather general direction, and it is easy to be misled. If you feel envious of rich people, and feel put down when you are considered poor, you may need to admit to yourself, if you haven't already, that you would like to be rich. However it may be that the money itself is not the real point. You need also to go beneath the obvious to find out what it is about money that you envy. Is it freedom? Is it being able to spoil yourself? Is it social status? When you discover exactly what it is that your envy or defensiveness are pointing to, you can go for what you really want.

You want the right to spoil yourself – how could you spoil yourself even without being rich? You want social status, how are you not allowing yourself to gain social status, when you could? You wish for freedom, what sort of freedom is already possible for you that you don't take? Choose a role for yourself to try out – pampered child, or important person, or free spirit – and find out how to play them well. Remember that good actors can create convincing roles with whatever props are available. When you feel confident about the role, you may decide that playing it to your satisfaction does require you to earn more money. If so, chapter 15 on Time and Money might be your next port of call.

OBJECTIVES AND IMAGES

The best role playing, whether in real life or on the stage, does not proceed from the outside in but from the inside out. A role is not an empty form, or an attractive image; it is a structure within which certain kinds of intentions and relationships are carried out. As the great director, Stanislavski[1] wrote: 'There is only one thing that can lure our creative will and draw it to us, and that is an attractive aim, a creative objective. . . . The objective gives a pulse to the living being of a role'.

Take the famous 'bedside manner' of a doctor. If, as a young medical student, you believe that all you have to do is to look and sound like a doctor, dress appropriately, use the right tone of voice, and generally mimic successful doctors, you would be taking on the role image, but not the inner objective that characterises the role. Meeting you, a patient might think, 'This doctor looks impressive.' But they might not feel any better themselves.

To really play the role accurately, however, you need to get into the intentions embodied in the role. Within the spirit of the doctor with a truly healing bedside manner is a powerful intention to convey to human beings in distress that they are being listened to, cared for, and understood, and that they can relax and trust their doctor enough to facilitate their own natural healing processes. On meeting this doctor, a patient might give a sigh of relief and feel. 'I can trust this person.'

The same is true of any other role. The appearance needs to proceed from the inner objective, and not vice versa. Arthur, for example, had always longed to be the life of the party. He watched other people who were good at this role, including his friend Alan, and tried to copy them, but it never seemed to work. Then he tried the imagework technique of imagining entering in to the body of Alan and asking himself 'As the life of the party, what is it I am intending to *do*?'

As he did so, he realised that he was not trying to be the life of the party at all but rather that his intention was to amuse and entertain everyone so that *they* felt relaxed and happy. Understanding this, Arthur discovered within himself a pleasure in, and a talent for, amusing others, and he began to look forward to parties as an arena for bringing out a facet of himself he hadn't known was there.

THE OUTER EXPRESSION OF ROLES

Once the inner objective is clear, like any actor you need to find the outer expression of that role. Most important is what Stanislavski called a 'through line of action', the pattern of action that expresses your intentions. Your active efforts to attain your goal are your through line of action. Furthermore, in the obstacle course of life you will come face to face with oppposing circumstances, and people with opposing through lines of action. The conflict between your through line of action and the counter-through actions of the world constitutes the drama of life.

Last but not least comes the outer appearance of that inner objective and line of action. How can you look the part? Here all the research you can do in watching how other people dress, what backdrops they look good against, and so on, becomes important. But the best test of how to look is still your inner eye: when you look the way your role feels, you are on your way.

TRANSFERRING SKILLS

Most skills involved in a new role are simply old skills in a new context. It is much easier to figure out where you already have the skill and to transfer it to your new role, than to try to learn a new skill. The through line of action then emerges naturally and powerfully.

Thus, Jimmy, who had been made redundant, desperately wanted to get a new job, and knew he should look like a 'confident man on his way up'. But every time he got to an interview, he felt scared and messed it up. When I asked him where in his life he had this feeling of confidence, he replied: 'When a friend comes to me for advice.'

We explored exactly how Jimmy operated when he felt confident – what he said, did, and felt. What was the initial difference between the two situations? In the interview situation Jimmy felt on trial, but when a friend came to see him he felt needed. 'If you felt the interviewer needed you, what would you do?' I asked. An action plan rolled out in no time which Jimmy could see himself carrying out. After all, maybe he was the man the interviewer needed.

SELF PRESENTATION: THE STRUCTURE OF THE EXERCISE

The exercise on 'Self Presentation' begins with the process of choosing a role that interests you and feels right. You may do this in a number of different ways: by noticing whom you envy, or what makes you feel bad, or what is stopping you from getting what you want, or what role would be the greatest challenge to you. The next step is to study the role as it is played by other people, watching how they play the role, getting into their shoes and finding out the inner structure of their intentions, and asking as many questions as you can. Where possible think of an aspect of your life where you already have the skills necessary to play the role and find out how you can transfer these skills. Then, using the idea of the cinema screen in the Life Change exercise of chapter 11, see yourself on the screen as you are and then as you will be in your new role, try out the role, find an inner guide, and look back to see how you achieved the new role. Finally, as usual, you appreciate, reflect, look forward at the implications for the future, and emerge. The format, in brief is:

Preparation: Clearing a space and relaxing
1　Choosing a new role
2　Studying the role
3　Transferring skills
4　Becoming the role
5　Finding your inner guide
6　Looking back
7　Appreciating, reflecting, looking forward, and emerging.

SELF PRESENTATION – BASIC EXERCISE

Preparation: Clearing a space and relaxing

1   *Choosing a new role*: The following are some ways you can use to help you decide what role you would like to play better.

a   *Turn on the green-eyed guide*: Look back in your mind's eye and think of the people that have made you feel envious. What qualities did they have? Give names to the roles they played.

b   *Rags to riches*: Think back to the last time someone made you feel really bad about yourself. Describe the image that you had of yourself. Give it a name. What is the opposite of this image? Would you like it? Give this a name.

c   *Fitting the part*: Think of a goal that you want to achieve but feel unsure as to whether you can manage. What sort of person could manage this? Give their role a name.

d   *The biggest challenge:* What role would be the most difficult in the world for you to play? Would you like it? Why not try it out in your imagination? Give it a name.

2   *Studying the role*: Having chosen one role, begin by making a study of it. You are the officially named researcher of that particular role. You are researching into the nature of the role, the scripts, the style, the clothing, and the backdrop that distinguishes this role, as well as the inner objectives and lines of action. Whom do you know personally, or whom have you seen, who can play this role well?

As you think of a person, imagine your spirit going up above them and all around them. What do you notice? Now go inside the person and discover: what is my intention or goal when I operate in this role? What is it that makes this role what it is? What is my characteristic line of action to reach my objectives? How do I deal with opposition? How do I make sure I look the part? Do this with respect to each person you can think of as a model for this role.

When you are involved in everyday interactions, start noticing people that play that role. Be guided by your attraction to them, or by your envy of them, to pick out the stars. Take it that they are doing something that can be learned, and start observing. What do they do? How do they dress? How do they move? Imagine your spirit going inside their body — how does it feel to be that person? What are you trying to achieve? What is the essence of this role — the feature that defines it?

Learn to ask questions. If your friends are among those you have defined as being better than you at the role, ask them about how they do it and why. They will certainly be pleased at being interviewed by an admiring researcher. Whom do you know who understands 'costume' and 'props'? Ask them to take you shopping. And do also ask your good friends to be honest with you about how you present yourself, in as specific a way as possible, and what, in their view, you might do differently.

3 *Transferring skills*: What is difficult about this role? Think of another situation or area of your life in which you are able to do this successfully. How do you operate in the old situation — what is your line of action? Now, how are these situations

different? If they were similar, how would you do the same thing but in the new situation? Work out your new line of action.

4 *Becoming the role*: (Note that Steps 4, 5 and 6 are a brief version of the Life Change exercise in chapter 11). Imagine that you are sitting in your private cinema. Allow an image of yourself to emerge on the screen as you are now in everyday life. How do you dress, move, interact with others, decorate your home, etc. What seems to be your main goal in life, judging from how you act? What name would you give this role? Do you like it? Thank the person on the screen for their performance, and move the image over to the left and off the screen.

Now, allow an image of yourself to emerge on the screen playing your new role. Observe it. Then enter into it – be the actor. Notice how you dress, how you move, how you speak, and what you say. Think about what your house is like, and what sorts of places you frequent. Notice how you feel about other people and how you deal with them. If you originally had a particular situation in mind – e.g. an interview or a party – imagine you are in the situation and play the role. Think of the situations or people whom you might find difficult to handle, and practise how you would deal with them. Ham it up, exaggerate it, so that you really get the point and then tone it down. If possible, get a friend to help you role-play it.

5 *Finding your inner guide*: Allow the name or image of an expert or guide to emerge that could be particularly helpful for you as an advisor for this

role. This could be a real person you know, a historical figure, or even a mythological one. Ask them how they see your present role, and what you need to do to play this new role. Get specific advice.

6 *Looking back*: As this new role player, look back at the person you were, or the role you used to play. How did you learn to play this new role? What inner and outer changes did you have to make? If you could give any advice to that person you were, what would you say?

7 *Appreciate, reflect, look forward, and emerge*: Thank all your advisors for their help, including those people you were most envious of. Think about what you learned from this process. Before and after emerging, look forward and consider whether there are any changes you would like to make in your life, and how you might go about doing it. If you played this role more often would you need to buy different clothes, have a different house, or choose different social networks? Or would you just need to walk differently and talk differently? You don't need to decide to change anything now – just wonder about it, and wonder whether any of these changes might be more fun than the way you live now. Plan to spend a few moments a day, or before important events, just picturing being that role and getting a sense of your line of action.

In future: Before walking into a situation that is important or difficult, sort out which role you intend to play, and get a quick image of playing the role and of your line of action before you walk in. It should be a role that you will also find comfortable, and will get you what you want in that situation.

And whenever you need to make a choice that is relevant to this role, wait a moment, and tune into that role player that you now recognise. Be him or her for a moment. Get a sense of what choice that person would make. Or just say: 'If I were x, I would . . . .' You can also speak to your advisor: 'What would you do, or what would you advise me to do?' You don't have to follow any of the advice, but if it feels good – take it.

IN CONCLUSION

Playing, including playing roles, should be fun. Learning to be successful on the social stage of life is a challenge to set yourself, not a life-or-death test of your inner worth. Indeed, the better you learn to play roles consciously, the less likely you are to be taken in by the performances of others, and the more you will be able to recognise and respect the authentic qualities that you really value.

It is essential to keep in mind also that stages have an off-stage, and while there is pleasure in putting on the role as you step onto the stage, there is equal pleasure in dropping it when you move off stage. If you can't drop the role when you wish to, it stops being fun and starts being an armour-plated defence system. So enjoy the performance, and the applause, but keep in mind that your friends want to be intimate with you rather than impressed by you. And never get so typecast into one role that it becomes the only role you'll ever be asked, or indeed able, to play.

In general, do select the parts you play carefully. Try anything once, but if you don't like it, then once is enough.

Successful actors like yourself do not need to take any part that is handed to them; they can pick and choose those that are enjoyable, promise a challenge, and provide the best medium to express the full range of their talents and spirit.

=== 15 ===

UNDERSTANDING TIME AND MONEY

Scarcity and abundance

I used to think of Time as a threatening stranger chasing me down dark streets. I always had too much to do, and went to bed with a sense of failure each night because I hadn't managed enough. In fact time was almost synonymous in my mind with external expectations and the threat of failure to meet them, even though I myself had chosen to do most of the things I was doing. There was always the fantasy that someone else, perhaps anyone else, would do it all faster and more efficiently. I avidly read interviews given by busy people to discover just how they managed, hoping that some of it would rub off. In the middle of a particularly horrendous period, I woke up one morning with such an obvious and straightforward solution that I marvelled that I hadn't seen it sooner: all I needed was two of me.

The other side of this drama with time was that, on reflection, it was clear that I did in fact manage to accomplish what I needed to accomplish, and meet the deadlines I needed to meet, despite the fact that I really had far too much on my plate. I noticed also that I had a habit of putting things off until I reached a moment of overwhelming anxiety when I was sure I had failed and it was all too late; I would then move into action, and finish what I needed too at the last minute. I also became aware that if by any chance it looked like I might finish

a project early, I became a bit worried, and I managed to mess it up or procrastinate in such a way that I would still only finish the project at the last minute.

CONFUSIONS, CONTRADICTIONS, AND CONFLICT

There are very few people that do not have some inner conflict, confusion, and contradiction built into their attitudes to time and/or money. Time and money are powerful signifiers in our society. They are deeply connected to self image and social status, representing as they do the expectations and rewards handed out by society. They are also viewed in an inherently distorted manner through the lens of our language and cultural values. Hence our relationship to time and money tends to reflect and magnify any confusion and ambivalence we have about meeting the world's expectations, and reaping the world's rewards.

As long as we are unconscious of the complex attitudes to time and money we have inherited from our society, of the inner decisions we made about them when we were younger, and of the ambivalent feelings we are playing out daily, and we can easily perceive the world as full of unalterable 'facts' and limitations that defeat us in some way. 'There are only twenty-four hours in a day, so what can you expect?' Or, 'I don't have enough money, and I never will.' As we become conscious of the underlying dynamics, we may also find our way to new attitudes that can change the 'facts' and enable us to transcend our limits.

SCARCITY AND ABUNDANCE

For example, the 'facts' about time and money which are built into our language, and reflect our Western technological society, are that money and time are both nouns – things or commodities – which are definitely limited. Both can be wasted, spent, lost, saved, managed, stolen, or conspicuously flaunted. Some people have more than others do, and it is possible to feel guilty and ashamed of having too much, or guilty and ashamed of having too little, or both. Depending on your social circle, being a 'have' can be as dangerous to one's self image and self presentation as being a 'have-not', and we may not be sure which is the frying pan and which is the fire.

There is also a complex relationship between time and money: time is money, and money is time, so that we pay for time with money, and when we have money we can buy time. On the other hand, some people seem to have too much time that they can't seem to convert into money (e.g. unemployed people), and others have too much money that never seems to guarantee the owner enough time (e.g. successful and overworked entrepreneurs). Furthermore, in some social spheres, as among certain self-employed professionals, the less time you have, the higher your social status is because you are seen to be in demand; others, for example where inherited wealth is valued, it is conspicuous leisure – having too much time – that represents real success.

Yet in my own experience, and that of many people I have worked with, the clarity that emerges from unravelling our relationship to time and money tends to point the way to seeing them not as commodities but as life energy that we need to acknowledge as our own and use consciously and appropriately to live well, to create well, and to contribute well.

Implicit in the understanding of time and money that emerges as we work through our ambivalence and confusion is almost always a sense of abundance rather than scarcity. Abundance doesn't mean in this case having too much; it means, rather, that there is always enough. It also doesn't mean that someone else has less because I have more; it means that there is enough for everyone. And as we sense that there is enough for us, we tend to find that we are as happy to give as we are to receive.

This feeling of abundance both reflects, and contributes to, a sense of self esteem and of trust in oneself and in one's possibilities to deal creatively with the world. We can begin to perceive ourselves not as saving, wasting, losing or conspicuously flaunting time and money, but rather as recycling them.

As usual, I hasten to say that this does not mean that we are totally free unconditioned beings, nor do I wish to imply that unemployed people should take responsibility for the fact that their firm made them redundant and therefore landed them in a situation with too much time and not enough money. Our time and money conditions are in many ways not under our control, and the distinction between 'haves' and 'have-nots' is built deeply into the fabric of our society. But there is no doubt that understanding our contradictions and becoming unambivalent is likely to open up new doors and new possibilities.

THE HOUSE OF TIME

During a particularly busy period in my life, when I was in the grips of my fundamental drama with time, one insight got me through. I was waking almost every night, worrying about whether I would finish what I had to do, or attacking myself for not having done enough. I kept feeling that the situation must be a challenge to me from which I needed to learn something, and yet I couldn't figure out what it was I could learn.

Suddenly it struck me that there was an inner magician inside that got things done. Like all good magic tricks, what he did was not magic at all, although it looked like this to the audience, but a simple skill. This was how I could always manage to get things done, even though it never seemed possible. While the magician worked confidently, however, it was the ever doubtful audience that woke me at night. As soon as I got the magician to reassure the audience, I began to sleep at night.

More recently, realising that my relationship with Time was still not all that it could be, and that Time couldn't be a limited commodity that I never had enough of, nor a menacing stranger threatening me with failure, I decided to create and visit a House of Time to get a new understanding of the situation.

My House of Time turned out to be a building of great grandeur, something like a cathedral. There I met Father Time. He was an amazing, awe-inspiring, magnificent figure. I almost cried at his grandeur and at the sense of ancient greatness about him. I suddenly understood on a deep level that he who had literally been there since the beginning of Time was not some trivial stranger.

I told him about my problem, and asked for his help. He responded thus: 'It cannot be that you don't have enough time, because you *are* time. Time is the days of your life. Your problem is really that you are always trying to trick time. You play little games, like hide and seek, with time, and therefore

261

with yourself. You need simply to decide how you want to use your time – or to put it another way – your energy. Once you have decided what you want to do, just open the file for that task and leave it open on the desktop of the imagination. It will get done, naturally. You will also find that you want to close some other files that have been open for too long: in particular the ones to do with worrying about not having enough time.'

This moving experience, on top of my previous understanding, fundamentally transformed my relationship to time. I now find that I think of time more like a hand flat against my hand, matching it absolutely.

It is my time to do with as I wish, rather than an external taskmaster and critic. I do not need to feel myself to be a failure each time I can't accomplish enough; I simply need to face the fact that for some reason I have chosen to fail to leave myself enough time. I also understand not only intellectually but also emotionally that time is not linear, and that the amount of time I have in clock terms has little to do with whether and how well I will get things done. The point is simply to open the file: to consciously intend to do the thing. The rest follows naturally, as it always has, despite all the dramas. On a deep level, I have begun to make my peace with time.

JANET'S HOUSE OF MONEY

In Janet's case, it was her relationship with money that needed urgent sorting out. Janet, a woman of great determination, wanted to earn a lot more money because she saw this as a means of creating for herself the life style, and the self respect, that was right for her. However she had a lot of odd ways of dealing with money about which she was uncomfortable: she spent too much one day, deprived herself of necessities the next, and generally had a sense of confusion and guilt hanging around whenever she dealt with money. In an imagework workshop on time and money, she decided to visit the House of Money.

Janet's House of Money was a beautiful building, with walls of shimmering gold which seemed to be made up of coins, and with an amazing light about it. She smiled happily as she looked around. But the first figure she saw there was a rather severe looking man in a suit sitting behind a desk. She was frightened to approach him. She then saw an old man with a beard, who looked a bit like Methuselah, and seemed to have a kind face.

Janet talked to the old man and found out that his name was Joseph. She asked him to tell her what her money patterns were and what she could do about it. When she switched roles and became Joseph, Joseph told Janet that her main problem was that she didn't believe that she would have enough money, and this had to do with the fact that she never knew how much she actually did have, and what she was spending. Her lack of clarity was dangerous to her. He reassured her that she would always have enough money, and didn't need to worry, but she did need to know exactly what she was doing.

Pleased and rather relieved, Janet now felt ready to approach the man in the suit, who was named Michael. Michael told her that she was a bit of a spendthrift, and in fact, in his view, would spend whatever she had. As the conversation unfolded, it became clear that Michael demanded that she keep exact accounts of what she was spending, but was unwilling to tell her how much money she had, because of his fear that she would just go out and spend it. He admitted that he had confused her into thinking that it was his money that he was kindly doling out to her in small portions, when it was really her money, because he didn't trust her to take care of it.

Janet began remembering the problems she used to have about pocket money as a child, and started to be angry. She demanded that he reveal to her how much money she had and put her in charge of her own money. After all, until she was given responsibility she was likely to act irresponsibly.

When she switched roles, Michael responded that he was willing to do it only on the condition that she saved 15 percent of her money, no matter how much it was. Janet almost agreed, but then stopped and rethought. Yes, she was certainly willing to plan to save money, but on her own terms.

Finally, after much discussion, Michael agreed to give her both information about and responsibility for her own money, and to trust that she would now act as an adult. She was delighted, and promised that she would work out her personal accounts before the week was over. She thanked Michael, and told him that she would be back to see him, because she wanted to use him as a consultant.

Image as Metaphor

There are many other ways of exploring our relationship with time and money, often by adapting the exercise formats in other chapters. Some ideas are listed below under Variations.

The Image as Metaphor exercise of chapter 5 is one particularly powerful way to approach the issues: through asking for an image that represents money or time and your relationship to them, you will find your deepest attitudes mirrored in the image that emerges.

Thus, Jake, who was considering making a fundamental job shift from the helping professions into the commercial world which paid so much better but might alienate him, was very troubled about what choice to make. He came up with an image of being a pile of coins which said, 'I am energy and power, and I would like the nice people to use me more. However, I am right near a sewage system, and people smell the sewage and think it is me. In fact, although I don't like to admit it, the sewage system does seem to have something to do with me, because when I try to move away it seems to follow me.'

Or Alan, who was devoted to his music, but didn't know how to publicise himself or to make money from his music came up with the image of a triangle (the musical instrument kind), that depended totally on other people to play it; he didn't even have any control over the sound he emitted because depending on where and how he was struck the sound could be discordant or musical.

As Jake and Alan worked through their images, they could begin to see a way to make decisions that reflected what they really wanted, rather than continuing to play out their unresolved conflicts.

Hindsight About the Future

By adapting the My Future Self exercise from chapter 10, it is also possible to learn from the future you how to go forward.

Alan put himself forward five years to a time when he felt good about the way he dealt with time and money. He discovered that now he had a successful music-making career. He spoke to the younger Alan, and told him that he needed to begin to take the initiative in his life. He could no longer be the triangle that waited to be struck by others. More specifically he told the younger Alan exactly what phone calls he needed to make, what letters he needed to write, and what attitude to take. He knew – because he'd done it already.

THE HOUSES OF TIME AND MONEY: THE STRUCTURE OF THE EXERCISE

To create your own House of Time or Money, the basic format is to allow the image to emerge of the House of Time or Money, explore it, find out who you meet there and talk to them, asking about their view of you and of your situation and their suggestions for the future. As usual, you end by appreciating, reflecting, and looking forward to how you will apply this. Thus the format is:

Preparation: Clearing a space, relaxing
1   Inviting the image of the House of Time or Money
2   Studying the image
3   Talking to the beings you meet

4 Moving toward resolution
5 Appreciating, reflecting, looking forward, and emerging.

The beings you meet may not be the ones you expect – my imagework students have found bleeding martyrs, beggars, children and dogs as well as wise people inhabiting their Houses of Money and Time. Remember that whoever you meet is both an advisor and an aspect of you. Treat them with respect, but don't be afraid to argue if you don't agree with them. Sometimes it is only through a challenge that you can find your true position.

THE HOUSES OF TIME AND MONEY: BASIC EXERCISE

Preparation: Cleaning a space and relaxing

1 *Inviting the image of the House of Time or Money*: Allow an image to emerge of the House of Time or the House of Money.

2 *Studying the image*: What does it look like? Let your spirit go up above and look down upon it, and then move around to the sides and underneath. What do you notice from the various perspectives? Now enter inside. What is your feeling as you enter this House? What can you see, smell, hear, or otherwise sense around you? Whom do you meet there?

3 *Talking to the beings you meet*: Approach whomever you see there. (If there is more than one being, then talk to each in turn.) Consider him or her as an advisor as well as an aspect of you. Ask for his or her view of your present patterns with respect to time or money, and for any advice that would be useful to you.

Then switch roles and become the figure, and respond. Have you heard what this person has asked you? What do you notice about this person who has come to visit you in your House? How does he or she operate habitually? What advice can you offer him or her?

4 *Moving toward resolution*: Explore further. If there is a disagreement between you, make sure to negotiate clearly. As far as possible, end up with a practical agreement between you as to what you need to do next.

5 *Appreciating, reflecting, looking forward, and emerging*: Thank the being or beings. Before and after emerging, reflect on the meaning of what you have experienced, and be clear about what you have learned regarding your present attitudes and behaviour and future possibilities. Look forward and plan exactly how you will operate. Remember that if these beings have been helpful you can continue to use them as consultants whenever you feel confused.

VARIATIONS

Image as metaphor: Begin by saying: 'I would like to allow an image of an animal, a plant, or an object to emerge that somehow represents money (or time – whichever you choose) and my relationship to it at this moment in my life.' Then work your way through all the steps outlined.

Using hindsight creatively: Suggest to yourself: 'I'm on a space ship and I'm going off the face of the earth. I return to earth at a time in the future, five years (or any other period of time that seems useful) from now. It's five years (or *x* period) from now and I feel good about how I deal with time or money. What do I feel good about? How did I manage it?'

If you can't get an image of feeling good, start with: 'I feel terrible about how I've dealt with time or money', and look back at where you went wrong; then you should be able to check on positive image and compare the two.

Now, look back at the person you were five years ago. What exactly have you done since then to achieve your present state, whether positive or negative? What advice could you give him or her that will make the years ahead easier? Does he or she understand? If not, try to ensure that they do.

Ambivalence: Choose either time or money, and decide whether you tend to feel, or feel at this moment in your life, like a 'have' (you have enough/too much time or money) or a 'have not' (you are deprived or never have enough).

1 Be this 'have' or 'have-not'. What is it like to be you? Describe yourself. Complain bitterly if appropriate. Exaggerate this position to get the full flavour of it.

2 Allow an image of someone who is the opposite to emerge on the cushion opposite you (a 'have-not' if you are a 'have' or vice versa). This may be a real or an imagined person. How does this person look to you. What do you want to say to them?

3 Now switch roles and become this opposite person. How is it to be you? How does the person opposite you (the original Self) look to you? Continue the conversation, switching back and forth.

4 On the side of both of you, on a third cushion, is a wise observer who can look at this interaction and understand what is going on. Be the observer and see what you notice.

5 Return to the original interaction now, and come to a resolution.

6 Reflect on what you have learned and what its implications are for the future.

Life change: Consider what change you would like to make in your relationship to time or money. Now find out what it would mean to make that change:

1 Imagine that you are sitting in your own private cinema. Allow an image of yourself, as you are now, to emerge on the screen, before you have made this change. What do you notice? What do you feel? Appreciate this person for doing their best in a difficult world.

2 Allow an image of yourself to emerge as you will be after you have made this change. Go up to the screen and step into the picture. How does it feel? Spend a day as this person. Look back and see how and when you solved it: How did you get from there to here?

Time limits: What you would do if you really had to face clear limits: you have a day, a week, a year, or five years to live. How do you want to spend your time and money? Now come back to your present life. How can you do more of those things that are important to you even though you don't know how long you have to live?

Unlimited time and money: What if you had all the time and money in the world? Life is forever and your money is infinite. What would you do now? How would you use your time and money? Now come back to your present life. How can you map back what you have just learned onto a life with boundaries?

The past: Allow an image to emerge of yourself as you were at the time when you first had this feeling about this problem (e.g. when you first felt stressed by time, or pathetically poor). What is going on? Relive the experience.

Now imagine that the wise and mature you can go back and help that younger you. What can you suggest to help this younger you deal with the situation differently. Let the younger you try it out. Now come back to the present and see how you can do this in your life now.

IN CONCLUSION

Time and money are too important for us to allow ourselves to be dominated and limited by the distorted views of society, and by our own ambivalence. Once we have come to terms with time and money, and have sensed that they are forms of energy that are available to us as and when we need them, to use for purposes that we can identify with and respect, we have gone a long way toward righting our relationship, not only with ourselves and our own creativity, but also with society.

BEYOND THE PERSONAL SELF

Wise beings, other dimensions

My first real introduction to imagery outside of the special world of dreams was through the strange and funny images that used to come to me when I lay in bed in that semi-conscious 'hypnagogic' state between waking and sleeping. For example, I thought 'I can't bear it' and saw a polar bear; after writing an essay for college that was getting too long, I saw myself folding over a large omelette/essay into a small frying pan.

In that half world of semi-consciousness, I would some-times even see things in the room that I knew weren't there. The black spider-like insects hanging in the air were the most frightening. But as I realised that the images were not going to hurt me, nor were they a sign of impending madness, I came to feel more friendly toward them. Getting up my courage, I actually reached out and touched one. To my amazement, it powdered in my fingers, in precisely the way it would have if it were made of some real fragile material. The next time I had one of these images, I did the same, with the same dramatic effect.

This set me thinking about images – could images just be products of our imagination? Or do they have some kind of palpable reality? Indeed, are they perhaps messages thrown up not just from our personal unconscious but from another dimension beyond this one which is just as real but follows different rules?

This chapter has a speculative quality about it because we are delving into areas that are open to a great many interpretations, and that many people have strong beliefs about one way or another. But the aim here is not to find or to impart some absolute 'truth', but to encourage you to challenge the limits and boundaries that hold you back from extending yourself, and your images, to the full. By trying the impossible you may at least find yourself accomplishing the improbable. You may also begin to gain access to a dimension, or a part of yourself, that gives you a sense of peace, love, wisdom, and harmony that can transform and deepen your experience of life.

THE REALITY OF IMAGES

Images do of course have a real power in our lives, serving as they do as our guiding thoughtforms, so that by changing our images we can change the shape of our lives. But, if they actually had some objective reality too, it would mean that we could also have direct contact, both receptive and active, with other people's images.

If so, perhaps people leave behind image fields which we can intuitively tune into and gain understandings from when we sit in their seats, walk into their houses, or touch their personal belongings. More generally, by being receptive in any way to images from or about other people, we can gain real information that exceeds our own knowledge. Or get help from people who have skills we need. Or, more actively, communicate with them in a way that does not depend on speech, touch, or physical proximity, and even heal them if they are ill by healing their images in our minds.

Moreover, perhaps images not only allow us to make contact with other people, but also serve as a window into another dimension or dimensions beyond everyday reality. It may be that there are sources of wisdom, power, and love that transcend our own understanding, so that by imagining a wise loving being, we can make contact with this greater wisdom and love.

Equally, time and space may, in other dimensions, no longer be real boundaries so that all living things, objects and events, whether present, past or future, are connected to each other. By imagining the future we can tune into it and even affect it – a possibility we have already discussed in previous chapters. And by tuning in directly we can learn not only about people, but also about objects and events that may be physically out of reach. Indeed, if, as some people believe, animals, plants and objects each have a kind of living form or spirit, we can 'talk to them' in our imaginations and learn from them in the same way we do with people.

All these can be regarded as ways of going beyond the personal self, or, in other words, of discovering the realm of the 'transpersonal'. A world view that includes the transpersonal also often involves a belief that we are not struggling alone in an indifferent world. We live, rather, in the context of a universe, or a higher being or beings, or a higher self, that can be trusted to be essentially benevolent and that is protecting us, guiding us, or in some sense acting for us and for others, at least in the long run. If we are going to deal with images in a transpersonal way, it is safer to do so within such a framework, so that the power of images is not seen to be our own personal power, and thereby misunderstood and misused.

DREAMS, VISIONS, INTUITIONS, AND COINCIDENCES

There are many documented stories of dreams or visions that tell the future; of people or animals who intuitively sense events, including illness or death, that happen to people who are far away; of miraculous coincidences that do not seem attributable to chance; of psychics who tell of things that they could not possibly have guessed; of healers who heal plants, animals, or people; and of people having sudden great insights which they experience as coming from outside them and that turn their whole world around. There are also countless people who have a palpable experience of a benevolent higher presence in their life. Anyone who has any interest in these matters at all will have heard of, and experienced, out-of-the-ordinary events of one kind or another.

Dismissing all these events and experiences can be considered to be as much of an act of faith as accepting them. It does seem difficult to argue against the premise that at least some people do sometimes reach beyond limits that we consider absolute in our everyday reality.

Even so, should we consider these experiences to be special gifts for which we can feel grateful if and when they drop in our laps? Or could we all have such experiences all the time if we only trained ourselves properly? My guess is that if strange and wonderful things can happen occasionally, we can probably find ways to encourage them to happen more often. In so doing, we are at the very least continuing our search to reach, and utilise, the parts of us that we hardly know exist.

MEETING WISE AND LOVING BEINGS

I myself started speaking to wise people in my imagination out of sheer disappointment at not meeting them in real life. I always seemed to find that a person I admired would die or retire just when I thought I might study with them. The last time this happened, I was hoping to study with Frank Lake, a pioneer in helping people to re-experience their own birth, when I read in a journal that he had just died.

Instead of wallowing in frustration and regret, I decided to talk to him in my mind, and ask him to help me to do in spirit what I could no longer ask him to do in person. With 'his' help, I went through an unforgettable experience of feeling myself regressing to the moment of conception, and experiencing that moment as a brilliant flash of light and as a kind of whole-worldness in which I was the world.

Did I really put myself in Frank Lake's hands in a way that went beyond my psychological belief or desire to deal with my disappointment? Perhaps that doesn't matter so much. What is clear is that by opening myself up to the possibility that I could do so, I was able to accomplish what had hitherto been beyond my own apparent limits.

Meeting wise people, whether real life ones or ideal beings, is a sort of established 'tourist attraction' in transpersonal tours of the inner world. We all want and need more wisdom, love, and strength than we have. Can we gain them by reaching beyond ourselves and contacting people who have something to offer us, or indeed ideal beings who represent these qualities?

There is no doubt that we can gain insights and have profound experiences that go beyond the everyday by talking in our imagination to people or beings with exceptional or ideal qualities. It is harder to know whether we are reaching beyond ourselves, particularly when we cannot ever know what the real limits of 'ourselves' really are.

It may be that by talking to a person whom we admire or creating an ideal type and believing in it, we are encouraged to extend ourselves and reach a standard that we normally would not dream of as long as we think of ourselves as ordinary middle-of-the-road citizens. Thus the wise person we imagine is a way of bringing into consciousness that 'everyday unconscious' of unrealised potentials discussed in chapter 3, just as heroes of all descriptions inspire people every day to reach beyond their normal limits and accomplish what they believed to be impossible.

To go further, perhaps we are gaining access not only to a personal everyday unconscious but to a 'superconscious,' akin to Jung's collective unconscious. It may be that we all are on some level wise, powerful, good, and luminous, or have a higher self or a spiritual dimension that guides us in positive directions, but we are separated from this higher level or self by a kind of veil. In this case, it would seem that personifying a wise, loving, or powerful being helps to lift that veil to reach parts of ourself that we do not normally communicate with. It is then rather like looking into a mirror that shows us who we are at our deepest, best, and most fulfilled. We recognise in that wise being a reflection of an aspect of ourselves that we cannot yet see directly.

I like Sufi leader Pir Vilayat Khan's story of how he went on a 'guru hunt' in the Himalayas. He walked three days in the snow and ice, catching pneumonia, and finally found the wise man sitting in the cave. The wise man signalled to him not to come in, so Pir Vilayat Khan sat in the snow meditating. He opened his eyes to see the wise man smiling at him. 'Why have you come so far to see what you should be?' asked the wise man. Pir Vilayat Khan answered, 'In order to become what I am, I need to see myself in another.'[1]

It may be, however, as many people believe, that transpersonal experiences really *are* ways of going beyond the personal self, not just of discovering an aspect of ourselves. Perhaps there is in reality some more general or universal source of wisdom, power, goodness, and light in the universe that goes beyond our personal existence or our personal selves, even beyond our higher selves. There may also be a dimension beyond our everyday existence in which past, present and future are one and which accounts for an ability to see the future. The wise person or spirit we experience in our imagination can then be seen as a kind of symbolic focus through which we can experience this whole source or dimension that transcends us.

The more common belief may, on the other hand, be the right one – that there really is a personal God that we can talk to through prayer. Or, as others believe, perhaps there really is a group of wise beings, or spirits, or angels, or evolved spiritual Masters, beyond our own dimension who can appear to us, and who will help us if we are willing to reach out and ask.

These views are not mutually exclusive. In fact it seems not unlikely to me that all of these are true in some way or other: we *do* have greater everyday potentials than we realise; we *do* have a spiritual or universal unconscious that we need to contact; there *is* a dimension beyond for which our images can serve as a symbolic focus; and there *are* wise beings or one Source or Being. The full truth, I believe, lies beyond our present understanding, so that all of these are ways of saying the unsayable, or conceptualising the not-yet-conceptualisable.

It is crucial to remember, too, that when we talk to wise beings, we do not get a 'pure' response, but one that is expressed through our own language, limits, and even prejudices. Thus, as we evolve so do our transpersonal experiences.

Whatever way we choose to interpret the basis for experiences that seem otherworldly, it does seem to be the case that we have the potential to be wiser, more loving, and more powerful than we know, either in our own right, or by means of our ability to communicate with a source or sources of wisdom, love, and power. And, rather like having a reference library at home, maybe it doesn't matter so much if we can answer a question by ourselves, or if we have to consult with the experts, as long as we can find the answer and use it well.

COMMUNICATING ACROSS PERSONAL BOUNDARIES

One feature of abilities that go beyond everyday reality is that they don't depend on the five senses, or indeed on physical proximity. There is little doubt that there can be psychic communication between people, and between people and animals, particularly when they are closely connected, or members of the same family. Children have a way of picking up unconscious and conscious thoughts of their parents, identical twins often know what is happening to their twin, and animals, even more commonly than people, can react to the moment of distress or death of a loved person who is far away. After five years of not communicating with a friend, I picked up the phone to call her and her phone was busy because she was at that moment calling me. Everyone has examples of such 'coincidences.' If communication that doesn't involve either words or physical presence happens naturally, it must be possible also for us to consciously choose to receive and send messages using only a sixth or intuitive sense.

We have already begun in earlier chapters to explore the possibility that we can receptively tune into other people to learn about their feelings, thoughts, health, or any other aspect of their body, mind, and spirit. We can focus on the person, and ask for an image to emerge that represents them or what they need to know at this moment, as suggested in the Applications section of chapter 5. Or, as discussed in chapter 6: we can physically switch roles and sit in the seat and therefore in the image we have of another; or we can imagine entering into the body of the other, and sense what it feels like inside; or we can communicate with another person's 'higher self' and discuss what is going on with them that they might not themselves be aware of. Some of these processes may work at least in part because of an ability to tune into the image fields of other people. All are ways of expanding our receptivity to what is going on with another person beyond that which we consciously know, and perhaps beyond that which we could learn with the normal use of our five senses.

We can also use imagework actively to send messages that are difficult or impossible to send through the normal channels. I remember doing this right after my daughter Chloe was born. I was going through a difficult patch in my life and felt unable to give her the pure loving she needed. I used to talk to her silently, spirit to spirit, telling her how much I loved her, and that I was sorry I was depressed and couldn't actually express my love enough.

We seemed to establish between us a deep connection: I was even able to ask her silently not to wake up and wake me before I'd had a little sleep – and she always complied! Even years later, we seemed to have this connection, and not only did she say odd things that I had been thinking about but hadn't told her, but I noticed also that when I woke in the night, nine times out of ten Chloe would be awake too, though she was in another room and we couldn't possibly have heard each other. Who woke whom, I still don't know.

When a student of mine who had just had a baby worried about the fact that he was too busy working and studying to have enough time with the baby, I advised him to do the same: 'Talk to the baby and explain; don't say it out loud – just communicate.' Two years later he told me that not only did this relieve his own anxiety, but he still seemed to have a special connection with that child so that they were able to communicate without words.

I now make it a practice to use this form of silent communication whenever I am concerned about my relationship with someone, or about their health or wellbeing, but cannot use the normal channels of spoken or written communication, because they are too young to understand the words, or too far away to hear, or just likely to be unwilling to listen. I tune into them, picture them, talk to them and tell them what I want to say to them, and listen to their response. Sometimes I also send a ray of healing love, if that feels right.

I always feel better afterwards, and it does seem to me that when we meet again they look different and our relationship has subtly changed. Whether this is because I have changed in relation to them, or they have too, I cannot say for sure, although my own feeling is that we have both been touched by the communication.

I find this approach particularly useful if I am so tied up with another person's negative feelings, illness, or problems, that I have somehow taken their bad feelings into myself. I worry about the person, and yet the worry harms me without helping them. Instead of continuing to feel bad, I actively send healing energy or a loving message to the person and this 'action' seems to bring me peace. This is because when we send energy out actively, it is much more difficult to take anything negative in. So at one and the same time we can protect ourselves and offer something positive to the other person.

RECEPTIVE AND ACTIVE IMAGEWORK FOR HEALING

By combining the receptive and active approach for the purpose of healing, one can receptively get an image of another's state of mind and body, and then actively heal the image, and hopefully the person. This is, in a sense, an extension of an exercise suggested in chapter 11 on health and illness in which you heal yourself by imagining around you a circle of loving people who are sending you rays of loving and healing energy.

This healing procedure, or something similar, is an established practice among healers who do distant healing. The ability to heal in this way is based on the assumption, common in various forms in many religions and cultures, that images are palpable realities, though of a different order from people, events, and things, and that working with images can have a real effect on whatever or whomever they signify. Of course healing is a complex science, and this process that I am suggesting is only a small part of it.

When I use this method myself, I try where possible to check later with the person I have been trying to heal if they have experienced any change. When I have had a particularly real feeling during the healing, one which I now recognise and distinguish from other feelings, the person usually has undergone some kind of positive change, generally a short time after the actual imagework.

For example, one day, sitting in the bus going to work, I was feeling worried about a friend who was going through serious emotional difficulties, and was feeling totally powerless to help her. I decided that the only thing I *could* do for her was to imagine her, send her my loving energy, and heal her in my mind, and so I did. Later we talked of this and she told me that at about the same moment, she had experienced an important turning point in her therapy. Most recently, when I was trying to 'be with' a client who was going through a serious operation, I sensed her tension and tried to relax her in my mind. I am sure I was not the only one who was sending her their wishes at that moment. She told me later that she could feel people thinking of her, and that her whole body suddenly had a warm glow.

It is actually a very good idea to make a practice of checking whether your experience has had some kind of external effect or not. You can do this more or less subtly, and, if it is not appropriate, the person need never know why you are asking. Besides being an encouragement to you, this is also a way to begin to distinguish between those experiences that have a real transpersonal power, and those that are simply pleasant and wish fulfilling. If you continually gain feedback, you are offering yourself a training, because you can begin to recognise the different feelings that acompany effective and ineffective healing work.

WHOSE POWER IS IT?

Talking of healing sometimes leads people to ask whether we can equally harm people by 'black magic' or 'voodoo', which also involves using an image of the other person to affect them. A standard answer to this is that when we are in touch with the level of consciousness at which we heal people, we cannot or do not want to harm others. I am not, myself, sure that this is always true, and people have been known to go into trance states to carry out actions with the intent to harm. But I do believe that if we go deeply enough into ourselves, we will find that we are connected with everyone and everything in the universe, so that to harm another is really to harm ourselves.

It is important to remember that any healing you do is not with your own power, but rather happens *through* you. You, are essentially acting as a channel for the healing power that is universal and doesn't 'belong' to anyone. To prevent feelings of omnipotence which can lead, like all absolute power, to corruption, it can be a good idea to do any healing by explicitly invoking a higher spirit that heals others, or acts through you to heal. You may wish to pray to God, or, depending on your beliefs or inclinations, address your request to any benevolent and healing being or god who has special meaning to you.

Remember also that the final result of the process, if any, is not under your control. Indeed, according to Alice Bailey, a well known healer, mystic, and medium, healing a person can sometimes lead to the release of death rather than to health if that is appropriate.[2]

TUNING INTO OBJECTS

I make it a practice also to talk to objects and living things that have meaning to me. A walk through a museum is like a visit with friends – I have special statues, paintings and photos that I talk to, ask advice of, and get messages from, quite discreetly of course. A walk through the park can be equally chatty, with trees being the particular objects of my attention.

When I was in Egypt, I sat on a hotel balcony opposite one of the great pyramids and tuned into it. These pyramids seemed to me to be vast brooding beings, rather like dinosaurs left over from an earlier age, still having the potential of waking up and exploding. I could sense also that the pyramids must be a kind of sacred and magical shape, a belief that I later found is shared by many experts. Even now, I sometimes imagine surrounding myself with a pyramid, and this centres me and heals me.

I tried to get a sense of what the pyramids were really for. The surprising message I got 'from the pyramid' was that they were not primarily burial places for the pharaohs, but almost the converse – the body of a pharaoh was needed in order to make the pyramids complete. They were built, it seemed, for a magical, mystical purpose as a kind of ritual monument. The process of building them was itself a sacred ritual, and the final step of this process was to put into it the body of a dead pharaoh, i.e. the body of a divinity, and to seal it off. I must admit that I haven't found this theory in any of the standard books yet – but perhaps the Egyptologists haven't talked to any pyramids recently.

Sometimes rather than talking, I let my spirit 'go into' a statue or tree to get a sense of feeling or seeing the world from their point of view, just as I would do with a person. Again in Egypt, I tried to tune into one of the sphinxes of the temple at Luxor by letting my spirit go into its body, expecting to find a deep quiet peacefulness and wisdom. Instead, I had the feeling of fire, like a fiery angel with flaring and flaming wings, one of the Seraphim perhaps. As the sphinx, I saw myself and said: 'You are always seeking to be somewhere else or something else or to get somewhere as if life is where you aren't yet. The opposite is true. I have been standing here for centuries and people come to me. If you stood truly still for a moment, the whole world would rush into you as if into a vacuum.'

I cannot say whether any of these objects and living things do in reality have a spirit that goes beyond my own self, although it *feels* as if they do, but I do know that this process has been a way for me not only to gain important insights, but also to feel more at home in the world.

THE HOUSE OF TRUTH

Another way to gain understandings that go beyond your everyday ones is to use the notion of a House of Truth or a House of Peace or House of Healing or the like, a place that represents the quality you want to meet.

I, for example, have a House of Truth I visit, where I have a special throne of truth; as I sit in it, I find myself sinking into a knowledge or truth that I need to face. I also have a guide there, a very beautiful Egyptian goddess of truth called Ma-at, who wears a single ostrich feather, Ma-at is considered to personify all the elements of cosmic harmony established at the beginning of time – including Truth, Justice, and Moral Integrity – and is said to judge us after our death by weighing our heart against a feather.

It was from Ma-at that I learned about the concept of a 'point of transformation' that you will see in chapter 17 on problem solving. As I sat in the House of Truth, Ma-at appeared and told me that I was sitting with my head down, refusing to look at the realities of the world around me because they seemed too painful. She asked me to look up and around, and see the true nature of the world.

The world is indeed, she said, full of negative events, relationships, and feelings which could give rise to great pessimism and sorrow. But at the centre of all this negativity is a point of transformation – the potential for everything to turn into its opposite. This point of transformation is another word for hope, and is what makes it possible to look honestly at the realities around us. It is to this point of transformation that we must address our attention and our energy if we wish to have a positive effect on the world. I was deeply moved by this experience, which helped me to find a way to be honest with myself about the brutal realities of life and yet remain hopeful and effective.

VISIONS AND ILLUSIONS

In our everyday reality we have logical and scientific rules that help us distinguish between the subjective and the objective, between science and myth, between rationality and super-stition. When we leave the world of everyday reality, we enter a realm in which no one has taught us the rules; most of us have not undergone a spiritual training that could be considered the equivalent of our more conventional education. How can we tell truth from illusion?

This is particularly problematic if we mix up, as we are not unlikely to do, visions from our universal spiritual unconscious with fantasies from our personal unconscious. People who are considered mad often seem also to have transpersonal visions; perhaps when the filters between the conscious and the personal unconscious fall away, so do the filters between the normal self and the higher self, or between the self and that spiritual dimension that goes beyond the personal. But, conversely, no matter how sane we are, when we contact our spiritual unconscious it can be difficult to distinguish between transpersonal visions, and personal wish fulfilling fantasies.

The safest way to operate is to accept messages that seem to come from another dimension only when they feel right to you in the here and now everyday reality. It is also crucial to be particularly wary of any understandings that make you feel 'high' with your own power, omniscience and magnificence, rather than giving you the awareness that you are part of a powerful, wise and magnificent process. Not only is this state a negative one in itself, but you are also likely to find yourself knocked down into a hopeless 'low' when you find that you cannot heal every sick person, discover every hidden secret, or accurately predict the pools.

In Jung's terms, through the collective unconscious you may be in touch with an inner archetype or universal symbol, like the God archetype, which gives access to deep and ancient understandings. But if, instead of recognising that there is a God archetype in all of us, you identify with the archetype – and think you personally are God – then this is what he calls 'inflation', and can lead to paranoia rather than enlightenment.[3]

Alice Bailey gives a good tip: If you have a so-called transpersonal vision in which you personally are at the centre of the story – saving the world for example – it is probably illusion.[4]

MEETING A WISE AND LOVING BEING, and RECEIVING AND SENDING MESSAGES AND HEALING ENERGY: THE STRUCTURE OF THE EXERCISES

In this chapter I outline two major exercises: Meeting a wise and loving being, and Receiving and Sending Messages and Healing Energy. Under Variations you will also find an exercise on the House of Truth (or Peace, Love, Healing, or whatever quality you wish).

There are many guided imagery exercises based on the idea of meeting a wise and loving being. Typically the being is on top of a mountain, or in a cave, or in a deep wood, or on the other side of a river. The wise loving being may be experienced as other than yourself, or ultimately as a reflection of your deepest self. In this exercise, 'Meeting a Wise and Loving Being', you walk through a wood, and up a mountain, and wait there for the wise loving person with whom you communicate, and through whom you also discover an aspect of yourself. When you say goodbye, you can plan to meet each other again and then, as usual, appreciate the gift, reflect on its meaning, look forward to see its relevance to your life, and emerge. The basic structure of the exercise is:

Preparation: Clearing a space, and relaxing
1 Summoning the image of the wise person's domain

2 Finding the wise being
3 Interacting with the wise being
4 Finding your own qualities
5 Saying goodbye
6 Appreciating, reflecting, looking forward, and emerging

The second exercise, 'Receiving and Sending Messages and Healing Energy', encourages you to let go of the normal boundaries between people, and between people and other living things, objects and events, and to be open to sending and receiving information and energy through non-physical means. Once you have done this, you can tune into a person or object or plant or animal, and get a sense of what is going on with them, or ask them to teach you a skill or guide you through an experience, or tell them what you need to, or send them loving energy. You can also get a picture of their, or someone else's, emotional and physical health, and try to heal them. Again, as usual, you would then appreciate, reflect, look forward, and emerge. The general format is:

Receiving and Sending Messages and Healing Energy
Preparation: Clearing a space and relaxing
1 Summoning a dimension without personal boundaries
2 Receiving and sending messages
3 Healing
4 Appreciating, reflecting, looking forward, and emerging

MEETING A WISE AND LOVING BEING: BASIC EXERCISE

Preparation: Clearing a space and relaxing

1 *Summoning the image of the wise person's domain*: Imagine that you are walking along in a

beautiful wood. Feel the ground under your feet. Notice the wild flowers, the sounds of the birds and insects, the feeling of the breeze on your cheeks, the way the sunlight dances on the leaves, the smell of the pines. As you walk along allow yourself to experience a sense of well being, of being connected with everything, and of deep peace.

You can now see a mountain ahead of you. You reach it and begin to climb, feeling the effort of the muscles in your legs as you go up hill. You continue to walk, until there is no path, and you are clambering up the rocks. As you get near the top you notice that there is a strong field of light that seems to be resting at the top of the mountain. When you reach the top, you find yourself immersed in this light. You sit for a moment and view the world around and below you.

2 *Finding the wise being*: From the distance you will see a wise and loving being who is ready to listen to you and to help you. At first he or she is a luminous point in the distance. You begin to walk towards each other.

If you don't see anyone, realise that this time you are meant to be your own wise person, and to find what you can from within yourself. So ask for an image to emerge of the wise loving person in you.

3 *Interacting with the wise being*: As you come close to this being, use all your senses to understand and experience his or her qualities. Does he or she have a particular light? A particular magnetic power? A special form of joy, wisdom, knowledge, love, peace, clarity, freedom or innocence?

Look in his or her eyes and sense the message there for you.

Now talk to the being, first greeting him or her and asking for their name. Say anything that feels right, ask any question, talk about any problem. Listen for the answer, and just continue the conversation, both verbally and non-verbally, for as long as it seems right.

4 *Finding your own qualities*: As the conversation ends, begin to tune in with your whole being to the wise person, matching your energy to theirs, your wavelength or vibration or state of mind (however you conceive of these) to theirs, your sense of being alive to theirs. Begin to experience their qualities in you, as if the wise person is a mirror to show you who you really are. Feel your own light, joy, power, wisdom, knowledge, love, peace, clarity, freedom or innocence.

5 *Saying goodbye*: Thank the wise loving being, and take leave of him or her, in any way that feels right. Ask also how you can meet again. Coming back down from the mountain and through the wood, notice any difference in the way things look or the way you feel.

6 *Appreciating, reflecting, looking forward*: Appreciate the gift, emerge, and reflect on the meaning of the messages you got from the wise person, as well as the value of the experience itself. Be aware that in future, when you need help or advice or caring, you can return to speak to this wise being, or to that wise being who is the real you.

RECEIVING AND SENDING MESSAGES AND HEALING ENERGY – BASIC EXERCISE

Preparation: Clearing a space and relaxing

1 *Summoning a dimension without personal boundaries*: Try either of these: Alternative A: Say to yourself: I'm going to count down from ten to one, and with each number I'll feel more and more deeply relaxed, more and more in touch with a dimension in which everything and everyone, past, present, and future, are connected with each other and I can send and receive images, messages, and healing energy from and to anyone by simply deciding to do so. Ten, nine, deeper and deeper, etc. Alternative B: Imagine that you are in a spaceship going out of the dimension of time and space that we know. You land in a dimension in which everything and everyone, past, present, and future, are connected with each other and you can send and receive images, messages, and healing energy from and to anyone by simply deciding to do so.

2 *Receiving and sending messages*: Allow your mind and emotions to become quiet. Allow an image to emerge of a person about whom you want information or with whom you want to communicate, or else a person, living or dead, who has some quality, skill, knowledge, or experience, that you would like to gain.

Look at the person's image, make a deep connection with it, and wait for other images or thoughts to appear. Try letting your spirit go up above, below, behind, in front, and underneath the image to explore further. Tune into the person, matching your energy, wavelengths, or vibrations or state of mind (however you conceive of these) with the person's. Talk to the person, using words, images, or non-verbal communication; you may wish to ask them for information, or tell them how you feel about them, or request them to teach you something or guide you through a learning experience. Wait for their response.

Try also to step into the body of the person, sensing what it is like to be them, and gaining the skill or knowledge you need through this direct experience. See the world, including yourself, from their point of view.

When you are ready, thank them, and say goodbye, arranging if appropriate how to meet again. You may also wish to send the person your love and best wishes.

You can do exactly the same thing with an object or a plant or animal. You can either do it in its presence – studying, talking to and 'going into' the real object, plant, or animal – or by inviting an image of it.

3 *Healing*: Think of a person whom you are concerned about – perhaps someone with a health problem or an emotional difficulty. This may or may not be the same person as above. Ask for images related to that person's emotional and physical health. Scan your image of their body from head to toe, noticing any abnormalities, such as dark, broken, ill-seeming areas. Enter inside their body and sense what it feels like.

When you locate any problem externally or internally, try to heal the image in whatever way feels right. You may wish to ask a healing, loving being to send a ray of love and healing. Or you yourself can send a healing light, or reinstate the natural light of the person. Or you may actually straighten out a twisted muscle, or untangle the web of tangled threads in the emotional body. Conclude in the same way as in the Life change Exercise in chapter 11 by putting the image of the healed person in a bubble or balloon, asking for the healing to be, and also 'releasing' it – knowing that it is not all up to you, and that you need to release the healing into the lap of the universe, God, the spirits or whoever or whatever goes beyond you. You can simply say, 'I ask for this to be and I release it', and then send the bubble off to disappear from sight. You can also add, if you wish, 'And it is so' – in the dimension in which past, present and future are one, this healing has already happened and exists in potential, only waiting to be actualised.

3 *Appreciating, emerging, reflecting and looking forward*: Give appreciation in whatever way feels right and to whomever it feels right to give it. After emerging, reflect on the meaning of your experience and on its implications for the future.

QUICK TUNING IN

Tuning in to someone can take only a moment, and can be done in or out of their physical presence. I suggest that whenever you get a chance, you add this to your normal communications with people: tune into their image or spirit and send them a message or a loving energy. Thus whether tucking a child into bed , or going to see a friend, or thinking of someone you are worried about, pause a moment, tune in, and send your message or energy. You never know what good you can do that way, and you will certainly be doing yourself some good.

VARIATIONS

Going to the House of Truth (or Love, Peace, Wisdom, Power, Healing, etc.): Allow an image to emerge of the House of Truth (or whatever quality you want to explore). What does the House look like? Let your spirit go up above and look down upon it, and then move around to the sides and underneath. What do you notice from the various perspectives? Now enter inside. What is your feeling as you enter this House? What can you see, smell, hear, or otherwise sense around you? Is there a special place for you there, or special tools or instruments for you to use? Find out, and if so, explore them or try them out.

Approach whomever you see there. Find out who they are, and talk to them about your life, and what you need. Ask for their response. You may just listen to what they have to tell, or you may wish actually to switch roles and become them, or continue the conversation or conversations as long as appropriate. Thank the being or beings. Remember that if these beings have been helpful you can continue to use them as consultants whenever you feel you need their help.

IN CONCLUSION

The realm of the transpersonal is not, so to speak, everyone's cup of tea. But the awareness that everything we experience may have an added dimension to it that goes beyond the obvious can add to the magic and mystery of life even for the greatest sceptics. At the very least, it can remind us of all the vast potentials of this everyday reality that are just waiting to be discovered. And at best, it can give a deeper meaning to everything we do, and a fuller sense of who we are and where we are going.

PART FOUR

Finding Your Own Way

=== 17 ===

A DO-IT-YOURSELF
SUMMARY

Resolving problems, improving
skills

Some years ago, my sister Shira talked to me about how, whenever she faced a really difficult problem, she told herself, 'Every problem has a solution', and with that reassurance was able to calm down and figure out what to do next. I tried this myself and found it gave me a kind of 'Pause Before I Panic' key to problem solving. But then I began to have doubts. Does every problem have a solution? Surely not, any more than every illness has a cure.

What every problem does have, in my view, is not a *solution*, but a *point of transformation* and a *resolution*. There is always some kind of lever, or way through, or perspective, that can move us forward: this is the point of transformation. Once we have found this point of transformation, we open the way to resolution, a clarification of a confused picture that has kind of rightness about it. Another word for point of transformation is hope. Another word for resolution is peace.

When we look for a solution to a problem, we tend to be aiming for a predetermined endpoint that we would define as 'desirable'. When we seek the point of transformation and the resolution, we are simply trying to find the situation's own internal dynamic and clarity, whether or not this dynamic takes us where we thought we wanted to go. In the words of the *I Ching* or *Book of Changes*, the ancient Chinese book of wisdom, 'a light will develop out of events, by which the path to success may be recognised.'[1]

When you are stuck in a relationship problem, for example, the point to transformation may involve a new acceptance of yourself and your partner that enables you to stay together, or a new attitude that enables you to let go of each other. Either can give you a sense of resolution, and enable you to move forward. In the same way, for someone who is seriously ill the way forward may be towards health, but it may also be towards accepting the inevitability of death.

So perhaps rather than talking of solving problems, we need to talk of transforming and resolving problems. How do we transform or resolve problems so that we can move forward toward new choices? This question applies equally to problems that are traditionally referred to as personal, or business, or creative, or professional, or academic. A problem is a problem: it is any situation where we find some difficulty in moving forward.

PRISON BARS

Julie was a very popular management consultant very much in demand both professionally and personally. She took her commitments very seriously, and tried to meet everyone's needs, yet found that she wasn't leaving herself enough time to be on her own, or to spend time with her partner, and ended up stressed and tired rather than feeling good about herself. She kept looking at her diary, wondering how she could organise her life differently. How could she meet the expectations of others and still take care of herself?

She asked for an image to represent her relationship to expectations, and found that a prison bar emerged, with her self behind bars. The bars didn't reach all the way up to the ceiling nor quite down to the floor, and there was a window in the cell, so she reassured herself that things could have been worse.

What could she do? Julie decided to melt down the bars and turn them into a lovely sculpture. And so she did, feeling quite pleased with this instant and creative solution. But in a few moments, she realised that she wasn't happy with this solution; in her attempt to solve the problem in her usual efficient manner, she hadn't allowed herself a real resolution. The sculpture was pretty but it was still made out of iron. She needed a change of a totally different order.

Suddenly she found herself trying the bars out, and discovering that they had never been locked. This was Julie's point of transformation. She pushed the bars open and walked out into a field where she found herself singing, dancing, and painting. This felt like home to her, and she was relaxed and delighted. She had that sense of resolution now.

As Julie mapped the image back onto her life she saw that there was no way she could reorganise her timetable so that her life looked better – even when bars look like beautiful

299

sculptures they are still bars. She needed to look at what she really wanted to do or have at the centre of her life, and then everything would fall into place around it.

Julie suddenly realised that what she yearned for most of all, and was giving no time at all for in her attempt to meet everyone's expectations, was to express her creativity. She eventually decided to move to the country, and do what she had really always wanted – write books. She still sees her friends and runs courses, but only as and when it fits into her own overall plan for her life. And when she does, she laughs a lot more than she used to.

Laughter, indeed, often accompanies the moment of transformation, as we let go of our tension and confusion, and even see the funny side of the problem we have been struggling with. When one of my imagework students, Boris, was faced with problems, he tended to go to his House of Truth, where he met such distinguished figures as Socrates, Jung, and other eminent gurus. One day, when his relationship with his lover seemed devastatingly confusing and painful, he visited his House of Truth hoping for a word of wisdom. To his surprise, instead of a great philosopher or psychologist, Hollywood producer Cecil B. De Mille appeared.

Boris was disappointed, but still asked the producer what he should do about his relationship. Taking his cigar from between his teeth, and blowing cigar smoke out of the corner of his mouth, Cecil B. De Mille said: 'Gee kid. You think your life is a Hollywood production number. It's only a B movie.' Boris laughed uproariously, recognised his habit of dramatising situations, and promised that he would not take his life quite so seriously again.

No solution was offered, but this was indeed a point of transformation. With his new light touch, Jonathan was able to look at his situation afresh and resolve it himself.

THE STRUCTURE OF PROBLEM RESOLUTION

The first step toward resolving problems is a kind of leap of faith. By this I mean that we need to pause and have the trust that every problem does have a point of trans-formation – all we need to do is find it. This trust reduces anxiety and allows us to 'put on our thinking caps'. As we pause, we need also to take a moment to relax and focus deeply on the problem.

The second step involves finding another way to look at the problem, or as many other ways of looking at it as we can. If the problem were soluble as it stood, you wouldn't have a problem. The question we need to ask ourselves is: 'how can I reconstruct this problem in such a way so that it does admit of a satisfactory way forward?' remembering that even the notion of 'satisfactory' depends on your perspective on the problem. Every technique of imaging you have used can come in handy here.

The third step is to identify the point of transformation, the way forward, the handle, which can lead to clarity and resolution. There may of course be more than one of these, in which case you need to choose the most satisfactory one, which again depends on your perspective.

It is important to emphasise that although I have described this in terms of steps, this is not necessarily an orderly sequen-tial process. The moment of resolution, in particular, often follows a period of waiting, which allows your creativity to bubble away inside you through what has been called an 'incubation' period. The moment of insight may then come during a bath, or after you 'sleep on it', or while you are busy doing something totally different. The skill is then to grasp it with both hands, say 'Eureka' – and follow it through.

This all sounds pretty simple, and in principle it is simple. In a sense, it is the trust that makes it simple. A great deal of the difficulty we have with problem solving has to do with anxiety, or, in other words, the numbing, or incapacitating, or panic-making feeling that we are stuck with the problem, and the problem is stuck with us – forever.

HOLISTIC, CREATIVE PROBLEM SOLVING

To this simple structure, we need to add one more not inconsequential rider: we don't want to resolve problems any old way. First, moving forward can sometimes mean creating a new set of problems that are worse than the old, particularly if we take account of the effect on other people and situations rather than just on ourselves. Thus Ellen, in chapter 8, felt that she had solved her marriage problem by leaving her husband suddenly without really saying goodbye, but the mess and confusion she left behind her not only caused her partner a great deal of pain, but in the long term did not allow her to resolve her guilt or feel good about her new relationship.

Secondly, moving forward on a problem may be a first-aid measure that represents a habitual approach and doesn't move us forward as human beings, which is a shame. Julie, the management consultant, could have reorganised her diary so that she had a bit more time for herself, but she would have found herself still stressed and unhappy – just slightly less so.

So to the notion of transforming problems we need to add two more concepts: holistic and creative.

A holistic approach to problem transformation is one that takes account of the whole context and network of people and events within which the problem is situated and which the problem will affect. To do this we need to consider the problem from as many points of view as we can, because this is the easiest way to identify implications that we would not see from our own limited perspective.

The problem of extending a motorway through a town, for example, can be perceived in very different ways from the point of view of the house owners, the motorists, the local government, the conservationists, the pedestrians, and the bicycle riders. A marital problem is likewise a different problem for the husband, the wife, the children, the family system as a whole, the neighbours, or, indeed the husband's and/or wife's lover.

To create a holistic solution, you would need first to consider all of these points of view, and then return to your own perspective, and choose the way forward that seems right for you at the time.

A creative solution to a problem is one that varies our habitual mode of thinking and responding and represents a novel approach to the problem. In so doing we are expanding the transformation possibilities not only of the problem itself, but also of ourselves as problem solvers.

Your habitual approach might be to consider the practical rather than the emotional results, or the long-term rather than the short-term effects, or the straightforward safe path rather than the daring risky one, or the complicated rather then the simple one. Someone else might come up with a radically different approach to the same problem, not because their material interests or point of view differ, but simply because they have a different habitual approach.

To reach a creative solution, you need to increase your potential avenues of approach, and consider the problem in a new way. The solution that emerges when you have done this, perhaps not immediately, but after an 'incubation' period of waiting and allowing the unconscious to take its time, is likely to have that quality of beauty or rightness about it that creative people talk of as the hallmark of a creative break-through.[2]

Imagework is ideal for holistic and creative problem solving because it gives us the ability literally to vary our perspectives dramatically, and because the metaphoric and intuitive power of imagery expands manifold the number of potential methods of approaching problems.

This chapter has a do-it-yourself flavour because it is intended mainly to remind you of the various methods you can use to solve a problem, so that you can construct an exercise that suits you out of these. The general approach I suggest for problem solving is as follows:

1 Clear a space and relax
2 a Put the problem in perspective
  b Put yourself in perspective
3 Allow an image to emerge, and deepen and explore it, until you find the point of transformation, or the way forward.
4 Appreciate, reflect, look forward, emerge, and carry through

---

PROBLEM RESOLVING MADE EASY(EASIER): BASIC EXERCISES

1 *Clear a space and relax*: The first step in going forward is to stop. You need to take the moment or moments necessary to carry out one of the relaxation methods in chapter 5, or any other one that works for you, even though it may be a one-second process.

This has two functions, First, it encourages you to have the trust that you will find a point of transformation, and helps you let go of the need to solve it which inhibits your curiosity and creativity. Your attitude will be: 'I wonder what will emerge?' rather than: 'I've got to solve this quickly or else.'

Secondly, it enables you to use that non-critical, free associative, and yet highly concentrated mode of awareness that facilitates not only imaging but any kind of problem solving. It stops you from just giving the first habitual answer 'off the top of your head', and encourages you to focus deeply and use more of your resources. I find that just taking this focused approach is sometimes enough to shed light on the problem, and to lead me directly to a new view of the situation, a point of transformation, and a resolution.

Remember that if you are using a count-down to deepen the relaxation, you should use words that are relevant to the task, e.g.: 'I'm going to count down from ten to one and with each number I'll be more and more relaxed, more and more in touch with my resources, more and more able to define and resolve my present problem.'

2a *Put the problem in perspective*: Where is your problem? Is it all round you? Is it inside you? Weighing down on your head? Wherever it is, try putting it somewhere else and taking another perspective. The most effective place probably is to begin by picturing it and putting it outside you. If it has more than one part, you may put an image for each aspect outside you. Then walk round it or them. Take an aerial perspective. Get under and look underneath. Each of these will yield a new insight. At the very least, it will 'put the problem in perspective'.

2b *Put yourself in perspective*: Allow your spirit to go out and look at yourself from above, the side, below, etc. Get a sense of what is going on for this person (you). What can you notice about his or her energy, relationship to the world, relationship to the problem, or whatever else occurs to you. Give any messages to that person that would be helpful.

3 *Allow an image to emerge, and deepen and explore it, until you find the point of trans-*

formation: This is the opportunity for your do-it-yourself creativity. The following is a summary of some of the ways of using imagework for problem solving:

a   *Use an image that represents the problem: The metaphoric approach*: Here we allow a metaphor to emerge, and really focus on the metaphor. This approach is given at length in chapter 6, but following is a short summary:

Suggest to yourself: 'I'd like to allow an image to emerge of an animal, a plant or an object that somehow represents this problem, (or name the problem) at this time.'

When the image emerges, study it, then enter into it: become the image. Find out what it feels like to be this. Ask yourself questions like: 'What is going on right now? How long has it been this way? Was there a time when it was different; if so, when and how? What's next? What do I need to do to take a step forward? What feels right?' (In other words, get the present, history, and future of the image.)

Try also looking at the image from above, the sides, and underneath, to see other perspectives. If you can't see a way forward you may try saying: 'It's *x* time in the future, and I've solved my problem. What did I do?' (more about this later).

Now look back at the problem. Map your understandings back onto it.

It is also possible to think up three or four aspects of the problem: e.g. a writing project or problem might be subdivided into the structure of your chapter, the first paragraph, the ending, and the point of it. Then allow three or four images to emerge, watch them combine and recombine, talk to each of them, view the scene from different perspectives and finally make sense of the story that emerges, as in the case of the dog, the carrot, and the samovar that you can read about in Appendix One.

b *Use an image that represents the problem: the analogic approach*: Here we explicitly choose, as an analogy to our present problem, a situation or problem that we have successfully resolved, or perhaps never even saw as a problem, and compare and map back throughout to find out what we can learn from it:

Think of the problem. What is difficult about it? Think of another situation or area wherein you are able to do this successfully. For example, supposing you're a student, and you can't manage and organise your studies for an exam: think of an area where you *are* able to manage and organise. If you can't, think of someone else who is good at managing and organising. Or, supposing you find that you don't know whether to go forward or to hold back. Think of a problem in which you are good at knowing whether to go forward or hold back. Now map back, noticing the features of the successful situation and problem, and think in each case of the equivalent in the present situation, and how you could do that differently. (e.g. 'I'm good at managing and organising a party.' Look at: the feeling, the way you use food, the way you use your own talents, the structure of how you do it, etc. and relate to the original. Don't just choose obviously relevant points; the kind of spice you use in cooking may be exactly relevant to writing the essay).

c *Use an image that represents other problem solvers*: Here the focus is on other perspectives upon the problem: someone else who might take another point of view, or have an understanding or skill or resource you don't have:

Allow an image of someone else to emerge on the chair opposite who has expertise in this area, or who might be able to solve it differently or better than you can. (This could be Einstein, your mother, a wise person, Hercule Poirot, your lecturer, your child, or the best health consultant in the world). Picture them clearly. Tell them about the problem. Switch roles and be that person. Find out how you see it and what you suggest. Continue the conversation until you feel you really understand.

It is possible to do this more than once: ask a number of different kinds of experts what their view is; perhaps a friend who you know supports you, an expert who you know might have objective answers, and a child who might take a totally novel perspective.

It's not actually necessary, once again, to see the person in the seat and switch seats if this makes you uncomfortable. It does simply make the process more effective. But you can imagine the person and listen to what they have to say. It may also be a good idea to combine this with going to a place that is relevant: you may associate wise people with mountain tops, or financial advisors with offices, and this may be where you go to meet them.

Remember, too, that if the person is saying what you would expect, you probably haven't really gotten into the image. There should be something surprising about it. Otherwise you may simply be conjuring up a caricature rather than a real image.

For a quick inner consultation, do also try saying to yourself: 'If I were *x* (the best therapist in the world; the best advisor in the world; my own health consultant; Einstein, etc.) I would ... ' and then see what comes up.

d *Use an image that represents another time frame*, e.g. after the problem is solved or the decision made, or before it ever happened. Because images are spatial rather than temporal, you can tune into any time, past, present or future and experience it as totally in the present. This means that you can tune into the future and gain the benefits of hindsight. It also means that you can tune into the time before you had the problem; this is particularly important with emotional problems, sometimes allowing a sense of freedom for the first time. There are many exercises using time and time lines in a variety of ways, but here are a few:

(i)   Allow an image of yourself to emerge as you will be after you have solved this problem.

(If this is difficult try the space craft idea in chapter 10: imagine you are in a space craft and moving off the earth. You come back to earth at a time x years from now when you feel good about this problem. What is happening?) Look back and see how and when you solved it.

(ii)   If the problem is a more general life one, e.g. where am I going, what do I really want, simply go forward in time, as in chapter 10, by giving yourself the instruction: 'It's five years from now, or I'm eighty-years-old, or whatever, and I feel good about my life. What do I feel good about? How did I manage it?' (If you can't get an image of feeling good, start with 'I feel terrible about my life', and look back at where you went wrong, you should then be able to do the positive one and compare the two. Or try the spacecraft again).

(iii)   Imagine before you a line that represents time. Allow the past to be on your left and the future on your right. The line may represent your life, or the time from the beginning to the future completion of a creative project, or the beginning and the solution of a problem. Step on it and move back into the past, including before the problem emerged, and forward into the future. Have conversations between the selves that emerge, offering each other resources. Step off the line, and get a sense of the whole story line, and of the critical points and events. Consider how the critical event that is about to come up needs to be shifted so that it makes a better story, or so as to resolve the problem effectively.

e *Use an image that represents a place where you can go to solve the problem*: There are a number of different types of internal environment that might make it easier for you to solve the problem. Here are some of them, and you can be creative here too:

(i) Allow an image to emerge of a House of Truth, or a House of Money, or a House of Time, or a House of Health, or a House of Sleep, in other words, any image which seems to represent the quality that you need to solve the problem or the subject of the problem. This is a good place to look at the problem and you will probably find experts there. You might even try the House of Jane, or Alan, or whatever your own name is and see what happens there.

(ii) Allow an image to emerge of an Ideal Creative Workplace. What does it look like? Find out what tools it has – perhaps a magic screen, or a magic spring that washes away impurities, or a calendar with dates in the past, present, and future, or whatever. Wait for the door to open and for two guides to emerge, a male and a female, who are there to help you. Greet them, get to know them, ask for what you need, and thank them for whatever they offer.

(iii) Go to the sanctuary that you created in your relaxation exercises in chapter 4.

(iv) Imagine yourself on a swing, perhaps a swing you used as a child. As you swing on it, ask it to propel you to the best place for you to explore and resolve your problem. Allow yourself to be propelled out of the swing and to travel through time and space and land somewhere. Where are you? Continue the exploration.

f   *Use an image to represent you doing your best or getting what you want*: This is most useful when you want to improve your skills, or your situation. Allow an image to emerge, either on a screen, or however is best for you, of yourself as you are now. Notice how that person operates and accept him or her as they are. Then let that go, and allow an image to emerge of yourself doing the thing you want to do perfectly, having the attribute you want to have, or getting the thing that you want. Notice how that person is operating, they step into the image and be the person and explore and accept the feeling. Finally, step back out, put the image in a bubble, ask and intend for it to be, and release it into the lap of that which is beyond your conscious personal controlling self. Now sense the way forward.

4   *Appreciate, reflect, look forward, and emerge*: When you have finished your imagework, as usual, appreciate your conscious and unconscious, use your conscious rationality to understand and map back your insights onto the situation you are in, look forward to see how you plan to follow through and emerge. You then need to use your will and perseverance to follow in the footsteps of the image or insight.

IN CONCLUSION

To resolve a problem, or to find a way through a difficulty, or to make an important choice, or to improve a skill, you need to vary your perspective and approaches as much as possible. You can use an image of the problem, of another problem solver, of a time when the problem has been solved, of a place where problem solving is easier, or of a way of operating that is perfect for you. There are literally as many perspectives as you can imagine. When you finish playing around, come back to your own perspective and decide what your best solution is, and your own best way to move forward into the future.

CONCLUDING NOTE

You have by now gone some way on your voyage into the world of the imagination. Some of the territory has no doubt been strange, painful, frightening and confusing. Perhaps your hopes have, on occasion, been dashed and you have been tempted to give up. Yet at other times you have probably been astounded by the depth of your understanding and vision, and by the vast possibilities inherent in being you that you had not yet dreamt of. Perhaps this is a good time to look back and see how far you've travelled, and to look forward to the challenges and changes ahead.

Do enjoy the process of exploring the world of the imagination as a pleasure in its own right, recognising that your inner world deserves as much respect as the outer world. Keep in mind, however, that the main function of the imagework is to help you to live better here and now.

People often talk of the 'path' of self development. But self development in general, and imagework in particular, is not itself the path of life: it is the means by which we stay on our path.

We walk along happily for a while, and then find ourselves, for external or internal reasons, feeling confused, lost or uncomfortable – we have been knocked off our path. We turn inward and develop a new resource or attitude in ourselves so as to get back on. That works fine for while, until we find we have fallen off the other side of the path. More imagework to get back on the path and walk on it in a new way.

We walk along some more and suddenly realise we are in a cul-de-sac. What choice point did we miss? More imagework to find our way to a crossroads and make a choice that leads us onto an open path. More path. More imagework. Getting knocked off the path or going into a cul-de-sac is not a failure but just a part of the learning process, as long as we keep in mind that we do have the resources to find our way back to a path that is right for us. And each time we do so, it will get easier and easier, and the experience of walking on our path deeper and more satisfying.

Do share your new skill with others. If you have not done so already, consider forming an imagework group with like-minded people at work or in your personal life. Use imagework in the classroom, in the boardroom, or in the hospital. Talk about and teach it to your children, your friends, your colleagues, or your clients. Make sure it no longer seems any odder to people to consult an image before making a decision than to draw up a balance sheet of pros and cons. It is time for the ancient language of imagery to come out of the closet and to take its rightful place in our everyday lives.

Appendices

APPENDIX ONE

THE DOG, THE CARROT, THE SAMOVAR AND THE FISHING BOAT

When I began to write this book, the way ahead was still shrouded in darkness, and I used imagework to get myself started. I decided that I needed an image for the book as a whole, the content, the structure of the first chapter, and my own approach. I allowed images to emerge, watching them develop a relationship to each other, observed them from a variety of perspectives, spoke to them, and generally explored their meaning.

The images that emerged were the dog, carrot, and samovar, after whom the first chapter is named, and a fishing boat. As the images moved around and settled down, I saw the rather mangy but bright and lively dog sitting in the boat, enjoying eating the carrot, and waiting for the samovar to boil. I then discovered that there was a man sleeping at the bottom of the boat. The dog suddenly got an urge to surprise the man, and took the boat out to sea himself.

The man woke up, furious, yet helpless, because he hadn't even any oars to get back. He finally reconciled himself to the fact that he was on his way, with a companion he would not himself have chosen (he preferred sleek house-trained dogs) and even decided that the dog was actually a lot of fun. He offered the dog another carrot and a cup of coffee, realising that the dog had actually been boiling the samovar for him, and they planned the journey together.

When I talked to the dog, who seem to represent the first chapter, he 'told' me exactly what needed to go into the chapter, and gave me the headings in order. What he gave me was such an excellent set of guidelines that even when I strayed from it, I seemed always to come back and end up with exactly what he suggested.

The carrot, which seemed to represent the content of the book, offered: vitamin A to see, or create images with, at night; crunchiness, or the crunch of basic theory that gives a structure; and flavour, given by lots of personal examples – until then I had expected to use only examples from clients and students and not from my own life; a bright warm orange colour to the writing; and the smell, like no other, which was the smell of self discovery.

The samovar, which was an old Russian hand-me-down, (and in fact was the one that used to belong to my Russian grandfather in New York), seemed to be myself, and I needed: water – my own transparent creativity rather than the contents of other books; my own energy source so that the water could boil and bubble, and coffee – the ingredient that would make it tasty and wake us all up.

The man was probably the book as a whole, still sleeping in the bottom of the boat, which seemed to represent the process of writing the book.

Armed with all these insights, suggestions, and proposed structures, I started to write. The funny thing is that the dog not only provided me with the chapter structure, but really did trick me by pulling the boat out to sea before any of us expected it. Having set myself the task of doing the first chapter, I couldn't understand why it was taking me so long. I discussed the draft with a friend, who pointed out that what I had written was by no means simply a first chapter – it was probably a quarter of the book.

Like the dog, the chapter was neither sleek nor house trained, but it became the basis for planning the rest of the book. And I was certainly very pleased indeed that my boat was really on its way.

APPENDIX TWO

THE SNAIL'S STORY

This is the full text of what emerged for me as I followed the exercise in chapter 6:

1 *Summoning the image*: The image that emerges is a snail. I notice that my image is not very exciting, and wish I had something more dramatic to tell you. But I accept it and I thank my unconscious, knowing that this will yield more than it seems at present.

2 *Studying the image*: I see the snail moving along a vast expanse of grass. It looks really tiny and the grass looks so high. I feel it to be moving so slowly, and in that sense to have such a great hopeless task trying to get anywhere, but I don't know if the snail sees it that way. Whatever sound it makes, cannot be heard. As I move and look at it from above, I suddenly notice that there are other snails in this vast expanse of grass, but that this snail cannot see them because they are quite a distance away in snail terms. The others seem to be aware of this snail, and are somehow encouraging the snail, athough it is unaware of all this. Looking from the sides of the picture I sense that the snail has already come a long way, and that the way ahead is not so far. When I put myself into the earth and look up, I see how very vulnerable the snail is, and it seems awfully brave to be soldiering on as it does. I wonder if it ever gets a rest.

3 *Becoming the image: deepening and exploring*: I become the snail. I do find it quite painful to move across this vast expanse

of grass. The essence of being me seems to do with stillness – deep inside I am very, very still, and yet I also need to keep moving. I like the protection of the high grass around me; it makes me feel safe and as if I can do things at my own pace and in my own way. I love the view of the blue sky above me, or rather the patch of it that I can see. It seems to give me hope whenever I look up. I also like the smell and taste of the grass. My immediate environment feels in that sense very natural and nourishing to me. But I do feel rather lonely and a bit threatened by how far I have gone and how far I need to go.

I smile a bit to myself though, because I have a little secret: although I look like a snail, I am a very deep, wise being, and that is nice to remind myself of. But as I say this, I get the picture of being crushed by a foot, and I realise that even though I may be a deep wise being inside, I am still physically vulnerable to being treated like a snail and stepped on carelessly or even cruelly.

There are no other snails near me, but I sense that there are others in the world not too far from me, and every now and then I seem to get a kind of intuitive message, rather faint and dreamlike, that encourages me by letting me know that I am not alone and that it is worth going on. It's almost like the snatch of a far away song, or temple chant. Perhaps we will all meet up at the end of the trip. I hope so.

I notice that there is a wonderful grace in my movement, and I enjoy feeling my body as it moves. I also notice that while I am not good at going fast and far, I do have the time to feel my immediate grass-environment in a wonderful sensuous way and that seems totally pleasurable as long as I don't worry about my goal. I make sounds, but they seem to be a kind of ultrasonic sound that cannot be heard except perhaps by those other snails. I also have another sound – a yelp – that is a bit louder, and that is what I make when I fear or feel physical danger or pain.

As I reflect a bit more, I feel that deep down there is a kind of helplessness and hopelessness too, a kind of feeling that because I move so very slowly, I'll never never get far enough to make this all worth it, and yet I can't simply stay here. I sense that there is something wrong with my expectations of myself and of life, because by the nature of being a snail I cannot meet them. I wonder if other snails do it differently, and how it is for tigers and gazelles.

4 *Getting a sense of the history*: I sense that things have not always been this way. And yet funnily enough, it feels almost like there is a distant memory of a previous life – as if there was a time when I was a lion or tiger or other wild beast and ranged the jungles and the forests and couldn't imagine ever being so small and slow, indeed would have looked down on anyone who was.

As a snail, in this life, it feels as if there was a time when I was even smaller and weaker, when my journey was just beginning, and I stood at the beginning and nearly wept at the enormity of the task, and in those first days or months or years kept giving up and saying – this is impossible, I can't go on.

Then, it feels as if a few years ago I looked back and realised how far I had actually gone, complaints and all, because I had been moving while I was complaining and fearing. And at that point, three or four years ago, I took courage, and held my head up high, and said: 'I will survive, although I don't quite see how, because I can see how far I've gone even though I didn't believe I could.'

And since then, although that hoplessness is still there sometimes, it doesn't feel so heavy and deep, and there has been a joy growing, even an enjoyment of the travel itself, and a secret satisfaction at how much I can get to know the feeling of the grass because I move so slowly. I have a feeling that I have speeded up in my travels these last few years because I move with more energy, and less fear and confusion.

To confirm this, I let my spirit go up above me and look down upon me, and I can see that the distance I travelled in the last three or four years seems about a third of my total distance. It does amaze me a bit to have speeded up that much, because it felt so much easier and less fraught than before.

5 *Getting a sense of my possibilities*: I cannot see what's next. I feel I have to plod on forever, and although it has its compensations and pleasures, I am aware of the hopelessness of this. What stops me? I feel my nature and size stop me – I am not built to do anything else, and the world is vast.

What if I could change – how would that be? If I could change I'd learn a snail locomotion technique so that I could zoom along at great speed but remember to roll around in the grass as I go so as to get maximum pleasure from the feeling of the grass. I try that and it feels wonderful.

I look from above, and I see that the snail doesn't realise that there are actually wheels under the ground, like a vast conveyor belt, or one of those moving platforms at the airport, and that it could get on one of these and be carried along with great pleasure and majesty. I whisper to the snail to find the right tracks and get on them.

Now I put myself back into the snail, and imagine it is five years hence. How does it feel? I realise that I have travelled light years in that time, by snail reckoning, and I have done that not by effort, but by constantly improving my little motor, finding the right moving tracks for me, and generally enjoying the process. I've also come closer to the other snails, and we're now within shouting distance to each other, and we really enjoy our play as we roll around on the road, and also share any new tricks as soon as we figure them out. Every now and then I even get close enough to give one of the other snails a big hug, and that glow that we get from the hug lasts for miles.

I look back to that time five years ago (the present), and I realise how stuck I was in believing that snails can't have fun and can't move fast and the grass is so vast that there is no hope. As soon as I shifted my belief I transformed myself totally.

What about the stillness I wonder? And I realise that the stillness is there now because I don't have to force myself to move by effort, but rather that my whole being bounces along in a harmonious, integrated way and the effort is put into finding better devices, not into forcing myself to move.

6   *Appreciating*: I tune back into the snail in the present. As the snail I seem to be smiling and feeling 'raring to go'. I don't yet have my motor inside me, but I sense that I will, and so I can let go of some of that hopelessness at the enormity of the journey. I am curious as to how I will change and look forward to it. And I particularly love the idea that I will be able to roll around with other snails instead of trudging along always in my own little path. I thank my unconscious for the lovely gift.

7   *Reflecting*: As I map the snail back onto my life I realise how strongly I sense the inner stillness which seems to go against my need to keep moving in life, and how deep is the hopelessness that the tasks I set myself, or life itself, always seem so vast. I am protected by the grass in the sense that I sit here at my desk writing this book, and this protects me from the world. But I can also sense the loneliness in this creative work. I know as I look back how much I've changed in the past few years and how far I've gone, and I'm surprised at the level of the hopelessness that is still there in the snail and at its feeling that it is so slow, particularly when everyone else always tells me how speedy and quick I am.

I can see that the way forward has to be by a different means – fitting a motor in me, which means tapping into my real deep engine and will, rather than forcing myself to do things, and also finding the paths in life that take me along fastest rather than always doing things the hard way. And I see now that this must involve getting closer to the people that I feel are on the same path, rather than being content with sending them distant messages.

The emphasis on fun in the life of the snail seems also an important one for me to look at – I love the idea of rolling-around forward rather than, say, zooming forward, as a mechanical object like a train would do with more efficiency but so much less pleasure. I'm touched by the idea that I can keep my stillness and still move and need to think more about how the snail does that.

I'm also moved by the idea that in a previous life I was bigger and more powerful and more speedy, and I am grateful for having this opportunity to try out the idea that small is beautiful too. I sense I must have been very proud, too proud, in ways that are hurtful to others. I imagine that this does not refer to a previous life literally, but to another aspect of myself that I sometimes live out.

I smile as I remember that the only other time I had an image of myself as a snail was when I was working on my difficulty in passing a driving test. I had almost passed my previous test when at the last moment I bumped into the crash barrier in the parking lot of the test centre. The image of the snail that emerged after that seemed to be about moving slowly but surely, with caution until the last moment. Unfortunately, I failed the next test for going too slowly! How helpful it would have been for me then to have had the motor in my snail.

8 *Looking forward*: What is the motor? How can I have it in my life? I draw the conclusion that it has to do with finding my own inner drive, and that every time I become self-judgemental and try to meet expectations I move into that slow but persistent and slightly hopeless mode of the original snail, whereas picturing what I want to do and going for it regardless of whether it is 'good' or 'bad' gives me that active motor feeling.

I realise that the purpose of the original snail is to meet some internal expectations to keep going on this path and to 'get there'; while the purpose of life for the motorised snail is to express herself fully, whatever herself is, and whether that is particularly 'nice' or 'perfect' or 'acceptable'. In other words, I need to really confront my 'shadow' – that aspect of me that isn't so nice but is me nonetheless – before I can really have a motor.

I also realise the importance of sensing which projects feel like they are on the moving platform and take me along, and which feel more onerous. I subject my plans to the 'moving platform' test – does this feel like a moving platform sort of experience? Luckily, writing this book feels very much like one – so here I go.

Four months later

As I revise the book, I notice how important the image of the snail has been to me over the past few months, how often I've tuned in to check how the snail is doing, and how central it has been in my life to let go of expectations and to find my own inner movement. Right now, as I tune in to the snail, I have the feeling that the snail is moving with a lilt to it, in short scurries almost, and then it stops and looks round, and then starts again. It feels more like being a cute little mouse than a snail now.

I don't mind now how far I have to go, since I need to keep moving all my life, so what's the difference? I enjoy trampling the grass a bit as I move. I know I haven't yet made contact with the other snails, but they seem closer, and I can actually hear them calling to each other and me. I don't yet dare to call. Perhaps I'm afraid my little self-contained life will be shattered. But I know that I will, soon.

One day, when the sun is shining, and they've moved even closer, I'll just call out and move over and join them so that we can play together. After that it'll be easier. I'll be able to go on my way, but when I feel lonely, I won't find it difficult to call them because I'll know that they want to welcome me.

Do I have my motor? Yes I do! But it's set on a very low power while I get used to it. How did I get the motor? It was there all the time, but had been set at 0. I had felt so overwhelmed by life that it hadn't occurred to me that there might be some power inside me too. Now that I know that I've got my own motor, life seems more fun – my power jousting with life's power, neither of us trying to win, but just having a good time.

APPENDIX THREE

COMMUNICATION PRINCIPLES

The following principles of communication are a useful framework within which to conduct imagework conversations, and are particularly relevant to chapters 7 and 8 on relationships and chapter 9 on talking to the child within. They are also ideal for conducting your 'real life' relationships. Try any or all of them the next time you get stuck, and you will soon see how powerful they are.

If the examples below sound stilted, this is just because of my effort to make the point clear. Once you've understood the principle, do find a way to say it that is natural to you. There's nothing worse for communication than people that sound like they have stepped out of a textbook on good communication.

'I' messages and not 'You' messages
This is one of the most important and difficult roles to follow. The basic principle is that you stick to describing your own experience and feelings, rather than labelling the other person. You say 'I feel' rather than 'You are.'

The most common reaction when someone has hurt you is to name-call. For example, you might find yourself saying 'You are totally insensitive', or 'You don't care about anyone else but yourself and never have', or 'You're a really mean pig', or whatever your style of address is. The most dramatic and damaging can be those that begin with 'You never', or 'You always'. This name-calling serves a protective function because we believe that we are not allowed simply to state feelings unless we can justify them. Blaming the other proves that we ourselves, or our feelings, are acceptable and legitimate. But it is a dangerous protection, both in our internal conversations or our external ones.

It is not useful in our internal conversations because the feeling is the primary thing, and these accusations simply protect us from having to deal with and get through the feeling. It is not useful in our external conversations because nobody likes being attacked, and not surprisingly, they either defend themselves or attack back. In fact, this is the major background structure of most rows.

So go back to saying, 'I feel hurt' or, 'I feel angry' rather than 'You are mean.' Where possible, let the person know what specific action or attitude makes you feel that way. A useful structure goes something like 'When you do/did x, I feel/felt y. I would like you to do z instead.' Thus for example: 'When you ignore me, I feel really hurt. I want you at least to acknowledge my existence even if you don't have time to talk', or 'Last week when you showed up drunk, I got really furious at you and didn't want to see you again. I'd prefer you to cancel the appointment rather than come to see me when you're drunk'. As we will see later under Accurate Listening, it is also a good idea to ask them why they acted in that way: to find the image or view of the world or of you that guided their actions, so that you can get a handle on how to help change the interactions that are painful or unproductive.

Negatives and Positives

It is important to remember that in any relationship that is at all important, you are almost certain to have both positive and negative feelings. Where, for example, the dominant feeling is anger or resentment, it is crucial to unlock the loving feelings too. Where one feels only loving, the angry destructive feelings need to be looked at. If your relationship was totally unambivalent, you probably wouldn't be looking at it or working on it now.

Try the following basic formula: 'I resent you/hate you/am furious at you for doing/being x.' (Try making up five to ten sentences that begin like this). 'I appreciate you for y.' (Another five or ten sentences).

Discovering the feelings behind the feelings

Remember that the feelings that are obvious to you are not always the original ones; we often have feelings that we are relatively comfortable with and go back to when we are faced with ones that feel unbearable to us. Thus for many people, anger conceals and takes over from helplessness, which is too painful to face. Or fear may conceal and take over from anger if we have learned very early that it was dangerous or bad to be angry. Learn to look behind the feelings to see whether there are any others concealed behind.

Ask yourself 'What is behind this feeling?' Or picture the scene in which you started to feel your present dominant feeling, and locate the feeling that you had immediately before; this is likely to be the original feeling. Thus for a moment you may have felt shocked and hurt, and then immediately furious. The shock and hurt is the feeling you need to explore first. So ask yourself: 'What did I feel just before I felt this?'

Accurate listening (sometimes called active listening) and assertive communicating

Accurate listening means trying to really understand what another person is telling you without having to agree with it, like it, or follow the implicit demands. This is more difficult than it sounds, because most of us have long ago developed the habit of blocking out communications that are threatening to us in some way, usually because they imply to us that we need to do something or feel something that we don't want to do or feel.

Half an hour spent sitting and listening to conversations between mothers and toddlers in a toddler's play area should convince you of how early it starts. 'You have no right to be

331

angry.' 'You can't possibly be hungry'. 'How dare you say that to your mother?' 'You're being silly now. There's no reason to feel that way.' All these communications say that the child's feelings are not valid. What they really mean is: 'I don't want you to be angry'; 'If you're hungry I'll have to feed you and I don't want to feed you'. 'I feel angry when you don't appreciate me.' or 'It makes me guilty when you feel that way.'

Accurate listening is only possible when we separate the listening from any implications. In other words, we make a commitment to really hear and understand and even empathise with the point of view of the other, but make it clear that we may still hold a totally different point of view or wish to continue to make demands that are unacceptable to the other. This is also the basis of assertion: I understand your point of view, and I still have a right to mine.

Often people will not tell you their point of view unless you ask them. So make it a habit of asking them what view of the world leads them to do what they do, say what they say, or feel what they feel; even if you don't agree with them, they must have some reason, and if you understand it, you can both work together to adapt to each other. Even if they are telling you that you are an incompetent idiot, it doesn't hurt to find out what makes them think that: you may be surprised at the response, and you will be impressed at how much easier it is to change their view once you know where it is coming from. Thus here is a typical interaction:

> Jean: I am furious at you for hurting me.
> Jerry: You have no right to be furious at me. Look at what you did to me. You deserved everything you got.
> Jean: How dare you say that to me after all I've done for you?

Try replacing that typically unuseful communication with the following assertive communication using accurate listening:

Jean: I am furious at you for hurting me, Jerry. When you hung up the phone on me, I felt humiliated. Why did you do that?

Jerry: I can understand your being angry at me, and I'm sorry I hurt you. I really didn't mean to. But I was hurt too when you refused to help me at the moment I really needed you, and I just got so angry I slammed down the phone. I do want you to agree to be more helpful in future.

Jean: I didn't realise how hurt you were feeling. Sorry about that. I know you would like me to be more helpful, and I don't blame you. But I don't think I am cut out to be the helpful type you want me to be. What do you suggest we do?

In other words, you start by accurately reflecting the point of view of the other and then you clearly state your own viewpoint. You don't have to agree. By acknowledging and listening to the other person, you change the whole tenor of the interaction from a stone throwing match to a team effort. You then state your own view. You end, where there is a disagreement, by asking for their suggestion about how to proceed.

Let me report my first experience with accurate listening with my son Ari who was them about five. We'd just gone for a walk, and two minutes after leaving the house he said: 'I'm hungry'. My spirits sank, and I felt angry, because having just started out on the walk, I didn't want to go right home. Normally the conversation would have gone:

Me: 'How can you possibly be hungry?'
Ari: 'I am hungry, and I want to eat.'
Me: 'Well we're not going home now.'
Ari: 'Yes we are, we're going now.'

However, I decided to try accurate listening:
Me: 'You're hungry.'
Ari: 'Yes, are you?'

Me: 'A little.'
Ari: 'Oh.'
And we continued on our way.

One last word: I cannot emphasise strongly enough that accurate listening and assertive communication are not a technique but an approach and an attitude. Accurate listening means that you really do try to listen and understand the other's point of view and acknowledge it as valid. Stating what you want assertively means that you really do feel that you have a right to your point of view and your needs as well. Otherwise this just becomes one more method of manipulation.

Separating me from you

Most of our important relationships are confusing because to some extent we lose the boundaries between ourselves and the other. As a result, our feelings or actions seem to be a direct consequence of the other's feelings. We then say 'You make me feel x' or 'I have to do x'. This is also one reason we don't like to do accurate listening; 'I don't want to know how you feel because then I'll have to feel/do x.'

Be clear about what you want and feel, and what the other wants and feels. Then be aware that there is no direct umbilical cord between you, even though it feels like there is, and that you can each learn to choose how you react to the other. Try to change your language so that it reflects the fact that we do not literally cause each other's feelings, and that we do each have an independent choice. Thus, try this approach: 'I need this and I would like you to give it to me' (but you may not); 'You expect this and I may choose to do it' (or I may not); 'You feel this and then I feel that' (but I could learn to react differently).

Negotiating clearly

Another reason we need to wipe out the point of view of the other is that it seems so absolute. Jean imagines that Jerry wants total devotion, when a smile might be all that is required. Or Jerry imagines that Jean wants to be phoned every day, and

Jean does want this, but would settle for once a fortnight and still feel pretty good. So it is important for each to be specific about what they want from the other, and specific about what they are willing to give the other:

> Jerry: I resent your always rejecting me when I need help. I want you to be more helpful. (This is not specific enough.)
>
> Jean: What do you mean by helpful?
>
> Jerry: When I ask you for help, I'd like you to be willing to go out of your way for me. Like when my car is broken down, or I'm ill, I really need some help, and I'd like you to be willing to offer it to me if I ask for it.
>
> Jean: I couldn't make that kind of commitment.
>
> Jerry: What would you be willing to agree to?
>
> Jean: I'm willing to really listen when you ask for help, to be sympathetic, and to let you know whether I can help you and if so, how. I don't want to be tied down to having to help you, and that's probably why I sound so unsympathetic.
>
> Jerry: That sounds okay. Let's try it.

Locating what you have in common

No matter how great your differences are with the other person, it is usually possible to find out what you have in common, and then to see the differences as variations in approach to the same goal. Thus when you are arguing vehemently with your spouse about your child's education, remember to state: 'We are both concerned about our child's education. We just seem to have a different view of what's best.' Or when you are at loggerheads with your employer about the firm's policy, remember to point out: 'We are both really committed to the success of this company – that's why we're arguing. We do have a different view about how to get there. Let's see how we can understand these different views and work together.' As soon as you do that, you will find something of the tension between you relaxes and you can begin to cooperate rather than simply battle.

IN CONCLUSION

Communication rules are ultimately ways of being honest with ourselves and others. They should help us to be listened to, and help us to listen to others and to ourselves. They are not techniques of getting our own way, although we are much more likely to get what we want when we use them – and so is the person we are communicating with.

When I run seminars on assertion, I start with the assumption that we need to find a way to be assertive and effective communicators which does not rest on the hope that other people have not read the same book, and therefore will be impressed and give way. In other words, if we want everyone to be assertive, effective communicators, we cannot create a model that is based on winning. The following four principles result from this assumption, and are relevant to all the communication rules above:

a I have a right to be who I am, feel what I feel, believe what I believe, and want what I want.
b I don't necessarily have a right to get what I want.
c You have a right to be who you are, feel what you feel, believe what you believe, and want what you want.
d You don't necessarily have a right to get what you want.

NOTES

Chapter 1

1. Jung, C. G. (1969) 'Commentary', in Wilhelm, R. (trans.) *The Secret of the Golden Flower* (Routledge & Kegan Paul), p. 123.
2. Samuels, M. D. and Samuels, N. (1975) *Seeing with the Mind's Eye* (Random House).
3. Simonton, O. C., Mathews-Simonton, S. and Creighton, J. (1980) *Getting Well Again* (Bantam).
4. Freud, S. (1953) *The Standard Edition of the Complete Psychological Works*, J. Strachey (ed.) (Hogarth Press).
5. Jung, C. G. (1953) *Collected Works* (Pantheon Press).
6. Clarke, J. (unpublished) *Jung on Active Imagination*.
7. Assagioli, R. (1965) *Psychosynthesis* (The Viking Press); Ferrucci, P. (1982) *What We May Be: The Visions and Techniques of Psychosynthesis* (Turnstone Press); Leuner, H. (1969) 'Guided Affective Imagery (GAI)', *American Journal of Psychotherapy*, vol. 23, no. 6.
8. Perls, F. S. (1969) *Gestalt Therapy Verbatim* (Real People Press).
9. Bandler, R. and Grinder, J. (1979) *Frogs into Princes* (Real People Press); Luthe, W. (1969) *Autogenic Therapy*, (Grune & Stratton); Rossi, E. L. (ed.) (1980) *The Collected Papers of Milton H. Erickson on Hypnosis* (John Wiley); Silva, J. and Miele, P. M. (1978) *The Silva Mind Control Method* (Souvenir Press); Simonton, O. C. *et al.* (1980), op. cit.; Wolpe, J. (1969) *The Practice of Behaviour Therapy* (Pergamon Press).
10. Perls, F. (1969), op. cit.
11. Bandler, J. *et al.* (1979), op. cit.
12. Silva, J. *et. al.* (1978), op. cit.
13. Spangler, D. (1975) *The Laws of Manifestation* (Findhorn Publications).

Chapter 2

1. Elisabeth Kubler Ross (1977) Public Lecture, Conference of the European Association of Humanistic Psychology.
2. Jung, C. G. (1917) *Collected Papers on Analytic Psychology* (Moffat Yard), p. 468.

3. Klopfer, B. (1957) 'Psychological Variables in Human Cancer' *Journal of Projective Techniques*, vol. 21, pp. 337–9; Jaffe, J. T. and Bresler, D. E. (1980) 'The Use of Guided Imagery as an Adjunct to Medical Diagnosis and Treatment', *Journal of Humanistic Psychology*, vol. 20, no. 4, pp. 45–60; Simonton *et al*. (1980), op. cit.
4. Jung, C. G. (1961) *Memories, Dreams and Reflections* (Random House).
5. Perls, F. (1969), op. cit.
6. Shachtel, E. (1959) *Metamorphosis* (Basic Books).
7. Flavell, J. H. (1963) *The Developmental Psychology of Jean Piaget* (Van Nostrand).
8. Cole, M. and Scribner, S. (1974) *Culture and Thought* (John Wiley); Mead, G. H. (1934) *Mind, Self and Society* (University of Chicago Press); Whorf, B. L. (1956) *Language, Thought, and Reality* (MIT Press).
9. Gazzaniga, M. S. and Ledoux, J. E. (1978) *The Integrated Mind* (Plenum Press); Springer, S. and Deutsch, G. (1981) *Left Brain, Right Brain*, revised edn (W. H. Freeman).

Chapter 3

1. Galyean, B. (1983) *Mind Sight: Learning Through Imaging* (Centre for Integrative Learning).
2. Reich, W. (1973) *The Function of the Orgasm* (Farrar, Strauss & Giroux).
3. Galyean, B. (1983), op. cit.; Goldberg, P. (1983) *The Intuitive Edge* (Turnstone Press).
4. Sheldrake, R. (1988) *The Presence of the Past* (Collins).
5. Zdenek, M. (1983) *The Right Brain Experience* (Corgi Books).
6. Whitmore, J. (1982) 'The Use of Imagery in Sports Education', *Scottish Journal of Physical Education*, January, pp. 7–13.

Chapter 4

1. Wilhelm, R. and Baynes, C. F. (trans.) (1950) *The I Ching or Book of Changes* (Pantheon Books), p. 16.

Chapter 5

1. Houston, J. (1982) *The Possible Human* (J. B. Tarcher).

Chapter 8
1. Leftwich, A. (1988) 'Death at a Distance: Reflections on the Poltics of Grief', *British Medical Journal*, vol. 297, 24–31 December, pp. 1684–5.
2. Siegel, B. S. (1986) *Love Medicine, and Miracles* (Rider).

Chapter 10
1. Simonton, C. *et al.* (1980), op. cit.

Chapter 12
1. Desowitz, R. S. (1987) *The Thorn in the Starfish: The Immune System and How it Works* (W. W. Norton).
2. Siegel, B. S. (1986), op. cit.
3. Ibid.
4. Jean Houston (1982), op. cit.

Chapter 13
1. Schachtel, E. (1959), op cit.

Chapter 15
1. Stanislavski, C. (1961) *Creating a Role* (NEL Mentor Books), p. 49.

Chapter 16
1. Khan, P. V. I. (1982) *Introducing Spirituality into Counselling* (Omega Press).
2. Jung, C. G. (1953), op. cit.
3. Bailey, A. (1953) *Esoteric Healing* (Lucis Trust).

Chapter 17
1. Wilhelm, R. *et al.* (1950), op. cit.
2. Goldberg, P. (1983), op. cit.